The
Sacristy
Manual

SECOND EDITION

G. Thomas Ryan

With revisions by Corinna Laughlin

LITURGY
TRAINING
PUBLICATIONS

Nihil Obstat
Very Reverend Daniel A. Smilanic, JCD
Vicar for Canonical Services
Archdiocese of Chicago
July 6, 2011

Imprimatur
Reverend Monsignor John F. Canary, STL, DMIN
Vicar General
Archdiocese of Chicago
July 6, 2011

THE SACRISTY MANUAL, SECOND EDITION © 1993, 2011 Archdiocese of Chicago: Liturgy Training Publications, 3949 South Racine Avenue, Chicago, IL 60609; 1-800-933-1800, fax 1-800-933-7094, e-mail orders@ltp.org. All rights reserved. See our website at www.LTP.org

Illustrations: cover by Tracy Walker, i2i Art Inc.; interior by Kathy Ann Sullivan

Printed in the United States of America.

Library of Congress Number 2011933759

19 18 17 16 15   2 3 4 5 6

ISBN 978-1-61671-042-2
SACMNL2

Table of Contents

Preface

Like the work of sacristans, this manual is full of details. Small items can deter or facilitate public actions. Particular customs in the sacristy can do one of two things for the liturgy: help it to be the act of the whole Church, or keep it the province of clerics. Correct attention by sacristans to liturgical details is fundamental to healthy liturgy.

Checklists and procedures, ordos and norms impede our liturgy or become trivial if our attention to them is not deeply rooted in a commitment to the liturgical life of the local Church. We need more than intellectual assent to the Church in her actions. We need a passion for the local community as sacred reality, a passion for the communal rites as sacred interactions, a passion for the shared physicalities—from grand architecture to the tiniest artifact—as sacred art.

While reflecting on these basic beliefs and requisite details, I visited a parish across town for Sunday Eucharist. I had never been in the building but had read about its fine architecture. Upon entering, it became obvious to me that something strange was in the air. I joined a cluster of people standing to the side of the sanctuary. They were staring at a life-sized marble statue of Saint Anthony of Padua, toppled from its pedestal, and headless. The image of the baby Jesus in Anthony's arms had been similarly mauled. The stone showed evidence of powerful thrusts of the axe wielded by the one who had stolen the heads. This was surely the act of a deranged person, we might say, but amazing in its power to render speechless an otherwise intelligent, articulate group of city dwellers.

The statue had been no artistic match for the far superior architecture of the church; furthermore, it had been placed a bit too close to the altar area. Decapitated, it made such thoughts impertinent. The parishioners felt violated. Their sacred art had been desecrated; their house of prayer had been profaned.

In the presence of these primal emotions, I recalled a moment from my youth in a large urban parish where the church and parish school were the central points of energy. One day, while gazing from our back porch, my friends and I saw smoke rising from the church. We rushed to the sacred place, a haste made more purposeful by the shrill sounds of sirens as fire engines sped down the streets.

Police blocked our access, but we were all altar boys and knew well the back alley that would provide us with an unobstructed view of the smoking church. When we got there we saw the priests carrying out the treasures of our community's prayer. Their varying degrees of clerical dress bespoke their haste as they carried out the monstrance, some black boxes we knew encased chalices, and smaller containers that we guessed were for the sacred oils. We heard that the hero of the day was Father Hankins, the priest who had taught us our Latin responses. He had just rescued the Blessed Sacrament. We knew that this was a priest's duty, no matter the risk to life and limb. In hushed tones and nervous laughs, we thanked God that Father Hankins had survived.

With grave solemnity and fear we awaited the collapse of our church. What a relief—and momentary disappointment—that the fire was doused and all was well within a few minutes. Everyone went back home, figuring out how to make the final story more exciting than a ten-minute fire. Still, it was exciting—to see the sacristy saved, the Blessed Sacrament rescued.

Over the past few decades, liturgical reforms and progressive teachers have helped most Catholics pass beyond the understanding of the parish church as the sacred throne room for the tabernacled Lord. We know that the church complex is sacred because the people who meet there are sacred and are engaged in sacred rites. Yet, the physical elements that are within—from the reserved Blessed Sacrament to the chalices, from the altar to the various statues—are not just neutral matter.

When parishioners lose their church building to fire, when statues are decapitated by vandals, when vessels are stolen or strewn about, the reactions are primal, strong, far beyond the "rational." One could remind members that chalices can be replaced for a few hundred dollars, that the building can be rebuilt in a more glorious and energy-efficient way, that Saint Anthony (of all the saints) will find his head again. But if you were to say these things out loud, you would sound foolish. The emotions surrounding any violence to the place of worship tell us that the very objects of our common prayer are strong symbols of our life together. The building itself, even when empty, is a sustaining symbol of our identity. The given parts of a church complex come to represent the topography, the cosmology of the sacred for the local community. How fitting it is that the sacred assembly, the church, has lent its name to the building itself.

Our attention to the details of the sacristy and our passion for full community meet here. We tend to the implements and artifacts worthy of a sacred people. True, they are mortal things—everything in the sacristy is either consumed and replenished or conserved. Yet the importance of these things is what makes our ministry in the sacristy so rewarding. Because the community of mortals needs frequent interactions, our work is never ending. Because the requisites themselves are transitory, our ministry of providing and preserving is year round. If the community finds its immortal future through the physical interactions of sacraments, then our attention to the physicalities of those sacraments makes this sense of sacredness possible.

The first chapters of this manual form an introduction, setting the later details into this framework of church and liturgy. Part Two is a long tour through the different parts of the church complex, showing the relationship of the items in the sacristy to the actions and places of community. Part Three describes the sacristy's holdings and functions; it is a review and background for experienced sacristans and a suggested program for those building a new sacristy. Finally, Part Four is a series of checklists for major feasts and rites. These are just lists—the principles and norms are found in the main body of the manual.

Sacristans may want to use the various chapters for reading or for group study. Then the checklists can be referred to as events are scheduled. In any construction or renovation, and even in the preparation of decorative programs for parts of the parish church complex, the pertinent chapters provide some framework for shared discourse.

No single sacristy manual can be all inclusive. For example, the various documents that set norms for sacristies are not reprinted here. The central ones are found at the front of each official liturgical book, like the *General Instruction of the Roman Missal* at the front of *The Roman Missal*. (These documents spell out the shared rites that our work must support.)

As a server during the 1950s in Saint Gregory's parish in Dorchester, Massachusetts, I looked over the junior curate's shoulder to see the notes that he consulted. They were the richly detailed notes of a young commentator, Frederick McManus. I owe much to this generous man, this high school classmate of my father, this man who introduced so many of us to the reformed Holy Week, this capable administrator under whom I served at The Catholic University of America, the man who epitomizes the best of the local Church from which I come, the Archdiocese of Boston. I also praise and thank all of the sacristans with whom I have been privileged to work. Richard Butler—gifted pastor and pastoral liturgist and another Bostonian—also has been a docent and support to me. To them, and to all who have taught me that we can come to know the Lord through the concrete details of the sacristy, this volume bears witness.

—G. Thomas Ryan

Part One
Preparing for the Sacred Mysteries

Chapter One
The Church

The Action of the Church

"For these sacristans, that the preparations they make for the celebration of the liturgy may remind us to prepare our hearts for worship. . . ." This petition, from the blessing of sacristans (*Book of Blessings,* 1853), captures the essence of sacristy work. The joys and concerns, the moments of energy rush, the hours of painstaking details—all are part of this ministry of preparing the action of the church.

The word *church* comes from Greek words for the "gathered people" or "the Lord's holy congregation." When two or three or a thousand Christians gather, we constitute much more than a gathering of volunteers who have chosen to work together. We are a gift of God, the people gathered together by Christ, the Risen One, through his Death and Resurrection. Jesus himself spoke of his Death and Resurrection as the building of a temple; his Apostles, speaking of the Lord's Death and Resurrection, also have been described as Christ becoming the perfect temple and building a temple of living stones. The First Letter of Peter summons every parish: "See, I am laying in Zion a stone, / a cornerstone chosen and precious; / and whoever believes in him will not be put to shame" (2:6).

The Action of Christ

The congregation—or, better yet, the holy people, the temple of living stones—is engaged in the action of Christ. We pray as a community through, with, and in Christ. Liturgy is the act of Christ. This may sound like mere abstract theology when some members of our community seem to resent liturgies that take more than 45 minutes. Jesus, the perfect temple, may seem far away from the boredom or inattentiveness of some congregations. Yet we nonetheless cling to this affirmation: The liturgy is the act of Christ.

Millions of God-fearing worshippers know this. Gathering Sunday after Sunday, we know the holy power of Christ. We know that this power is at work in a holy meeting of ministries. We look forward to being shaped by an interaction with fragrance and oil, water and ashes, bread and wine. Our best and most memorable liturgies may or may not be marked by brilliant preaching, splendid music, and artfully arranged furnishings. But they are invariably marked by the profound interaction of holy people and holy signs and symbols. Even if we do not use these exact words, we know that our mystery is not like the "mysteries" of pagan temples; it is not a mystery of divine magic and secrets. In the Christian mystery we perform revered actions together.

The mysteries we celebrate are not an escape from the world; rather, they equip us to live in the world. Christ's action was and is one of saving the world. If we "leave the world" at liturgy, it is not an escape but a plunging deeper into the promised transformation of this very flesh, this very world.

The thousands of alienated Catholics who, despite their distance, seek ashes one day each Lent are not looking for a fast cure. They come forward for some signal of their identity, as mortal beings called to new life. The ashes, worn back to work or home, signify involvement with the coming transformation of the world.

In this way, week after week, the material elements of our holy gatherings, the vessels and elements prepared by sacristans, provide the matrix in which we interact. Water, fire, oil, ashes, bread, and wine are the archetypal elements that form the environment of our interaction. These elements accompany the many artifacts that facilitate such basic actions as cup-sharing, lamp-lighting, incense-burning, moving in procession, and committing our deceased to the earth. Catholics and many other Christians find that words are not enough for the sacred interactions that occur on Sundays and feasts. We need these elements and artifacts, too.

Our rites are far more complex than those public rituals that take place in schools, sports arenas, and city halls. But the complexity of our rites does not exist for the sake of complexity. Our ancestors never sat down to see how difficult they could make the work of future sacristans. The complexity comes from the rich variety of rites that respond to the many needs of the Christian community. We welcome new members through the Sacraments of Baptism and Confirmation, and recognize the call of God through the Sacraments of Marriage and Holy Orders (vocation). We minister to the sick in body and spirit through the Sacraments of Penance and the Anointing of the Sick (healing). We bury our dead. And, day after day, from birth to death, we receive food for the Christian journey through the celebration of Eucharist. Through liturgical time and feast days, the Church acts as Christ. We are Christ's holy people, the new temple of living stones.

A Building for Action

From the earliest centuries, the people of Christ have found appropriate places to house these sacred actions. To distinguish themselves from people of other religions, they were quite careful from the beginning to say that they had "no temple" but Christ, that their buildings did not contain their God. Gradually, the name of the people—"gathered people," "ecclesia," "church"—came to denote the building in which the people met to perform their actions together. Thus, the building was called "church." Our official liturgical books and the origins of the name itself suggest the felicitous nature of this double meaning: Even the name of the building reminds us of the people gathered there. Church buildings exist for the sake of the Church people, for the God who called this people into being, for the holy interactions that mark the passage through time.

In tracing our history, we might ask: Is the church building the "house of God" or the "house of God's people"? The question can be answered with a resounding "Yes!" It is both. The church building is the house or temple of God because the Church assembly is the house or temple of God. God is not contained by these walls; we do not come to the church complex to see a magical epiphany or pageant of the Risen One. Instead, we gather so that we can engage—with Christ—in the liturgical rites of our community. The intensity of these rites and the holiness of our union in Christ are what make this place holy.

When empty of its members, a church of stone should stand as a constant sign of the living stones who are now in the world, preparing the world for its transformation. And, just as surely, the church is also a sign of the generations gone before us, those who worshipped here, the communion of saints.

When enlivened by the presence of its assembly, a church building provides shelter and images for liturgical actions. If Christianity were just a set of beliefs to be transmitted, then a classroom would do. If the holy people became holy and remained so by sheer will power, then there would be no need for a public place. If we did not believe in the Incarnation, then all things of the flesh would be merely peripheral. But we are a holy people who find communion and identity in our public interaction. We cannot be Church without each other, without water and oil, bread and wine; we would find it difficult to be the Church without our churches.

This relationship of the people and their place for liturgy comes to beautiful and intense expression in the Rite for the Dedication of a Church. For example, the rite calls for the interior walls to be anointed at 12 (or 4) places. Crosses and candles can later be installed at these points along the perimeter. Those illuminated by Baptism will gather here week after week; the lights will embrace them in their gathering and lead them to recognize their identity.

The Second Vatican Council devoted much attention to the need to make liturgical architecture responsive to the liturgical actions that take place within it. Those old enough to remember the days before Vatican II (or who have visited spaces that have not been renovated in the wake of the Council) know that older church interiors were ill-suited to the reformed rites. Some buildings looked more like palaces for pageants than places of worship. Others looked like throne rooms for the reserved Eucharist. Many older buildings needed renovations to make them suitable for the sacred action of the liturgy. Some renovations went too far; others not far enough in adapting older buildings and spaces for the new rites. But the most successful renovations created space for ministers and the congregation to move and interact.

Yet church buildings need to be more than functional. If buildings of wood, stone, metal, and glass are to remind us that we are living stones, then they should look like something more than a fortress or a commercial sales hall. Architecture, furnishings, and decor play an important role in our churches. The *General Instruction of the Roman Missal* (GIRM)—the document that gives authoritative directions for the celebration of Eucharist—offers a summary in article 288:

> For the celebration of the Eucharist, the People of God are normally gathered together in a church or, if there is no church or if it is too small, then in another respectable place that is nonetheless worthy of so great a mystery. Therefore, churches or other places should be suitable for carrying out the sacred action and for ensuring the active participation of the faithful. Moreover, sacred buildings and requisites for divine worship should be truly worthy and beautiful and be signs and symbols of heavenly realities.

The Local Church

In the Church community, the local church building, one comes before these "heavenly realities." In this very place, in nooks and crannies, in the midst of this community of this altar, God and church are engaged in a saving interaction. This manual provides background information and set-up lists, explanations, and advice; readers must then adapt these guidelines in light of local conditions. Though written with the Catholic parish in mind, this book can be used and adapted for monasteries and chapels and for other Christian communities.

Local conditions and the adaptations they require should not be seen as burdens. In each local Church, with all of its unique qualities, the fullness of Christ is present. The people who come together here—relatives and neighbors, strangers and friends—are the "gathered people," the "temple of living stones."

Chapter Two
History of the Sacristy

Before Christianity

Sacristies are privileged places where the liturgical rites are prepared and where the treasured objects that facilitate that prayer are stored. Every place of public assembly has side chambers that shelter the objects used by the assembly. Archaeologists have identified many sites with these support rooms along the sides of both ancient temples and theaters. The Bible contains many references, especially in First and Second Chronicles, to side chambers at the Jerusalem Temple. These rooms were used by priests and other officials to store treasures and cultic materials, to receive and distribute gifts. The *Septuagint*, an early Greek translation of the Bible, used the term *pastophoria* to designate these auxiliary rooms.

Early Christian Centuries

An early Christian document from Syria used the same term for the side rooms in its description of an ideal worship site: "First, let the building be long, with its head to the east, with its vestries on both sides at the east end, and so it will be like a ship" (*Apostolic Constitutions,* II.7). Long before the civil legitimation of Christianity in 313, local communities met in specially designated and equipped buildings for liturgy. Sites now identified as early churches throughout the Mediterranean basin show that the communities utilized several interconnected spaces: Eucharistic hall, baptistry, atrium, catechumeneon, and auxiliary rooms not unlike our sacristies. For example, in 303 the church of Cirta (a regional center in present-day Algeria) was closed by the government. A list of possessions confiscated from the sacristies has survived in the local court's proceedings. They describe the chalices and lamps that were taken, but they also tell how the church's ministers took the books from the sacristy and hid them.

Documentary evidence of such ministers is rare. Every Christian congregation must have had some ministers in preparing the environment, but the work of preparing the environment and the artifacts has always been quiet and untrumpeted. Yet we know that, among the ministries related to the early sacristies, there were both porters and sacristans. A porter (*ostiarius*) tended the doors, and in later centuries rang the bells and performed other works of liturgical preparation. This ministry later became codified as a "minor order." Long before it was eliminated in 1971, it had become just a title conferred on seminarians. Yet, through all the centuries, every local Church has entrusted its keys to dedicated members who served as porters, as janitors, or simply as the first one up in the morning.

Sacristans were listed by writers (Jerome, for example) and by Church councils as "ministers of God." When recounting his life in the fourth century, Saint Paulinus of Nola wrote, "I call the Lord to witness that I longed to begin my holy service with the name and office of sacristan" (*Epistle 1*).

Such holy service is suggested by several stories told in the sixth century by Pope Gregory the Great (*Dialogues* Book I, Chapter 5). They sketch out examples of sacristans privileged to work in the midst of a sacred people on Sunday, and in the places of celebration and burial throughout the week. Holy sacristans are also cited as healers and wonder workers. Constantius of Ancona was known far and wide as a pious man. When the supply of oil for the lamps ran out, he took water, poured some into the lamps, fixed the wicks, and lit them as usual. They all began to burn as if they were fueled by oil. As Gregory noted, "you may gather . . . of what merit this man was, who, enforced by necessity, did change the nature of the element." Acontius is also said to have healed a girl who was paralyzed. In our rationalist times, we tend to be embarrassed by such stories, explaining them away. But the evidence of the early centuries tells of sacristans' holiness and of their respected work in relationship to the entire body of the faithful.

While taking great care to stress the holy nature of this work, leaders of the churches also passed on detailed lists to describe the practical work of sacristans. Isidore of Seville (seventh century) described the ministry as the care of security, access, vestments, sacred vessels, codices (books), oil, lamps, and candles.

Sacristans, Bishops, and builders developed various systems for organizing these materials and the rooms in which they were kept. A wide range of local names was used for these sacristies, often reflecting the particular items that were kept there. Rooms that held liturgical vessels and the elements for the Eucharist were often called treasuries—a name that conveys the esteem in which the Eucharist was held, not just the value of any precious metals that might have been kept there. Churches in some regions contained rooms equipped to store and distribute gifts (clothing and food, for example) for the poor. Such social services were deemed highly appropriate for a liturgical space, and the rooms took on names equivalent to "service center." Separate sacristies (or portions of rooms) were set aside for vesting and became known as vestries. Still other zones, separate rooms or not, were established for the reservation of sacred objects (especially the Eucharist for the sick and the holy oils). Before Christians ever began to use tabernacles in the main worship hall, the Blessed Sacrament was reserved in the sacristy.

One such system for organizing the sacristies is known from seventh-century Constantinople. The Great Entrance (Preparation of the Gifts) was a full and grand procession with bread and wine. Leaving a separate treasury building where the vessels were stored, the procession moved to and then through the assembly area of the church. The faithful were not lined up in pews; commentaries from that time describe them surging toward the arriving gift-bearers and then processing with them. This dramatic entrance, movement, and interaction with the assembly would be replaced in the medieval period by a brief appearance of the gifts as they were transferred to the altar table from a newly constructed sacristy (called a *prothesis*) next to the altar. The transfer of the side chamber, from a separate building to a zone immediately adjacent to the altar, signalled the end of participatory processions as well as a growing clericalization or privatization of the Mass (Thomas Mathews, *The Early Churches of Constantinople: Architecture and Liturgy,* Penn State, 1971).

Middle Ages

In the Eastern churches, it was fairly standard practice to have two sacristies. On one side of the altar was a *prothesis* for the preparation of Eucharistic elements; on the other side of the altar was a *diaconicon* for vesting and the storage of oil lamps and the like. Two separate rooms also became customary in Western churches. One was for the clergy (with vestments and Eucharistic vessels), the other for items tended by sacristans and other ministers (candles, flowers, incense).

In the eleventh century, a man by the name of Guy became sacristan in Anderlecht, a district of Brussels. His zeal for the care of the place for worship was so great that he was memorialized as a saint and as patron of sacristans. A remarkable number of legends about him grew up and spread. They tell us little about his humble life but a lot about the esteem in which sacristans continued to be held. The descriptions of his work and documents of that era indicate an important shift in the way that the role of sacristans was perceived. More and more, their role was being confined to the sanctuary section of the church complex. The sacristans' work was viewed more as a service to the clergy than to the whole assembly, and the rites were becoming more and more standardized.

Before and After the Council of Trent

The Middle Ages, the Renaissance, and the Reformation of the sixteenth century are not remembered with great fondness by liturgists. By then, liturgical actions had shriveled, and the liturgy itself was largely a pageant of clerics. As "low" Mass became the norm, the celebration was often colorless. After the Council of Trent in the sixteenth century, liturgies with minimal involvement of the faithful were codified and made even more universally standard. For hundreds of years before and then for hundreds of years after that Council, sacristans served the clergy and the sanctuary with lists that were virtually the same in Madrid, Paris, London, and in the American colonies.

By the time Christianity was brought to this continent, Catholics of the West (and other Christians who kept Eucharistic rites after the Reformation) were familiar with two sacristies. All but the tiniest chapels had one room for vessels and vestments, another for candles, vases and servers' robes. The first room was called, variously, the "priests' sacristy," the "secretarium," the "vestry," or the "sacristy." The second room, usually on the other side of the sanctuary, was the "servers' sacristy," the "second sacristy," or the "work sacristy."

Sacristies near the altar facilitated the changing of altar cloths and the provisioning of the credence table. This placement also served with the minimalist liturgical practices of the era—"processions" that just popped out from sacristy to altar steps, a sense that the clergy rather than the assembly were the beneficiaries of sacristy work, a sense that all of the sacred actions were unfolding at one end of the building screened off by a communion railing. Liturgists of old accepted this placement of the two sacristies. They even provided separate doors from the assembly area and from the exterior to the sacristies so that no one would need to pass through the sanctuary on the way to the sacristy.

The Decades before Vatican II

Many scholars and pastoral ministers formed a liturgical movement in the decades before the pontificate of John XXIII (1958–1963). They shared new research and fresh appreciation of the liturgical heritage. Patristics experts produced definitive editions of ancient liturgical texts and homilies; scriptural scholars adopted new methods of critical research; theologians began formulating a vision of Church that was more community-centered; pastors and catechists discovered the power of the liturgical year in structuring domestic prayer and religious education; daring pioneers envisioned a liturgy in the languages of the people; liturgists saw the power of the liturgy for reshaping the world. These were but a few of the trends in the air. They signaled that well before Vatican II many leaders within the Church had already agreed on the need for reforms.

In terms of the environment for worship, pioneering scholars and pastors of the liturgical movement highlighted the material forms of the community's interaction. They fostered participatory ceremony, art that followed the canons of beauty and liturgy, and the use of vesture and vessels that truly facilitated the "sacred action" of the Church.

Among the more progressive activists were church architects, especially in Europe during the rebuilding of cities after World War II. It was as if some architects saw the future and called the rest of the Church to it. They designed spaces for "Mass facing the people" before most had even heard of it. They foresaw the end of Communion rails, the end of tabernacles on center altars, the end of side altars for devotions, the end of birdbath-sized fonts. They embraced modern art, new technologies, an appreciation of the active assembly undivided by pillars and screens, and an aesthetic that preferred simplicity to gratuitous ornamentation.

Vatican II and the End of the Twentieth Century

Pope John XXIII was certainly mindful of the reform movements when he called the Second Vatican Council. Neither he nor any observer could have failed to notice the new and daring church architecture that had appeared in his diocese of Venice and in post-war France (where he was *nuncio*), not to mention in dioceses all over Europe. As Roman preparatory commissions sought out agenda items and drafted documents for the Council, leaders of the liturgical movement became active in their diocesan offices and at the Vatican. Liturgists were appointed as experts to the Bishops; the architects with the new ideas were also heard, as new norms for church buildings were debated. The Council itself only formulated the call to reform and its broad parameters. The actual reforms were left to Vatican commissions.

No document was issued then, or since, outlining the rearrangement of sacristies for the reformed rites, but a feeling of what changed can be gathered from the official liturgical books. Most notably, the *General Instruction of the Roman Missal* contains several sections on vesture, vessels, and other artifacts that relate directly to the work of sacristans. In and between the lines of these books, and in the currents of change that are often a step ahead of the documents, sacristans find both reform and invention.

The reforms are substantive, marking a return to the fullness of texts, ceremonial, and participation that seemed to mark the earliest Church. Sacristy work is seen as a service to the whole temple of living stones and to the whole church complex. The role is once more described in the terms of ministry and holiness.

Through the shifting forms of rites over the centuries, sacristans have always responded to their communities' needs—securing and cleaning meeting places, setting up and maintaining proper materials, providing images and decorations. Despite the paucity of historical sources about this ministry, the few that we have bespeak the holiness that can be found through the performance of these tasks. This is one job in the Church that puts to rest the foolish thought that spirituality rises as attention to the physical or material diminishes. It is precisely in these everyday, practical concerns where you will find the holiness of Christian people. Sacristans do not need time off from their work to find God. They need the insight to find God in the very act of preparing the way for public prayer.

The Current Positions of Sacristies within the Church Complex

The word *church* has come to mean the place in which we celebrate the Eucharist. But our parishes include a network of spaces—grounds, assembly hall, baptistry, sacristy, chapel for the reservation of the Blessed Sacrament, meeting rooms, reconciliation chapel, social hall, shrines, and so much more. Those who prepare the liturgy, and sacristans, need to think through the ways that the various spaces and their functions interact, because our celebrations of the liturgy will often take us outside the boundaries of the church proper.

Current Division into Two Sacristies

We inherited church buildings with two sacristies, usually located on either side of the sanctuary. We can still use two sacristies, but perhaps with a different division of materials and new locations. On this matter, the *Ceremonial of Bishops* (CB), issued by the Vatican for the Bishop's liturgies, is quite applicable to all parish churches. Article 53 states:

> The cathedral church should have a *vesting room,* that is, a suitable place, as close as possible to the church entrance, where the bishop, concelebrants, and ministers can put on their liturgical vestments and from which the entrance procession can begin.
>
> The sacristy, which should normally be separate from the vesting room, is a room where vestments and other liturgical materials are kept. It may also serve as the place where the celebrant and the ministers prepare for a celebration on certain occasions.

One simplification of this scheme for parishes is to store the vesture in the vesting room itself. This is the ideal form of two sacristies that will guide the advice contained in this manual. It will not be possible everywhere, but there is a surprising number of places where it can be done.

Note that the vesting room is placed close to the entrance, so that processions (and greetings following the liturgy) are facilitated. Besides these benefits for Sunday Masses, imagine the ease with which mourners and the remains of the deceased might be greeted at the entry. Consider how the full greeting at the door of bride and groom will unfold without peeking through the sacristy door and peering down the nave of the church.

The functions of the two support rooms should no longer be divided between clergy in one sacristy and servers in the other. The vessels do not need to be in the room of the clergy, with the flower vases in the lesser sacristy. The division of materials should relate to the rooms' functions within the building complex. The ordained and all of the other ministers who vest can do so in one vesting area, since they will form processions together. The Eucharistic vessels and all of the other materials needed for good liturgy can be maintained together elsewhere, closer to where they are used.

Chapter Three

The Sacristan

Ministry in the Sacristy

Not every parish or community has a volunteer or staff person bearing the title of sacristan, but in every place of worship many tasks need to be done before the liturgy can take place. The building must be opened and lit, cleaned and decorated for the feast. Bread and wine must be in place, vessels and vestments made ready, books and candles set out.

In some small parishes, the priest or deacon will often do most of this work, while in the larger communities a small army of volunteers and staff will get involved: pastor, liturgist, musicians, lectors and readers, altar servers, ushers, and extraordinary ministers of Holy Communion, not to mention the janitorial staff, altar guild, liturgy committee, decorators, and florists. Whether the parish is large or small, it will benefit by designating a sacristan: someone who can ensure that there is care and consistency in the preparations made for the liturgy, and support the pastor and liturgist in providing oversight of all those involved in carrying out the liturgy. The role of sacristan is an important ministry in itself, and designating a sacristan can help the whole community recognize that the liturgy isn't just something the pastor does, but something that we all need to prepare for.

Job Description for Sacristans

The role of sacristan varies widely from place to place, but the following job description includes the tasks most often assigned to sacristans.

1. *Supervise the calendar.* There should be only one master calendar for the church, with clear guidelines about who can schedule an event and commit parish facilities, personnel, and resources. Major solemnities and feasts should be added early so that their hours will be kept clear of other events, and certain restrictions should be made clear far in advance (for example, clear rules against scheduling weddings during the Paschal Triduum). Procedures for scheduling funerals and other last-minute events need to be made clear—and then followed by all concerned.

2. *Prepare specific liturgical times and liturgies.* Sacristans should help the pastor and liturgist prepare for liturgy by reviewing the liturgical texts and options, by reviewing previous years' files, and by noting sacristy-related questions. In liturgy preparation meetings, sacristans should take special note of any objects that need to be borrowed or purchased. They should prepare detailed checklists of the preparations for any given liturgy, especially for special events and major solemnities, and then carry out the preparations in a thorough and timely fashion.

3. *Establish standard operating procedures.* Sacristans, in collaboration with the pastor and other staff, should negotiate a clear flowchart of responsibilities for the daily and weekly operation of the sacristy.

4. *Maintain the church complex.* Every part of the building (including the exterior) needs regular maintenance and cleaning. The sacristan might be the one to enlist volunteers for this and negotiate the responsibilities of a custodian in relationship to other ministers.

5. *Prepare liturgical materials.* The *Roman Missal, Lectionary for Mass,* and other ritual books need to be prepared. Locally prepared texts such as the Prayer of the Faithful also need to be available. Vestments, vessels, and other materials need to be maintained, cleaned, or replaced as necessary.

6. *Maintain images and decorations.* Permanent and "seasonal" images need maintenance and cleaning. Sacristans are often responsible for planning and caring for flowers or other "seasonal" decorations. Whenever flowers are brought into the church complex, responsibility needs to be taken for their watering and disposal.

7. *Take inventory.* Sacristans set up and supervise the regular replenishment of materials like wine, hosts, candles, and charcoal. They also procure annual items like palms and the paschal candle. Every few years, the sacristan, working with the pastor and parish administrator, should take a thorough inventory of church property. This might include a review of insurance policies, appraisals of old objects, and setting priorities for acquiring new things or replacement items.

8. *Minister at major liturgies.* The sacristan is usually present at all major liturgies. Everyone involved needs to know who will be present and who will do what. Responsibilities include opening and closing the facilities, setting up objects, welcoming other ministers, participating in certain parts of the rite (ringing bells from the tower or lighting new charcoal at various points of the Mass), and returning all objects to their proper place after a liturgy.

9. *Train volunteers.* The sacristan is often responsible for training volunteers to do sacristy-related tasks like polishing brass, tidying pews, sweeping, dusting, and watering flowers. Sometimes the sacristan is also involved in training liturgical ministers—readers, extraordinary ministers of Holy Communion, altar servers, and ushers. The sacristan should be able to provide volunteers with the information they need succinctly and gently, and to instill in others a sense of wonder and reverence in the preparations they make for the liturgy.

10. *Perform other administrative duties.* The sacristan is usually responsible for preparing and maintaining a balanced budget, and for attending certain meetings of the pastoral staff or parish pastoral council.

Close Collaboration

When parishioners first get involved in the liturgy, and especially when they begin to participate in committee-based decision making, they are often surprised by the tension and discord that can exist within the parish community, even in the area of liturgy. Good pastoral leaders will help keep those involved grounded in prayer and reduce the tension, but should keep in mind that the Church deals with life-and-death issues; with signs and symbols that are central to faith, close to the bone and close to the heart of all involved. Friction and emotion are guaranteed. We must resist the temptation to pine away for a perfect Church where there is no tension, but instead realize that God is with us in our local church—flawed as it is. Within a community of frail and holy ones, sacristans need to be bridge builders among these varied groups:

PARISH MEMBERSHIP   Sacristans serve the entire assembly. This relationship should never become a them-and-us division, with parishioners as outsiders.

PASTORS   In some eras, the priest was the only one the sacristan needed to listen to. He would celebrate the liturgy in his own style, outfit the church complex according to his own taste, and make all major decisions without consultation. That model of leadership is far from the ideal for priests today. Both priests and sacristans need to look beyond their own tastes and leanings, and listen to the sound advice of the *General Instruction of the Roman Missal*, 352:

> In arranging the celebration of Mass, the Priest should be attentive rather to the common spiritual good of the People of God than to his own inclinations. He should also remember that choices of this kind are to be made in harmony with those who exercise some part in the celebration, including the faithful, as regards the parts that more directly pertain to them.

PASTORAL STAFF   Larger churches benefit from the work of other leaders—catechists, liturgists, musicians, outreach ministers, counselors, and others. Depending on local custom, a person in charge of a given area might bear the title of "minister," "director," or "coordinator." If there is a parish liturgist, then he or she is the usual liaison between the pastor and the sacristan. The sacristan and all of these ministers must have full and open communication with one another.

PARISH COMMITTEES   Most parishes have a parish pastoral council and a finance committee. Sacristans might attend some of these meetings, but most of their committee time should be invested with the liturgy committee, if there is one. There are no hard and fast rules in place for liturgy committees. In some places, they may prepare every major liturgy in great detail, while in others they take more of an oversight role, simply supervising the standard operating procedures. Sacristans have an important role here, especially when budgets and difficult decisions are under discussion. Sacristans also should work closely with building committees to ensure that the church complex is not only well maintained, but that it also functions efficiently as a place for the celebration of the liturgy.

ACOLYTES OR ALTAR SERVERS   Acolytes or altar servers are the traditional allies of sacristans. For centuries, they have passed on traditions about how to set up wine and water, how to fix wicks and otherwise deal with candles, and how to get the maximum smoke from a parish's thurible. The work of these individuals, and that of others who prepare the symbols and artifacts of ritual, is supervised by sacristans. Because sacristans and acolytes work together so closely, they must necessarily have great respect for one another. When young children are involved as altar servers, sacristans can be patient and firm educators, helping children show the proper decorum and respect during the liturgy and grow in their love and understanding of the Mass.

OTHER MINISTERS   Other ministers have roles in preparing for Mass. Musicians often take care of their area of the church as well as the microphones. Lectors and readers often ensure that the *Lectionary for Mass* is correctly marked. Extraordinary ministers of Holy Communion sometimes set up the various patens and chalices (and, at the end of Mass, wash them after they have been purified). Ushers often assume a great deal of responsibility—opening and closing parts of the complex, setting out materials, preparing the pews and chairs before people arrive. The roles of each group of ministers should be understood by all involved and should also be periodically evaluated and reformed if necessary.

SEXTON OR CUSTODIAN   A church complex can benefit greatly if the budget will sustain such a position. Parishes with both sacristans and janitors will need to define clearly the tasks of each position. An effective division of labor might have the sacristan taking responsibility for all liturgical items, with the janitor taking the lead on the physical maintenance of the church complex.

ALTAR GUILDS AND OTHER VOLUNTEER GROUPS   Whether they are called altar guilds, tabernacle societies, or some other name, for centuries church members have been volunteering to help maintain and prepare the items needed for worship.

Where clear guidelines for these groups are established and maintained, the members of such groups not only contribute to the liturgical life of the parish, but they also find great satisfaction in the work they do. In parishes where these groups do not exist, sacristans might set up new groups of dedicated volunteers. Rather than calling them "altar" or "tabernacle" societies, titles that relate more closely to their work might be chosen instead. For example, some might act as "environment ministers," seeing to the proper use and placement of church decor and furnishings. Others might work on "seasonal" or festival decorations—flowers, outdoor luminarias, and the like. Still others, perhaps under the heading of "housekeeping" or "maintenance volunteers," might clean the church complex on a regular basis, polish brass, clean votive lights, and the like. A "textile" or "vestment" group might take care of the vestments (cleaning and repair) or the linens (laundry and ironing).

DECORATORS   Some parishes have formed liturgical environment committees or have otherwise deputed certain individuals as decorators for the parish. These, too, will need to work closely with the sacristan.

ARTISTS AND ARTISANS   In procuring new materials, it is always good to consider artists and artisans who are members of the parish. The benefits of such collaboration are great, because at the same time it could lead to an awkward situation if you need to refuse the inferior work of a well-meaning parishioner. Having clear guidelines and a careful process of research, evaluation, and commissioning helps avoid this problem.

VISITORS   Visitors should be close to the heart of every sacristan. They should be welcomed during off hours and given tours of the church complex and the sacristy. School groups, and especially middle school-aged children, love to explore the recesses of the sacristy, where they can gain wonderful insights into the work that goes into preparing for Mass and the richness of the liturgical tradition. By making these opportunities available, sacristans can help to enhance the participation of these children in the liturgy.

VENDORS   The sacristan must get to know the vendors who supply the different items used in the sacristy, from vestments and vessels to hosts, wine, and candles. Sacristans should also get to know local suppliers. Some sacristy needs can be met by shopping wisely in nearby towns and at retail outlets other than at stores that specialize in church goods. For certain items, however, a general church goods catalog may be utilized; for example, when purchasing fine liturgical linens. Other items, like wine and candles, might be procured on a sort of standing order once a source has been found. In general, the specialized catalogs of vestment makers and vessel artisans are better sources of quality items than are the general catalogs that offer everything. When purchasing the major art and furnishings of the church complex—like an ambo or a baptismal font—the parish should not simply order from a catalog, but, if resources allow, commission an artist or architect to design a piece of work that responds to the needs of the specific community, and that can endure as a treasured part of the parish's heritage.

DIOCESE   The sacristan's relationship with the diocese normally will be centered around the worship office or liturgical commission of the diocese. These offices or groups can be enormously important to sacristans, because they will often have lists of reliable local purveyors of different items. They also often sponsor workshops, consultation services, and learning opportunities.

CIVIL AUTHORITIES   Awareness of safety codes is important for the sacristan. In some localities, permits are needed for outdoor fires, as at the Easter Vigil, as well as for street processions and outdoor sound systems (even when they're on church property). Codes also may govern the number of people permitted in the building, the ringing of tower bells, the use of candles—even the straw used in mangers and the use of cut Christmas trees.

Also, if decorations will cut across walkways, the legal egress specifications should be consulted. Attention to these kinds of things not only can lessen the risk of injury to persons, but also can reduce the potential legal liability of the parish, an important consideration in our increasingly litigious times. At the same time, if civil officials and the codes they administer seem unduly restrictive, then sacristans and pastors should be prepared to do some negotiating. This can be done by, or in consultation with, diocesan personnel or local lawyers.

Qualifications

Those who coordinate the ministries of a parish need to take the role of sacristan seriously to think carefully about the kinds of persons they will engage to assist them in this important work. Here are some qualifications:

1. *Sacristans should be regular and alert communicants, men and women who love the Mass, who sing with gusto, and who participate wholeheartedly in the liturgy.* Their regular participation should attune them to the flow of liturgical time and of the rites. They do not need to know everything about sacristy practice or be able to define every word in the specialized sacristy vocabulary, but they should know what they don't know and be willing and able to learn. Complementing this dedication to the liturgy, sacristans must be zealous in their commitment to fostering the growth of the local church. This happens not only through preparations they make for the liturgy, but also through the sharing of responsibilities with children and adults, and the friendly supervision of all aspects of the work. With the gifts of all members so central to the vitality of the church, the days when a sacristan could claim the sacristy as a personal fiefdom are long gone.

2. *Sacristans should be free to work at the great solemnities.* Prospective volunteers and paid sacristans must plan their schedules around the long hours of the Paschal Triduum. They will be needed on Christmas, as well as on days such as New Year's, Ash Wednesday, and Thanksgiving.

3. *Sacristans may be of any age and either gender. All that counts is the ability to perform and enjoy the tasks.* The role of sacristan was once reserved to the ordained. In our day, it has been taken over mostly by lay people. Now all are welcome—young and old, male and female—and the diversity of our individual gifts brings fresh approaches to this work.

In-service Training

LOCAL READING AND DISCUSSION   Sacristy volunteers, liturgy committees, and all the liturgical ministers should spend some of their donated time learning more about the rich liturgical heritage of the Church. Some topics to consider might be as follows:

1. *Liturgical reforms.* The history of the liturgical reforms of the last century or a general history of liturgy, using commentaries and Church documents such as *Sacrosanctum Concilium* (the Decree on the Sacred Liturgy of the Second Vatican Council) or *Sacramentum Caritatis* (Pope Benedict XVI's "post-synodal apostolic exhortation" of 2007), and accessible histories like Lucien Deiss's *The Mass* (The Liturgical Press, 1992), and commentaries on the Mass such as *At the Supper of the Lamb* by Paul Turner (Liturgy Training Publications, 2011).

2. *The rites of the Church, with study materials from the official ritual books.* Use the introductions at the chapter headings along with an outline of the rites or a sampling of the texts themselves. The *General Instruction of the Roman Missal* contains a wealth of theological reflection on the celebration of the Eucharist. The *Liturgy of the Hours,* the *Rite of Christian Initiation of Adults, Rite of Baptism, Order of Christian Funerals, Pastoral Care of the Sick, Rite of Marriage*, and blessings frame a parish's life and should be studied in turn over the years.

3. *The central furnishings and symbols of our liturgy.* The church building itself and the altar can be studied by using the dedication rite. Insight into the history of the local church complex can be gained by reading the homily and press reports at its dedication, and exploring anniversary books and archive copies of parish bulletins. The deeper meaning of the baptistry, ambry, chair, ambo, tabernacle, reconciliation area, doors, bells, chalice, and paten can be studied using their respective chapters in the *Book of Blessings* and *Built of Living Stones*.

4. *Images in the church complex.* Use the introduction and blessing texts at Chapter 36 of the *Book of Blessings*. The crucifix, Stations of the Cross, Advent wreath, Christmas tree, and Christmas manger can be studied along with their own orders of blessing. Liturgical arts in general can be studied from modern commentaries. Studies on the name of the church (saint or title of the Lord) will yield ideas about existing or future images.

5. *The liturgical year.* The document *Universal Norms on the Liturgical Year and the Calendar* provides general information about the various liturgical times, solemnities, feasts, and memorials. It provides guidance for when these times and observances are celebrated and a chart with observance dates. It is printed in *The Roman Missal* and can be supplemented by the local *Ordo* and other guidances that might be published or prepared by the Bishops' Committee on Divine Worship in the United States of America or by your local diocese. If parish leaders do not have such resources at hand, call the diocesan worship office.

FORMAL INSTRUCTION   Beyond local discussions, training can take place in several venues. The diocese or region may have occasional classes or workshops on the liturgy; the parish budget should allow for an ample number of ministers to participate in these programs. Art museums usually have classes or lectures on art history that can shed light on the evolution of liturgical art. Programs of continuing education in one's own city or town should be reviewed for worthwhile classes. These are often the best places to learn the technical side of sacristy work: the care of materials found in sacristies, and tips for floral arrangement and interior design.

VISITING   Even if there are few opportunities for continuing education at the parish level, and if the formal classes available in a particular region are limited, people's love of travel will provide a fruitful arena for learning. Alone or in groups, sacristy workers should visit other churches (especially those recommended by the diocesan office), which can provide "living" examples of good renovation and construction work, along with creative alignments of furniture. A visit to the local cathedral would also be a good idea. Viewing another church environment fosters fresh insights into the relationship of the various parts of the church and the dynamics of liturgy, and the local cathedral is "a model for the other churches of the diocese in its conformity to the directives laid down in liturgical documents and books with regard to the arrangement and adornment of churches" (*Ceremonial of Bishops*, 46). A visit to the local cathedral will also allow some items to be seen in their unique setting, such as the *cathedra* (the Bishop's chair) and the repository of oils for the diocese. Often, the art of the cathedral reveals much about the history of the diocese, as well as of the region.

Those who live in larger urban areas may be able to visit art museums with medieval collections, including liturgical items. Visits to such places, complemented by readings, can give ministers an awareness of the richness of our heritage and can offer clues to the evolution of the rites we celebrate today. Some few places have wonderful museums that feature liturgical items from our American heritage, including the Spanish missions of the West and Southwest, St. Augustine, New Orleans, the diocesan museums of Quebec and Montreal, the earliest churches of Philadelphia, and the sanctoral shrines of American saints such as at Emmitsburg and Auriesville. It is no exaggeration to say that by traveling to these places we are seeking ways to prepare for the holy city that is to come.

Chapter Four

Sacred Mysteries and Liturgical Art

The Local Church

The unique characteristics of the local church should guide sacristans and decorators in every part of the church complex. There are several ways to appreciate each church's character.

1. *The congregation.* The architecture and interior of the building are usually related to the kind of community that uses the building. In this manual, unless otherwise specified, the focus will be on parish church sacristies. Because of this, sacristans who work in other worship environments—convent chapels, monastic churches, campus ministry centers, urban "chapels of convenience," or hospital chapels—may have to adapt some of the ideas found in this manual to their specific circumstances. The sacraments and rites observed in a given church or chapel will vary as well. For example, Marriages and infant Baptisms are performed regularly in the typical parish, but may seldom be celebrated in some of the other worship environments mentioned.

One parish church in each diocese is designated as the place for the Bishop's chair (*cathedra*). This church, the cathedral, serves as the liturgical model for the other parishes (see *Ceremonial of Bishops*, 46). The questions specific to cathedrals will be handled in this manual under such headings as the Chrism Mass and Ordinations. In dioceses where such episcopal liturgies occur outside the cathedral, these notes should help the parish sacristans involved in preparations. Some parishes and shrines are visited by large groups of pilgrims during the year. Such transient groups, with their size and devotional interests, present special tasks for sacristans. Though some special accommodations may need to be made, liturgical principles should never be compromised. (Some of the more renowned of these centers, with exemplary liturgies and superb artistic quality, have been honored by the Holy See with the title of "minor basilica"—a term unrelated to the style of architecture bearing the same name.)

2. *The title of the church.* Churches can be named after the Trinity, the Holy Spirit, Christ (invoked according to a mystery of his life or a title in the liturgy, such as the Exaltation of the Cross), Mary (according to an appellation in the liturgy), one of the angels, or another saint (see *Rite of Dedication of a Church*, Chapter II, article 4). The term *titular* is used here, avoiding the familiar but imprecise term *patron*. (The Holy Spirit and the Holy Cross, for example, may be titulars of the Church, but they are not patrons.) The title has implications for the calendar (the annual solemnity for the local titular) and for decorations.

3. *The age of the church building.* The treasures sometimes discovered in the sacristies of old churches would amaze many finance committees. As custodians of the materials in a church, sacristans should discard old objects only after consulting reputable experts, such as preservationists or museum curators. Nothing should ever be sold or given away until its value and historical significance have been ascertained.

4. *Architectural style.* The exterior style, the architectural shape, and the interior decoration of a church edifice will have an enormous influence on the work of sacristans and other environmental ministers. Sacristans need to consider how each chapel, room, and hallway is decorated and how it serves the particular action for which it was designed. Further, we need to see how each place is connected to the other places, and how real people, whether at Sunday Mass or at a wedding or funeral, move between the places. Even if the areas of Word (ambo) and Eucharist (altar) are only a few feet away, we still need to understand the distinct functions of each place.

Sacred Mysteries

We must prepare the church complex for the sacred mysteries. But there are different ways to understand mystery. From the start, while pagans held to a sense of mystery that was atmospheric and unintelligible, Christians held that mystery is not an atmosphere, a trick of lights or candles, but a sacred reality, the Paschal Mystery of Christ's life, Death, and Resurrection. It is a mystery because we can never understand it fully; at the same time, it is a mystery in which "we live and move and have our being" (Acts of the Apostles 17:28). We are engaged in these sacred mysteries, and in the Mass we are not passive spectators but active participants in the mystery of faith.

Sacristans prepare for the sacred mysteries not by creating an atmosphere, but by enabling the ritual action, the action of the holy assembly in Christ. The arts can foster the sacred mysteries of Christian liturgy when they empower a congregation to be a truly active congregation, when they draw all present from word to Eucharist, or from word to font, or from the funeral Mass to the place of committal.

These actions embrace the material world and employ images and elements like bread and wine, fire and water. Unlike those who denigrate the senses and consider the spiritual to be separated from the physical world, we find our holiness incarnated. We find our very identity through beauty—through words, actions, images, and spaces that are beautiful.

When we come to know every zone of liturgical action, when we discover the unique life of this local church, then we are prepared to celebrate the sacred mysteries.

Art for the Sacred Mysteries

Before considering the varied parts of the church complex, we can consider the arts that serve the sacred mysteries throughout the building. Sacristans are often called upon to be the chief decorators for liturgical times and particular solemnities and feasts. At the very least, they must keep in close communication with groups entrusted with the environment and decorations. After the permanent, "seasonal," or feast-day images or flowers are set up, sacristans are usually in charge of maintaining, cleaning, or watering them. Throughout all phases of the decoration and/or design process, sacristans should be advocates for arts that enhance the liturgical action.

DISTINCT FORM OF ART   As wise commentators have been saying for centuries, there are many works of religious art and many decorations that do not qualify as liturgical art. Just because a painting shows Jesus, doesn't mean it's appropriate for the liturgy. Liturgical art is a distinct form of art. It is related in style, content, and placement to liturgical action.

By its presence in the given space (baptistry, nave, sanctuary, reconciliation chapel), a work of art should foster the liturgical action in that space. It also should express the ethos of the community's liturgical tradition. Over the centuries and in the current reforms, this has meant that Roman Catholic church buildings and artifacts should have an inherent beauty, be made from honest and natural materials, demonstrate a certain restraint (so as not to overwhelm the actions or distract from it), and avoid both private perspectives and gaudiness.

ANCIENT FORMS   Liturgical art is part of a long tradition. As our earliest Christian ancestors were sharing ritual practices in cities around the Mediterranean, and as these practices then spread to more distant frontiers, certain scriptures also were shared as the most appropriate for given days. Many Christian images developed at the same time, often based on Jewish or pagan precedents. These images were used to adorn catacombs, Eucharistic vessels, fonts, and ritual books. Just as the liturgical rites and scriptures were passed on from generation to generation, so too was this vocabulary of images. These signs and symbols and forms have come to bear particular emotions and meanings in our long heritage.

Liturgists of our own time have drawn on early Christian prayer texts and Lectionaries as important parts of the reform. This has not been motivated by mere antiquarianism, but by the need to recover the full tradition, by the need to see how rites looked before the clericalizing of the liturgy that took place in the Middle Ages. In the same way, liturgical artists can draw upon the ancient images and symbols. But these earliest texts, rites, and images are not simply copied by each successive generation. Rather, in every century, they have received fresh life from the technologies and tastes of the time. The lamb at Easter, the ox and ass at Christmas, the palm of martyrs, the great image of Jonah coming from the whale, the wondrous power of a tree of life—these are but a few of the ancient forms that have entered our subconscious, our literature, our folkways, our Western heritage. They sprang from our scriptures and liturgical actions, and they can continue to be the best way to decorate our holy places.

No one sacristan, whether new or experienced, can be expected to know all of our rich and varied tradition. Yet all should look about them to see and learn these treasured images of our faith. The visual arts call us to enter into and interact with our rich tradition.

CURRENT NORMS   The standards set by our own official liturgical documents foster art forms flowering from and serving the liturgical action. In 1952, the Holy Office in the Vatican forbade "second-rate and stereotyped statues" (*Acta Apostolicae Sedis,* 44,). Vatican II, in its *Constitution on the Sacred Liturgy* (CSL), called for the removal of all works of art that offend by "the deficiency, mediocrity, or sham in their artistic quality" (124).

Built of Living Stones (BLS), the justly popular and authoritative guide from the United States Bishops' Committee on Divine Worship, provides a fine summary of the demands made by liturgy on the arts (140–157). There are two components of true and worthy art: its quality, evident in its use of genuine materials to create "a harmonious whole, a well crafted work" (146); and its appropriateness for liturgy, its "ability to bear the weight of mystery, awe, reverence, and wonder that the liturgical action expresses . . ." (148).

ROOTED IN LITURGICAL ACTION: In 1963, Daniel Berrigan was characteristically prophetic as he commented on arts and the liturgy:

> With regard to the past, it would serve no real purpose here to detail the centuries of vapid, dissociate art which we are in the process of disowning. Since the late middle ages, religious art has been largely and progressively shunted to the studio and drawing room; it has become the adjunct of the prie-dieu, instead of the impassioned flowering of a public, virile, and believing mind. . . . If it served for anything, it was only to heal over the wounds by which Christians were marked, the wounds of their amputation from their greatest possessions, the altar and the word

of God. . . . Since the fourteenth century, the Western Christian community has been quite simply ill—not irrecoverably, but still seriously; and its religious art is the syndrome of its illness. . . . It was an art designed quite literally for the sick room. It kept alive Christian memories and hopes in a subjective, devotional way. But its cumulative effect was disastrous, because it beckoned (Christians) further and further into their sick reveries. It helped them forget that there had ever been realities like community, anamnesis, sanctuary action. ("The Spirit of Modern Sacred Art" in *Liturgy for the People,* edited by W. Leonard [Milwaukee: Bruce Publishers], 157)

His analysis followed in the tradition of the great commentators of this century's liturgical movement. Citing but two of the more obvious leaders, one can see their consistent cry for an end to vapid art and pious trash, a rooting of liturgical art in the communal traditions of word and altar, the actions of the sacred mysteries.

In 1930, E. A. Roulin wrote:

Everybody knows the sort of use that is made of pennons, banners and flags on certain feastdays to decorate, or rather to uglify, our churches, even the best of them. . . . Our churches are not worthily decorated by masses of these cheap bannerets. It would be better to abolish all this trashy stuff and to limit ourselves to a couple of great pennons or flags of good shape and proportions and made of silk or damask. Our folk would soon learn to appreciate them and to prefer them to those countless gaudy objects that are really only suited for a country fair. (*Vestments and Vesture,* Newman, p. 289)

Ten years later, Martin Hellriegel addressed the first National Liturgical Week: "Pious rubbish must scrupulously be kept from the church as unworthy of the King of Ages, unworthy of his chosen and kingly priesthood." (*How Firm a Foundation: Voices of the Early Liturgical Movement,* edited by Kathleen Hughes [Chicago: LTP, 1990], 126)

PURPOSES OF IMAGES   The liturgical art form that has been discussed the most over the centuries is the representational image. Leaders and thinkers in the Church have identified three purposes that representational images should serve (see *Book of Blessings,* 1258, 1293). Although you might think that ornamentation would be one of the three purposes, it is not; ornamentation purely for its own sake is not part of our liturgical tradition. The legitimate purposes of representational images are as follows:

1. *The formation of the faithful.* This might well be the most misunderstood reason for having images. Gregory the Great is often quoted referring to images as books for the illiterate. Later leaders called them the catechism of the unlettered. Gregory was not putting down the illiterate, but rather promoting the power and efficaciousness of images. In fact, images do teach people, and not just illiterate persons and children. From the smallest chapel to the most exalted cathedral, images teach lessons of history, scripture, cultural differences, and much more. We all need the education we receive from the truly artful images.

This educative function of images can be misunderstood if taken too literally. When looking at representations of the saints, for example, we will probably not learn their entire life story, but we will call them to mind, ponder their witness and example, and recognize the communion we share with them and with the Lord they served.

In the fourth century, Saint Augustine of Hippo used broader and more powerful phrases when he wrote that liturgical elements shape our hopes and desires, motivate us to transform the world, and seek the city that is to come. In 1948, in his important encyclical on the liturgy, Pius XII spoke of images in churches as stimulating the senses and drawing viewers to reform (see *Mediator Dei*, 167). When preparing images for churches, this is what we should be striving for.

2. *Assistance for memory.* This is quite similar to the formation function; the viewing of sanctoral images should always remind Christians of the communion of saints. In one sense, most of us have already been educated in this. All we need is a little prompting, a reminder from time to time that we are part of a broad communion. We have a holy past from which we spring, in which we grow, a holy future toward which we stretch.

3. *Facilitate veneration.* It is not enough to say that we stretch toward full communion with the saints in heaven. The future, the new Jerusalem, pulls us toward that great and holy end. It is not just our efforts, our education, our service to the poor; the fullness of justice and peace comes only from God. Images do not just decorate our places and form our personalities. They can draw us into a sense of the real power of God who is all in all. Through the centuries, we have not just learned lessons from what we have seen; to this day we can feel impelled to kneel in awe and wonder. Theologians and Church councils have called this being pulled from the visible (form) to the invisible (the prototypes). The experience of powerful images is not magical; the response is an expression of our deep-seated veneration for the holy. When cynics laugh at people who treat images as if they were living, it is a measure of the critics' fear. When pious ones kiss, touch, or place flowers before images, they are providing even further proof of the power of images for focusing prayers and desires.

In the Eastern Churches, icons are an integral part of the liturgy. In the Roman Church and in other Western Churches, images are venerated but rarely incorporated into liturgical action—the Adoration of the Cross on Good Friday being a notable exception. In both East and West, though, people transact all manner of holy business in church complexes. Catechesis, social service, and devout honoring of revered symbols are all part of the public work we do as people. They all form us in ways that lead to and from the Eucharistic banquet.

SIMPLIFICATION AND FOCUS It is no secret that representational images and decorations in churches are fewer in number since Vatican II. The reduction of images and their more careful placement are acknowledgments of their power and the concomitant need to keep them from drawing energy away from the sacred rites. The *General Instruction of the Roman Missal* (318) says:

In the earthly Liturgy, the Church participates, by a foretaste, in that heavenly Liturgy which is celebrated in the holy city of Jerusalem, toward which she journeys as a pilgrim, and where Christ is seated at the right hand of God; and by venerating the memory of the Saints, she hopes one day to have some share and fellowship with them.

Thus, in sacred buildings images of the Lord, of the Blessed Virgin Mary, and of the Saints, in accordance with most ancient tradition of the Church, should be displayed for veneration by the faithful and should be so arranged so as to lead the faithful toward the mysteries of faith celebrated there. Care should, therefore, be taken that their number not be increased indiscriminately, and moreover that they be arranged in proper order so as not to draw the attention of the faithful to themselves and away from the celebration itself. There should usually be only one image of any given Saint. Generally speaking, in the ornamentation and arrangement of a church, as far as images are concerned, provision should be made for the devotion of the entire community as well as for the beauty and dignity of the images.

This attitude, while specifically applied in this instruction to the area for the congregation, permeates all of the rites and Canon Law. Thus, the other places in the complex—baptistry, reconciliation chapel, chapel for the reservation of the Blessed Sacrament, narthex—also need to be clear in their focus, decorated with restraint and dignity. Where parishes elect to create a separate devotional area or shrine, this is never to be just a catch-all chamber for every image, ugly or beautiful, that the parish ever owned. In every corner of the community's house of divine praise, all elements of the environment must contribute to the sacred mysteries, to communal action.

OVERALL PROGRAM FOR DECORATIONS   Preparing, commissioning, and installing images and decorations is not, for sacristans, a regular privilege. Most often, we are presented with buildings that are in place, painted or decorated, equipped with some permanent images, and we are already in the habit of using certain "seasonal" decorations. All of these amount to what we can call an "iconographic program" or a "scheme of decoration." Whatever we may call it, every church edifice has one: it is the totality of what is seen—the order in which forms and colors appear, the congruence or dissonance of shapes and textures with the liturgical actions, the attractiveness or lack thereof, the ways that the images appeal to us or repel us. Too often the program has evolved with little concern for the whole. Pastors or decorators add this or move that; other improvements may be put on hold indefinitely or implemented with deliberate speed if a parish benefactor happens to be involved. This element of randomness is dangerous, because the iconographic program continually shapes and orders the Church's memory.

Before any changes are made in an iconographic program, sacristans and decorators need to appreciate what surrounds and forms each liturgical zone at the present moment. Only after such an appraisal has been made should additions and changes be contemplated. And in considering such changes, we need to devote primary attention to the architectural surfaces that shelter the congregation, to the central artifacts and images of the liturgy—worthy cups and plates for the Eucharist, a font of fine stone and dignified color, vestments and wall hangings of high quality fabric and rich color, a crucifix that the entire parish will cherish. There is still a place for images and temporary decorations such as flowers, but these are never as central to the liturgical space.

ARCHITECTURAL SURFACES AND PERMANENT DECORATIONS The most important work of liturgical art is, of course, the building itself. It is the most obvious starting point for identifying the current program of design. Because decorations should relate to the architecture of the building, those who decorate the building, or any of its interior rooms and halls, need to know their building very well. Scale is very important. It would be a mistake, for example, to hang little wicker baskets of pansies from huge, gothic pillars.

To know a building well means to be familiar with the full scope of rites that occur in a given space. This requires a careful review of the liturgical texts and ritual action that unfold in that particular area, whether it be the baptistry, the reservation chapel for the Blessed Sacrament, or the area for the congregation itself. For example, colors, shapes, and images placed in the baptistry should not overwhelm the brightness of the Paschal candle or obscure a wall-mounted repository of holy oils. Our liturgical tradition draws strength from and is complemented by icons, sacred images, architectural forms, and the liturgical furnishings themselves. No symbol brought in to convey a particular "theme" or pot of cut flowers should trivialize these all-important parts of the worship environment.

Knowing a building well also means knowing it surfaces—walls, supports, ceiling, and floor. They either add to or subtract from the liturgical experience. Never are their effects neutral. Usually such surfaces must be "hard," able to sustain a lot of action, rather than soft carpets or acoustical tiles. Soft materials dull the acoustics and just as significantly dull the ambience of public interaction. The finishes do not necessarily need to disappear in neutral tones. Exact specifications of color would best be determined in light of the architecture itself; stone and wood make different demands.

Lighting the Church Complex

Church lighting is normally handled by electricians and renovation committees, not by sacristans. There is another kind of lighting in churches, though; one that might be evoked by the rich word *illumination*. In the early Church, the baptized carried candles and were called the "illuminated." Ever since, candles have been elements of our liturgical interaction, and the tending of lamps and candles has been an important part of the work of sacristans. Now, as in every century, the illumination of the liturgical space is essential to its decoration.

HISTORY OF CANDLES AND LAMPS Long before Christianity, ritual candles were used at the Temple in Jerusalem and in the meetings of many other religious communities. They were used not only at night, but during the day as well. Night or day, the controlled fire of the wick flickered as an expression of religious emotions. Before the invention of matches, it was eminently practical to keep an "eternal" flame burning in places where candles were lit regularly. At places like the Jerusalem Temple this seems to have led to a ritual of keeping and honoring such a flame.

When Christians first began holding their meetings, those scheduled at night obviously were lit with some forms of oil lamps or groups of candles. One such occasion is described in the Acts of the Apostles 20:8. As Christian communities developed, the night was often marked by liturgical gatherings, principally the hours spent singing and praying in vigil before Sunday or an important congregation. By the third century, the lighting of the lamps at nightfall and its ritual form, the "lucernarium," gave rise to many beautiful prayers and hymns, some still present in our hymnals—*Phos hilaron*, for example.

Ritual candles and an eternal flame would have been familiar to first-century Christians, both at home and as a part of communal worship, and the same could be said of certain pagan groups. From inscriptions and drawings of the catacombs and ancient cemeteries and from extant homilies and commentaries, we know that two of the earliest uses of illumination in the liturgy were at tombs and in funeral processions, as well as other processions, such as when the *Book of the Gospels* was being carried. When the procession ended, the candles often were placed on floor-mounted stands. A stone inscription found at Aquileia (northeast Italy) shows some third-century Christians praying beside a lighted candle that rests on a floor stand not unlike many seen in modern churches.

The visions described in the book of Revelation show how candles figured in the religious symbols of these earliest ancestors in faith (Revelation 1:12, 4:5, 11:4). The use of such primordial forces as fire was never just utilitarian; humans always have used fire to express their emotions, their desires for fullness, and the power of life beyond. It was the same in early Christianity. Early Christians did not light candles only to be able to see or to create an attractive light. They interacted with these elements of illumination, carrying them in processions and thus forming what they called "liquid fire." They placed the flame by their beloved's tomb, passed light to the illuminated neophytes. In that interaction, they experienced the holy presence, the light of Christ, the joy that we so haltingly say that candles "signify."

The liturgy in later centuries was far less participatory. Members of the congregation saw liturgical fire and candles only from afar. By the late middle ages, the candles that once had graced processions were put on the altar. In the same era, when the Blessed Sacrament reserved for the sick was moved into a tabernacle in the public prayer zone, a lamp was placed by it. Some commentators began confusing this with the eternal flame that predated matches; some even began to see this late addition as the primary light and identifying mark of Catholic places. As the distance grew between the people and the liturgy, people treated candles as symbols to look at. The number of candles that were lit indicated what kind of Mass was about to be celebrated. Thus were people separated from the action, and new, more limited meanings were assigned to rich symbols of faith.

Despite this impoverishment, many Catholic and Orthodox Christians continued to light devotional candles before statues and icons. While these actions are more individual than communal, they did (and still do) involve choosing a candle, lighting it, placing it before an image, and spending some time in veneration. In a way, this act is a link with the primordial elements of ritual, with *lucernarium* lights, held by all, with processions of liquid fire.

Material for Candles   The principal candles in liturgy were always made of beeswax, were clean burning, and were obviously a product of nature. When formulating allegorical lessons, commentators could say, "The pure wax extracted by bees from flowers symbolizes the pure flesh of Christ received from his Virgin Mother, the wick signifies the soul of Christ, and the flame represents his divinity" (A. J. Schulte in the 1907 *Catholic Encyclopedia I*, p. 347). In the decades before Vatican II, various forces caused the Vatican to mitigate this requirement. Exceptions were made for missionaries. For example, in 1850, because beeswax was unavailable in Oceania, the churches there were allowed to use sperm oil candles. In 1904, the requirement was further modified so that beeswax need constitute only a majority part of the candle. This quickly created a market for candles that were only 51 percent beeswax. In our current *General Instruction of the Roman Missal,* candles at liturgy are called for, but their material is no longer specified (#307). In 1974, Vatican authorities wrote that candles should "provide a living flame without being smoky or noxious" (*Built of Living Stones*, 93), and that electric lights were not permitted as a substitute for candles. Bishops in each country were free to make further specifications. Although, it might be interesting for some to note that the translation of the *Exsultet* (Easter Proclamation) in the third edition of *The Roman Missal* does make mention of the wax of the candle and the work of bees who provide the wax: "accept this candle, a solemn offering, / the work of bees and of your servants' hands, / . . . we know the praises of this pillar, / which glowing fire ignites for God's honor, / a fire into many flames divided, / yet never dimmed by sharing of its light, / for it is fed by melting wax, / drawn out by mother bees / to build a torch so precious."

Over the decades, vendors have been aggressively marketing non-candle products, plastic tubes filled with liquid. The United States Bishops' Committee on Divine Worship has warned against such imitations for use at the altar. Their popularity, though, shows that some sacristans and pastors prefer this version of efficiency over natural and traditional elements. Whether called "candelas" or "liquid wax candles," whether their fuel comes from polyethylene squeeze bottles or sealed tin cartridges, even if called legitimate and worthy by vendors, they do not burn down and change shape, they are not new each year, and thus they cannot be used as paschal candles.

Meanwhile, candles of paraffin, molded stearin, or tallow have been used in liturgy along with beeswax. Sacristans should evaluate all of these options by setting up the various kinds, burning them, checking for smoke and smells. You'll pay more for 100 percent beeswax candles, but they continue to come highly recommended because they burn so slowly and fragrantly. Whatever your choice, remember that candles are not merely utilitarian, not merely a way to satisfy a rule. They are a primal element in our interaction in sacred mysteries.

Current Use and Placement of Candles   The reformed rites have simplified the numbers and placement of candles. Current norms and advice will be found in this book on the pages for the various places where candles are used and stored: in the place for the assembly (altar, p. 47; walls, p. 37; pews, p. 39), in the baptistry (paschal candle, p. 61; baptismal candles, p. 63), in the chapel of reservation (p. 76), in devotional areas (p. 80), and in the sacristy (p. 95).

Flowers as Liturgical Art

Flowers can be placed in any part of the edifice. Here are some general notes:

HISTORY   The first uses of flowers at liturgy were in the ancient cemeteries of our earliest ancestors in the faith. Like their neighbors of other religions, they buried their dead in garden settings. Even in those locales where catacombs were dug, the underground corridors and rooms seem to have been painted as gardens, and the land above was almost always a garden. Christians were quite explicit in linking garden settings and their belief in paradise. For example, Perpetua of Carthage, just before her martyrdom in 203, spoke of her paradisal vision (*The Passion of Perpetua and Felicity,* 11):

> [A] great open space, like a garden, having rose-trees and all kinds of flowers. The height of the trees was like the height of a cypress, whose leaves sang without ceasing. We crossed on foot a place strewn with violets, where we found (those) who were burned alive in the same persecution.

The narrative was written soon after Perpetua and Felicity were martyred. It was read with the veneration usually reserved for the Bible itself, especially in the churches of north Africa. With the pervasive link between paradise and the garden, it is not at all surprising that the tombs of martyrs and revered heroes received floral embellishments on their feast days. Many historians note that when the Eucharist began to be celebrated at these tombs, then flowers began to be used at rites other than funerals. The use of flowers in the places for liturgy, with or without tombs, may have sprung from a desire to express faith in paradise.

We have no ancient record of flowers being placed on the altar or in a pot before the ambo. On feast days, garlands may have been placed on walls and on columns throughout the building; the decoration of doorways and other architectural surfaces proclaimed the festival of paradise. On some of these same feasts and for certain rites, flowers or herbs were strewn on pathways of special importance. In all of the ancient accounts, we can recognize the appeal to the senses. Like our ancestors, we value the brilliance and visual power of flowers and plants. Unlike them, we tend to forget the power of scent. Venatius Fortunatus, an important hymn composer (sixth century), proclaimed that flowers in the liturgy had more scent than incense itself.

Redolent of paradise, flowers, and herbs were used throughout church complexes over the later centuries, but they were never at the altar. Aside from their use around tombs, they were an architectural decoration and scent for the floor, doors, walls, and support systems. In keeping with local availability, certain scents and shapes became associated with certain liturgical times. These were never codified in law, for the customs of Mediterranean lands were unlike those of England or Poland.

It was only in recent centuries, as Christianity was finding new expressions in the Counter-Reformation and in the "new world" of America, that flowers were removed from the place for the congregation and put on the altar. Some said, as they do now, that the presence of flowers called attention to this important place. But the result was sometimes to trivialize or obscure any sense of life-and-death action at the altar table, while depriving the congregation area of sights and scents that had been welcome.

THE PLACEMENT OF FLOWERS IN THE REFORMED RITES Two approaches to floral decoration can be seen in most churches. During the centuries and decades before the Council reforms, flowers usually were placed on the shelves behind the altar table. Echoes of this practice are seen when flowers are placed on remaining side altars and when vases are symmetrically placed on the rear wall or on an unused shelf or platform behind the current altar. Especially in renovated churches, where unused altars have been removed, another pattern seems to have become almost mandatory, that is, the placing of pots of flowers or green plants in one or all of these places: at the foot of the lectern or ambo, on the floor in front of the altar, in free-standing vases on either side of the altar and around the baptismal font. If the font is an immersion pool, the plants there seem to be intended to discourage people from sitting on the sides of the font or setting things down there.

Perched before ambo or altar, though, flowers and plants can minimize the importance of these sacred places. We need to remember that we are not designing a stage set; we are equipping a space for the action of all. As in all other parts of the decorative or iconographic program, we need to have our paradisal forms and scents support the sacred mysteries, the actions that unfold in the church complex. This implies an integrated approach to decorating the walls, the doors, the floors, the devotional shrines, and spaces around representational images.

On occasion, liturgical actions might be facilitated by a free-standing arrangement or tree, an iconographic statement in the entryway or by the image of the day's saint, a scent-sending call to a particular feast. More often, though, our use of flowers should be integrated into the rite itself. For example, at funerals, a bed of herbs might support a coffin on the sanctuary floor; when the congregation will go in procession, the route might be marked by flowers or branches. At all times, the use of plants and cut flowers presumes vessels and forms that connote public action rather than domesticated cuteness.

In addition to facilitating liturgical action, flowers can become sensuous signals of liturgical times. Local traditions can evolve, as they did in early Christianity, from patterns of availability and prevalent expectations. At Christmas, the scent of evergreens is pretty well set and needs little tampering. Lilies may be the scent for early Easter Time; roses, for the days of late Easter Time and on Pentecost (they were used in traditional Jewish Pentecost rites). Just as sacristans need to appreciate the need for integration of the visual program, they also need to coordinate the varied scents of incense and flowers with the liturgical time. It need hardly be added that artificial flowers, at any liturgical time, should be strenuously avoided: "The use of living flowers and plants, rather than artificial greens, serves as a reminder of the gift of life God has given to the human community" (*Built of Living Stones*, 129).

FLOWERS AT WEDDINGS AND FUNERALS The desire for flowers at these emotional moments is great, but the selection and arrangement of flowers still needs to be attuned to the liturgical action that will unfold. Every parish should devise guidelines that respect the feelings of families, while at the same time clearly defining what may and may not be done. Such norms must be communicated at the earliest opportunity to those involved in order to head off any impossible or unreasonable expectations. Weddings and funerals, like all the Church's liturgies, belong to the whole Church. They are the action of the Church, the action of Christ. They are not prepared and provisioned as if the church building was rented for a family reunion. Participants book such events at church precisely so that it will be the Church acting here, with all the richness of sacraments and liturgical times.

Funeral guidelines—about what is brought into the church complex and what is put at the committal site—will have to be communicated at a meeting with funeral directors. Many times, during the first visit after death, pastoral ministers can suggest that any floral remembrance from the family might take this or that shape conducive to the liturgy.

Marriage guidelines need to be understood by all who lead pre-marital catechesis and communicated to couples at the same time that they are scheduling the rite. The pastor, the catechists, or a special parishioner who acts as liaison or negotiator can assume this role of communication with couples and area florists. Couples need to know, from the very first moment, that the day they have in mind is this feast or in that liturgical time. If it is in Advent, Christmas Time, Lent, or Easter Time, they need to know how to respect the already-present ambience of austerity or festivity. Parish leaders should not be afraid to issue norms on placement, visual impact, and even the floral containers; for example, banning spray-painted cardboard.

With such once-in-a-lifetime events, some participants are always surprised by this or that long-standing policy of a church. Great tact is needed here, and a diplomacy that knows the liturgical parameters. The sacred mysteries deserve such care.

Inscriptions

Many churches have on their walls tablets inscribed with the names of donors or their beloved. Current liturgical books make no mention of this practice, but after the Council of Trent such tablets were generally forbidden. They did (and do) distract us from worship and obfuscate the common ownership of the church building by the Church community. New memorial inscriptions should be placed in less obtrusive parts of the church complex (a donor's book in the entryway or inscriptions along the foundation wall outside). Rarely, if ever, should they be visible in the congregation or on liturgical objects.

The one exception is the inscription called for in the *Rite of Dedication of a Church*, Chapter II, article 25. It should state the date of dedication, name (titular) of the church, and the name of the Bishop who led the congregation of dedication. This can be on the outside, in the entrance hall, or in an unobtrusive place on the interior walls of the place for the congregation. Unlike a private donor's memorial, this signals the heritage and holiness of this house for the whole local Church.

Part Two
Equipping the Church Complex

Chapter Five

A Place for the Congregation

A Place of Communion

The congregation, the faithful, the people of God, the gathering, the congregation —all these terms are used in Church documents to describe those who come together for liturgy. The variety of terms used reveals how important this gathering is, because when we come together in the church to celebrate the Eucharist, we are not a crowd or a miscellaneous group of people thrown together by chance. We are a unified body, coming together for a single purpose, and engaged in a particular action—the liturgy, the work of God's praise. While different parts of this action are carried out by various ministers, there should never be a sense that only those who are "doing something" are participating, while the rest are merely watching, like an audience at a theater. The congregation at Mass is not an audience. All present undertake the sacramental action along with the priest, and all share in the saving mysteries.

The liturgy does not happen only at the altar; it takes place in a complex of interrelated places, including the baptistry, reconciliation chapel, chapel for the reservation of the Blessed Sacrament, entrance hall, and social gathering areas. All these must relate to the place where the congregation gathers for thanksgiving and Communion.

History and Current Norms

UNIFIED, ORIENTED PLACES   This action of the entire congregation was at the heart of the earliest Christian liturgies, and the churches they built were gathering spaces that allowed for visibility, movement, and access. Our ancestors in the faith called the long, central part of the church building the "nave," from the Latin word for "ship," perhaps because it reminded them of the shape of a boat, perhaps for its metaphoric associations as well—the ark of Noah, the ship of Peter. By "nave," they meant the entire hall, embracing the place of the clergy as well as of the laity. Within this unified space, small screens, a few feet high and normally of stone, began appearing at an early date. Their purpose seems to have been to define areas for certain liturgical acts; for example, framing the area where the Word was proclaimed. But the separated space we know as the "sanctuary" did not yet exist.

The places Christians built for the celebration of the Eucharist—with a few important exceptions—faced east. They were, literally, "oriented"—the word comes from the Latin for "east." The East is, of course, the source of light. For the first Christians living in the Mediterranean world, the East had other associations as well. They looked for paradise in the East, and gazed eastward toward the cross of Christ in Jerusalem, in anticipation of the second coming from the East (Matthew 24:27).

The table that was both sign and source of their Communion was usually placed at the eastern end of the church edifice. Often shaped as a half-circle, and vaulted so that it formed a sort of shell or cave, this area (commonly called the apse) was considered the place of divine entry. The churches of the East preferred to use the language of the Incarnation to describe the Eucharist; it is no wonder that the images on their apse walls were often of the first coming of Christ, the birth at Bethlehem. In our Western tradition, early Christians focused more on the second coming, with many still-extant apses dressed with images of the new Jerusalem.

MEDIEVAL CONCENTRATION ON THE RETABLE AND TABERNACLE   During the Middle Ages, shifting liturgical practice led to changes in church architecture. As the congregation became more passive—no longer joining in responses, singing, or even receiving Communion frequently—the separation of clergy and lay began to be reflected in the arrangement of the liturgical space. Large screens appeared in church buildings of many regions. Far more than earlier decorative panels had done, these screens divided the place of Eucharistic action into two parts: the "choir" or "sanctuary" and the place for the congregation. The medieval fascination with vertical screens also can be seen in their placement near, or even at, the altar. In most Western churches, the retable, or reredos, reared up from behind the altar table. Their size and verticality resulted in most of the iconography being located at or near the altar, too; and it usually depicted Calvary, not Bethlehem or the second coming. The reredos was typically studded with shelves or niches for a variety of appointments. The cross and candles, once carried in procession, became frozen in place. The glorious cross, bejeweled and made of precious metal, was transformed into a "passion cross," with the *corpus* (the body of Christ) upon it. In other niches coffin-like boxes containing relics of saints might be enshrined. Later, when churches began reserving the Eucharist in public, central tabernacles took the place of reliquaries.

It is ironic that such constructs, meant to bring attention to the altar, more often served to distract from it. As the retable grew in importance, the ambo and Priest Celebrant's chair were phased out by the curtailment of ministries (deacons, lectors and readers, cantors) and the absorption of all liturgical action to the area immediately in front of the altar-retable. The tabernacle, rather than the altar, became the focus of attention in the church building.

CURRENT NORMS   The reforms of the Second Vatican Council restored the role of the congregation as full, conscious, and active participants in the liturgy, and our church buildings today should reflect this. Our liturgical spaces need to draw the congregation toward unified participation in the rites. The *General Instruction of the Roman Missal* states in article 294:

> The People of God which is gathered for Mass, is coherently and hierarchically ordered, and this finds its expression in the variety of ministries and the variety of actions according to the different parts of the celebration. Hence the general arrangement of the sacred building must be such that in some way it conveys the image of the assembled congregation and allows the appropriate ordering of all the participants, as well as facilitating each in the proper carrying out of his function.

> The faithful and the *schola cantorum* (choir) shall have a place that facilitates their active participation.

> The Priest Celebrant, the Deacon, and the other ministers have places in the sanctuary. There, also, should be prepared seats for concelebrants, but if their number is great, seats should be arranged in another part of the church, though near the altar.

> All these elements, even though they must express the hierarchical structure and the diversity of functions, should nevertheless bring about a close and coherent unity that is clearly expressive of the unity of the entire holy people. Indeed, the nature and beauty of the place and all its furnishings should foster devotion and express visually the holiness of the mysteries celebrated there.

And again in article 311:

> Places for the faithful should be arranged with appropriate care so that they are able to participate in the sacred celebrations, duly following them with their eyes and their attention. It is desirable that benches or seating usually should be provided for their use. However, the custom of reserving seats for private persons is to be reprobated. Moreover, benches or seating should be so arranged, especially in newly built churches, that the faithful can easily take up the bodily postures required for the different parts of the celebration and can have easy access for the reception of Holy Communion.

> Care should be taken to ensure that the faithful be able not only to see the Priest, the Deacon, and the readers but also, with the aid of modern technical means, to hear them without difficulty.

The place for the celebration conveys the image of the gathered people. The sanctuary and the places for the faithful express a diversity of offices and roles, but at the same time they form a coherent and organic unity. Rails, screens, or steps that divide, and decorative programs that embellish the sanctuary alone should be avoided.

The active participation of the congregation was the most important element in the Council's reforms. That is why the church building must do more than simply gather people. The disposition of places must enable us to act, not just see the Mass; we must be able to move in procession, receive the remains of those who have died, greet arriving brides and grooms, pray over the catechumens, interact with and be the Body of Christ.

The character and beauty of the place show the holiness of the mysteries and stimulate devotion. The iconographic program should promote greater participation and understanding and stir the senses to deeper devotion and passion for the reign of God.

Architectural Surfaces

The sacristan needs to understand the architectural elements that shape the place of liturgical action. The walls, ceiling, and floor should be considered, for they can facilitate the celebration of the liturgy and enhance communal identity or impede it.

WALLS   No element in the church complex is neutral. Even the walls themselves can help or hinder the liturgical action. The walls of the church building have an obvious function: to contain the congregation. The walls should not contain so much imagery or decoration that they distract from the focal point of the building, the altar of sacrifice. All images and colors, windows and fixtures should contribute toward unified action. The Stations of the Cross should not draw attention away from the altar.

The *Dedication of a Church and an Altar* envisions that the walls of the church be adorned with 4 or 12 crosses, candle holders and candles (see Chapter II, 22) . They mark the places of the anointing of the walls and serve as reminders of the consecration of the church to the celebration of the sacred mysteries. These candles have a long tradition that can be traced back to an understanding of the church as the image of the new Jerusalem (envisioned in Revelation 21:14 as having 12 foundation stones). If they were not installed at the time of dedication, later installation is not forbidden.

Yet these crosses and lights, important as they are, should not dominate, and should never compete with the one cross of this congregation, the one that is carried in procession and that stands by the altar for the celebration. When the candles are lit on great feasts, like the anniversary of dedication, this embracing light, these "blazing walls," will illumine the celebration of the Eucharist.

FLOORS   The most common impediment to the creation of an active space, and thus to the full engagement of the congregation in the spoken and sung responses, is the use of carpeting. It affects acoustics by absorbing sound, and it can also impede the movement of people who use wheelchairs, leg braces, crutches, or walkers.

In ceremonial books that accompanied the rites after the Council of Trent, green carpets were suggested for the sanctuary floor. More elaborate carpets were to go on the steps to the altar for high feasts. An old custom of placing oriental rugs on these steps was countenanced, despite warnings against profane symbols. In our own century, it was no accident that wall-to-wall church carpeting appeared first in affluent suburban parishes. They had the funds and they wanted to make their churches into what might be termed the "living rooms of the bourgeoisie."

The appearance of full carpeting and of other domesticating elements (baskets instead of brass vases, windowsills with green plants) was a reflection of the trend in the 1960s toward home Masses. During that period, priests and people alike were in search of some alternative to hurried Masses read in Latin before large congregations. In those first years of the "new Mass," it was a breath of fresh air to have an unhurried Mass with a small congregation in the intimacy of a home. From this it was an easy and natural next step to introduce domestic elements into the church building, and to envision the ideal church as an intimate living room.

Today, though, we recognize that this domesticating approach has its dangers. The parish is not a "family," nor do we need or even want the pillows and rugs and couches of our households when we gather as a Christian community for the prophetic Word and the Communion that promises a total transformation of the world. While what happens at Mass should transform our lives and make itself felt in the home of each member of the community, the church building itself need not look like a home.

Seating and Action Space for the Congregation

For the first thirteen hundred or more years of Christianity, there was no general seating for the congregation. Provisions were made for those who were too weak to stand, but most people stood (or at times knelt on the floor) throughout the services. The place for the congregation was open. Liturgical commentators described the communities surging toward the ambo for the homily, going to greet the arrival of the bread and wine, streaming with the gift-bearers toward the altar, pouring toward the altar for Communion. Some small barriers were created in larger churches to allow the movement of ministers through the assemblies, which were described as waves crashing against the sanctuary steps.

Only in the late Middle Ages, simultaneous with other shifts in the participation of the congregation in the Mass, did benches and chairs begin to be introduced in many churches, and with the passage of time it has become ubiquitous. Despite its prevalence, seating has never been (and is still not) required by liturgical law. It can be argued, however, that even more important than the pews and chairs are the open spaces used by the congregation: gathering spaces, aisles, as well as the space around the entrance and font, around the altar and ambo, and the devotional spaces and other chapels. When arranging moveable chairs or otherwise influencing these open spaces, sacristans should recognize the value of processions, the value of people assembling closely around font or altar. In many places, even with pews affixed to the floor, alternative seating arrangements can be envisioned and open spaces can be expanded.

Within the seating areas themselves, there should be plenty of room between rows of chairs or benches—to minimize the sense of enclosure, to permit the people to stand and face in various directions, to facilitate people to enter and leave frequently for processions (for example, to join the Communion procession), and for other interactions. The same approach should be taken regarding auxiliary equipment like hinged kneelers or kneeling hassocks, hymnal racks, or pew-end candles: they should allow as much movement by the congregation as possible.

If pew candles are positioned to mark processional passages or to embrace the whole congregation, they can contribute to a program of unified decor. They can be in position for more than weddings; they can be used for great solemnities like Christmas Time, Easter Time, Pentecost, and the dedication anniversary. And for variety, they can be decorated with greens or blossoms.

The Choir's Place in the Congregation

The same quest for unified congregations and undivided places of sacramental action must direct the position of choirs and leaders of song. The norms for the placement of musical assistants, debated through the decades of the liturgical movement and in the preparatory commissions for Vatican II, are most fully expressed in *Musicam Sacram*, 23, an instruction issued by the Vatican in 1967:

> Taking into account the layout of each church, the choir should be placed in such a way:
>
> (a) That its nature should be clearly apparent—namely, that it is a part of the whole congregation, and that it fulfills a special role;
>
> (b) That it is easier for it to fulfil its liturgical function;
>
> (c) That each of its members may be able to participate easily in the Mass, that is to say by sacramental participation.

The *General Instruction of the Roman Missal*, 312–313, offers similar notes regarding instrumentalists, and *Sing to the Lord: Music in Divine Worship*, the United States Conference of Catholic Bishops' 2008 document on music in divine worship, reiterates these values and provides even more detail (see #95–100).

More often that not, these principles have resulted in choirs being moved from the back loft to a position beside or behind the sanctuary. This zone, more or less prominent, depending upon its elevation, usually includes seating, a secondary podium for the leader of song, an organ console, music stands, and instruments, such as the piano.

When considering decorations for a given feast or liturgical time, we need to remember that this zone is to be conceived as part of the place for the congregation, not a part of the sanctuary, or a liturgical focus. Therefore, it should not be singled out for highlighting any more than the rest of the place for the congregation. Those who plan decorations should consider sight lines of the ministers of music, avoid obscuring such items as the hymn board, and take into account any existing organ case and its given decoration.

Chapter Six
The Chair for the Priest Celebrant

History

The chair for the Priest Celebrant may well be the most ancient liturgical furnishing, possibly pre-dating even the use of fixed altars. From our earliest history, Christians have associated chairs with leadership in the Church. The cathedral, which is the mother Church for Catholics in each diocese, takes its name from a chair: the *cathedra*, or chair, of the Bishop. The earliest chairs for Bishops varied considerably in shape and style, and even where they were placed in the church building, but they were always meant to call to mind the Bishop's leadership role. In the ancient world, the chair would have suggested philosopher-teacher or judge, and the Bishop had to take on both of these roles in the local church. Later, as the ministry of the priests became one of representing the Bishop outside of metropolitan centers, presidential chairs were designed for them. As the liturgy changed and ordained priests took on all of the ministries at liturgy, these chairs were radically altered or discarded and a chair was rarely seen except when the Bishop or another visiting prelate "presided" at a Mass celebrated by another priest.

Current Norms

Today, the chair for the Priest Celebrant is a focal point in the liturgical space, since from it he leads several key parts of the Mass. The chair should be strong and simple, with simple ornamentation. The *General Instruction of the Roman Missal* describes it as follows in article 310:

> The chair of the Priest Celebrant must signify his function of presiding over the gathering and of directing the prayer. Thus the more suitable place for the chair is facing the people at the head of the sanctuary, unless the design of the building or other features prevent this: as, for example, if on account of too great a distance, communication between the Priest and the congregation would be difficult, or if the tabernacle were to be positioned in the center behind the altar. In any case, any appearance of a throne is to be avoided. It is appropriate that before being put into liturgical use, the chair be blessed according to the rite described in the Roman Ritual.

The chair for the Priest Celebrant is normally movable, so sacristans and those who prepare the liturgy can collaborate with Priest Celebrants in reviewing various locations for it to find what works best in a given church building. It should always face the rest of the congregation, but the warning noted in the *General Instruction* is well taken. Often, a position behind the altar is too far from the congregation. Even though audio systems can amplify and carry sound, communication needs to be more than aural: the Priest Celebrant needs to be physically proximate to the gathered people.

The position of the chair will vary, depending on the design of the building. In congregational areas arranged with antiphonal seating (altar at one end of the congregation, ambo at the other) the chair is best placed at the ambo end. During the Liturgy of the Word, the Priest Celebrant is usually at the chair; during the Liturgy of the Eucharist the chair will be empty. Placing the chair at the ambo end of the congregational area also helps to keep the altar area free of anything but the actions specifically designated for it.

In a cathedral, there are two chairs; the *cathedra* (which is to be fixed and immovable, as a rule—see the *Ceremonial of Bishops*, 47) and the chair for a Priest Celebrant when the Bishop is not present. Both should be arranged in distinct zones that meet the criteria mentioned above.

Seating for Other Ministers

The *General Instruction of the Roman Missal* puts this simply, saying that the

> [S]eats should be arranged in the sanctuary for concelebrating Priests as well as for Priests who are present at the celebration in choir dress but without concelebrating.

> The seat for the Deacon should be placed near that of the celebrant. For the other ministers seats should be arranged so that they are clearly distinguishable from seats for the clergy and so that the ministers are easily able to carry out the function entrusted to them. (310)

The seats should be of a simpler design than the Priest Celebrant's chair, and should not be placed on either side of it. Instead, they should be located near their places of action—lectors, readers, cantor by the ambo, servers at the credence table, book-bearer accessible to the Priest Celebrant, extraordinary ministers of Holy Communion readily able to approach the altar. Any furniture that is not in use at a particular liturgy should be removed, keeping the sanctuary clear of empty chairs and unused kneelers.

Chapter Seven
The Altar

The Table of the Lord

EARLY CHRISTIANS   In each early Christian community there could be only one altar. The altar was the presence of the one Christ, the center point of the community's gathering for the sacred mysteries. This centrality was shown in different ways in various regions. In some places, the altar was like a table, with visible legs or supports. Elsewhere, the altar was an unbroken block of stone. In some places a roof called the ciborium rested on four columns outside the altar's corners, drawing attention to the altar. In a startling image of the identity of the altar with Christ, some communities began a practice that later became universal—carving five crosses into the table surface to represent Christ's five wounds. As writers of the early Church said, "the altar is Christ" (*Rite of Dedication of an Altar*, 4).

The positioning of the altar within the church building was often related to the tomb of a saint. Though a city like Rome had both its cathedral complex and its local neighborhood centers for worship, other gathering places were built over cemeteries, so that the Eucharist could be celebrated near the burial places of celebrated saints. Later, when many of these cemeteries had been transformed into parish or pilgrimage churches, permanent altars were positioned directly over the tomb of the most important martyr. In Rome, the great basilicas of St. Peter and St. Paul Outside the Walls are churches of this kind, built around the tombs of the apostles and martyrs. Homilists reminded their communities that the blood of the martyrs was rooted in the blood of Christ.

MEDIEVAL CHRISTIANS   In the Middle Ages, the altar receded from the Christian community. The table itself moved deeper and deeper into a sanctuary screened from the congregation. A huge retable, or reredos, reared up from the altar. As the ministries once exercised by deacons, lectors, and cantors were absorbed by priests, the altar table itself became longer, so that readings could be done from different ends, distinct from the Eucharistic action place at the center. At the same time, the number of altars multiplied, and it was not uncommon, at least in cathedrals and larger churches, to have multiple altars within the church, often with the Blessed Sacrament reserved in three, four, or more places.

This revolutionary change from a simple table to an altar with numerous and sometimes very large accessories did not go unchallenged. Sixteenth-century reformers called for a return to the much simpler practices of early Christianity—an uncluttered table at the center of the community, and once again free from all the trappings of retables.

CURRENT NORMS   With the reforms of the Second Vatican Council, the practice of the early Church was restored. The proclamation of the scriptures was moved from the altar to the ambo, so that the altar could be reserved for the Liturgy of the Eucharist. "High altars" were replaced with freestanding altars, which allowed the priest to move around the altar and to face the people during the Eucharistic Prayer. Side altars were also removed, so that the one altar could stand forth in the church as the preeminent sign of the one Christ.

The *General Instruction of the Roman Missal* clearly expresses the priorities of the Council reforms:

> The altar, on which is effected the Sacrifice of the Cross made present under sacramental signs, is also the table of the Lord to which the People of God is convoked to participate in the Mass, and it is also the center of the thanksgiving that is accomplished through the Eucharist. (#296)

> It is desirable that in every church there be a fixed altar, since this more clearly and permanently signifies Christ Jesus, the Living Stone (1 Pt 2:4; cf. Eph 2:20). In other places set aside for sacred celebrations, the altar may be movable.

> An altar is said to be fixed if it is so constructed as to be attached to the floor and not removable; it is said to be movable if it can be displaced.

> The altar should be built separate from the wall, in such a way that it is possible to walk around it easily and that Mass can be celebrated at it facing the people, which is desirable wherever possible. Moreover, the altar should occupy a place where it is

truly the center toward which the attention of the whole congregation of the faithful naturally turns. The altar should usually be fixed and dedicated. (298–299)

In keeping with the Church's traditional practice and with what the altar signifies, the table of a fixed altar should be of stone and indeed of natural stone. In the Dioceses of the United States of America, wood which is dignified, solid and well-crafted may be used, provided that the altar is structurally immobile. As to the supports or base for supporting the table, these may be made of any material, provided it is dignified and solid. . . . (301)

The practice of the deposition of relics of Saints, even those not Martyrs, under the altar to be dedicated is fittingly retained. However, care should be taken to ensure the authenticity of such relics. (302)

The altar table should never be treated as just any other table. It is not to be a storage place for notes or a prop to be shoved aside when a choir wants to perform. The ancient practice of bowing as we pass before the altar should be retained to honor this sign of Christ in our midst.

Altar Cloths

ORIGINS   The earliest Christians lived in a region where fine linen, especially linen from Egypt, had been highly prized for centuries. Ritual laws, codified in the book of Exodus, often demanded the use of this Egyptian cloth for screens, tabernacle hangings, and vestments. This same linen, or similar fabrics made from flax, were used for burial shrouds. It is no surprise, then, that primitive documents from the Mediterranean basin make note of the use of one fine linen cover for the altar—carrying rich memories of burial shrouds and of vesture for the most significant public rites. It was placed on the altar at the start of the Liturgy of the Eucharist and removed at its end.

LATER USAGE   By the year 1000, it seems that communities preferred to leave this cloth on the altar at all times. Local customs for such cloths continued to evolve, often multiplying their number on the altar. Eventually, churches of the Roman Rite followed the same code, using linen (or hemp) cloths on the altar. There were two white linen top cloths ("fair linens," long enough to hang to the floor on each end); two linen under-cloths for each altar (or wider cloths that, when folded, yielded two layers); and a chrismale (or "cerecloth," linen waxed on one side and of the exact dimensions of each altar's surface). The latter was the cloth that was placed under the other three at the dedication rite and could be used permanently. In addition, there were cloths for placement over all the other cloths when candelabra were used, and for each altar a "vesperale," or dust cover, that was placed over the other cloths between services. In addition, the front of the altar was adorned with frontals or *antependia*, often lavishly designed in the color of the liturgical time.

CURRENT NORMS   The regulations are much simpler in the Roman Rite today. Out of reverence for the celebration of the memorial of the Lord and for the banquet in which the Body and Blood of the Lord are offered, there should be (on an altar where this is celebrated) at least one cloth, white in color, whose shape, size, and decoration are in keeping with the altar's structure. When, in the dioceses of the United States of America, other cloths are used in addition to the altar cloth, then those cloths may be of other colors possessing Christian honorific or festive significance according to long-standing local usage, provided that the uppermost cloth covering the mensa (i.e., the altar cloth itself) is always white in color (see the *General Instruction of the Roman Missal*, 304).

Within these guidelines, there are many possibilities for the cloth used on the altar. Often, the cloth is of the exact dimensions of the table top. In other places, the cloth will be longer, hanging over the altar on all four sides. The fullest form of this kind of cloth hangs all the way to the floor and is termed "Laudean" or "Jacobean" (perhaps related to their usage in England at the time of King James). It can create an appearance of great dignity, while also serving to conceal a poorly made altar. But if the altar is well-made and dignified, it is better not to conceal it behind a cloth or antependium.

Some communities with strong, well-made altars have been rediscovering the fine practice of covering the altar only for the Liturgy of the Eucharist. This provides another ritual gesture for the preparation of the altar, and it allows the communal table to be present in all its strength. In the United States of America, under-cloths in a variety of colors and natural fabrics are permitted, and "seasonal" colors and natural fabrics other than linen can dress the table well.

Everything used at the altar should be chosen with an eye for its compatibility with the space and with other objects, but each also should have its own vitality and form.

Altar Cross

THE PROCESSIONAL CROSS   In ancient times, this was the basic Christian symbol used at the altar. After leading the community into their gathering place, it was prominently positioned for the rest of the ritual action. The cross has been the subject of mosaics and sculptures, of door reliefs and illustrations. Communities have depicted the cross as the instrument of death, the tree of life, the archetypal meeting of horizontal and vertical, and the symbol of the four directions. Surrounded by so many images of the cross, the earliest Christian communities nonetheless gave the place of honor to the one cross that led them in procession and that provided a focus during every ritual.

THE STATIONARY CROSS   By the Middle Ages, the clergy performed most of the ritual actions, and processions of the congregation were rare. Thus, processional crosses mounted on stands in the sanctuary gave way to crosses positioned at the center of the altar, just above the priest's head as he celebrated the Mass. Unlike many processional crosses, this cross generally had a *corpus* (the body of Christ) on the cross.

By the time of the Council of Trent, the style of the crucifix and its position at the center of the altar had become fairly universal. The ritual action associated with it was not the procession but the mandated glance priests gave to it during the Eucharistic Prayer. Certainly a processional cross was used from time to time, but it was no longer the principal cross of the liturgy. Though many other styles of crosses were used for devotions and decoration, the Roman Church continued to call for the altar cross to have a corpus attached. Pope Pius XII called for at least some trace of suffering to appear on the altar's crucifix (*Mediator Dei*, 62).

RETURN TO ONE CROSS   The reforms after Vatican II called for a return to the more ancient practice of using just one cross, carried in procession and placed near the altar. The latest edition of the *General Instruction of the Roman Missal* reemphasizes the importance of using a crucifix, rather than a simple cross, both for the procession and for the cross that remains near the altar during the Mass.

> [T]he cross adorned with a figure of Christ crucified, and carried in procession, may be placed next to the altar to serve as the altar cross, in which case it must be the only cross used; otherwise it is put away in a dignified place . . . (#122).

> [E]ither on the altar or near it, there is to be a cross, with the figure of Christ crucified upon it, a cross clearly visible to the assembled people. It is desirable that such a cross should remain near the altar even outside of liturgical celebrations, so as to call to mind for the faithful the saving Passion of the Lord (#308).

Utilizing the one cross, carried in procession and placed near the altar, has many benefits over the custom of affixing stationary crosses to the walls or suspending them overhead: There can be different placements for various liturgical times; ritual actions in other areas of the room (especially when all walk in the procession) and those by the altar are linked; the cross is more clearly appreciated as a ritual element than as an item to gaze at; the one cross is able to be touched or venerated by all on Friday of Holy Week.

This cross is a standard for processions and a sacred furnishing accompanying the altar; it is the primordial emblem shaping the community. Between services the processional cross can be left in its stand, near the altar yet far enough away to allow for free access to all sides of the table.

Altar Candles

The *General Instruction of the Roman Missal* says:

> The candlesticks required for the different liturgical services for reasons of reverence or the festive character of the celebration (cf. #117) should be appropriately placed either on the altar or around it, according to the design of the altar and the sanctuary, so that the whole may be harmonious and the faithful may not be impeded from a clear view of what takes place at the altar or what is placed upon it. (#307)

On or near the altar there are to be candlesticks with lighted candles, at least two, but even four, six, or, if the Bishop of the diocese celebrates, seven (see the *General Instruction of the Roman Missal*, 117). There is also to be a cross on or near the altar. The candles and cross may be carried in the Entrance Procession.

Before the reforms, the number of candles to be used was regulated by the then-familiar types of Mass (low, high, solemn high, pontifical). Today such distinctions no longer apply, for singing is now normative at all celebrations. Pastoral leaders and sacristans in each parish should review the universal and local calendars and determine which liturgical times and feasts call for more solemnity and festivity. The greater the solemnity or festivity, the more candles the parish should use. The ritual books suggest that whenever possible, the candles lit for the Mass should be part of the opening procession.

The option of placing candles on floor stands away from the table is highly recommended. This practice draws upon customs from the early Church. These two or more stands and candles obviously should be selected and arranged in a way that facilitates action, or at the very least so that they don't block sight lines or paths of action. In addition, they should complement the other furnishings of the area and relate well to the overall decor. It is not required that the candles be evenly split on either side of the altar, nor that they nudge right up beside it. Through the various liturgical times, we can find ways that make our sanctuaries more conducive to action; for example, by grouping the cross and candles to one side of the area, by arranging flowers and candles away from the altar, by placing a candle at each of the four corners of an altar platform, or by adding more candles for great feasts.

Credence Table

This table should be conveniently placed, but as unobtrusively as possible, and it should be large enough to do the job. The table will have to accommodate the vessels needed for the Mass—the basin and pitcher for the hand-washing, the cruets of water and wine, and the chalices to be used for Holy Communion. These usually remain on the table until needed, and then are returned there after Holy Communion to be purified by the priest or deacon. The need for many cups may suggest the use of trays that also must fit on the credence table. If the cloth will be placed on the altar during the preparation of the gifts, this will probably also be prepared on the credence table. The credence table should be large enough to be used at the most elaborate rites of the year.

Depending upon the alignment of the major furnishings and the sacristy, the credence can be off to one side of the sanctuary. There is no longer a universally prescribed side from which acolytes need to approach the celebrant at the altar. The credence table could also be behind the altar on a lower level. If the credence is behind the altar, however, it must not resemble a high altar, nor should it compete with the altar table for attention in any other way. The credence table can be a table a bit higher than a domestic table, or a large shelf mounted by a wall bracket, or even a large niche in the wall. Other than the requirement that the credence table be as unobtrusive as possible, there are no set rules governing coverings that might be placed over it. In congregational areas where the chair of the Priest Celebrant is quite removed from the altar, another auxiliary table might be near the chair to hold such things as *The Roman Missal*, water buckets for the sprinkling rite, hymnals, and intercession texts. Where the community fully surrounds the table, the credence table should be well away from the central axis, so as not to obscure the action.

Book Stands

There is no requirement that a book stand be used for *The Roman Missal* when it is placed on the altar, but some priest celebrants prefer this so that they don't have to lean over as they lead the congregation in prayer. A plain cushion, or a stand made of metal or wood, would be appropriate for this purpose. If a book stand is used, the acolyte should put it on the altar during the preparation, then remove it after Holy Communion. Freed from stands, candles, cross, and cloth, the altar can be seen for the sacred table that it is.

Many parishes also use a book stand for the *Book of the Gospels* when it is placed on the altar. This stand, too, is optional. The *Book of the Gospels* can simply be laid flat, or it can be propped against a cushion. Many parishes use a book stand so that the book can stand upright and be seen by the entire congregation. If such a stand is used, it should be of worthy materials—wood or stone, not plastic.

Chapter Eight

The Ambo: A Place for Proclaiming the Word of God

Every liturgy includes the celebration of the Word of God—Mass, Baptism, Marriage, blessings, even the Rite of Penance. The congregation is more than a mere audience addressed by reader, psalmist, deacon, or priest. Those who listen attentively also are called to act intently: to participate in the Gospel Procession by standing and turning toward the ambo, to join in psalms and acclamations, to pray for the catechumens being dismissed, to profess their faith, and to offer intercessions. In this interaction with the saving word, we all receive fresh life.

Original Places for the Word

Ancient synagogues had a raised area with a reading desk where the Word of God was proclaimed. Called a bema, it continues to be used to this day. In some of the old synagogues in America the bema is located in the middle of the congregation. As Christian communities designated specific buildings for liturgy, they usually continued the custom of using a raised and centered place for the proclamation of scripture. The early Christian bema (or ambo, as it is now often called) was distinct from the altar and *cathedra*. In Constantinople, it was usually located on axis with the altar, but considerably extended into the open congregational area. In Syria, extant sites show its location on a sort of island or platform in the middle of the nave. In Rome, a second ambo was soon added, and both were located well into the congregational area.

The Loss of a Specific Place

Through the Middle Ages, the ministries of lector, cantor, and deacon were absorbed by the Priest Celebrant, who conducted all the action at a wall-mounted altar. On occasion, rubrics specified the use of smaller lecterns, but these were always in the sanctuary proper. In a parallel move, synagogues were designed, especially in recent times, with the bema located near the ark at the end of the place for the congregation. In designing both churches and synagogues, architects began using many of the same theater-like floor plans, as assemblies simply sat facing the unified stage for all holy actions. The loss of the bema, or ambo, in both communities corresponded to the rise of spectator status for the congregation. Of course, there were exceptions. When sermons were given, and this was not at every liturgy, a pulpit near the congregation often was used. Yet these were often almost non-liturgical moments. The "real" action was reserved for the sanctuary.

Current Reforms

Today, the ambo has been restored to its place of importance in the Church's liturgy. The *Introduction to the Lectionary for Mass* (#32–34) describes this area of the church complex as follows:

> There must be a place in the church that is somewhat elevated, fixed, and of a suitable design and nobility. It should reflect the dignity of God's word and be a clear reminder to the people that in the Mass the table of God's word and of Christ's body is placed before them. The place for the readings must also truly help the people's listening and attention during the Liturgy of the Word. Great pains must therefore be taken, in keeping with the design of each church, over the harmonious and close relationship of the ambo with the altar.

> Either permanently or at least on occasions of greater solemnity, the ambo should be decorated simply and in keeping with its design. . . .

> In order that the ambo may properly serve its liturgical purpose, it is to be rather large, since on occasion several ministers must use it at the same time. Provision must also be made for the readers to have enough light to read the text and, as required, to have modern sound equipment enabling the congregation to hear them without difficulty.

Too many ambos look as if they were borrowed from a lecture hall. The ambo is not just a shaft with a book holder. It is a raised and rather large place, with a reading desk of dignified proportions. Even a small podium can look and function well if there is a wider space or open platform around it. On solemn occasions, candles and even flowers can be used around this place, demarcating the larger area, but not crowding up against the reading desk. *Built of Living Stones* suggests that before and after the liturgy "the open Book of the Gospels or a copy of the Scriptures" may be displayed on or near the ambo (#62).

Just as the early Christian ambos were often located in the midst of the congregation, and the medieval pulpits were outside the sanctuary, there is no universal decree confining the place for proclamation to the sanctuary. The location may be determined by values such as visibility, the need for a dignified space distinct from altar and font, the desirability of having the ambo fixed, and the local building style (see the *General Instruction of the Roman Missal*, 309).

Secondary Podium

The Church documents are clear that the ambo, as the place of God's Word, is to be reserved for the Liturgy of the Word, which includes the readings, the Responsorial Psalm, the homily, and the Prayer of the Faithful, as well as the *Exsultet* at the Easter Vigil. It should not be used for the leading of song or the making of any announcements, for which a secondary podium or lectern may be used. Some Priest Celebrants use a third podium at the chair. This is not a good practice. The prayer texts are not proclamations, and the use of such a podium further diverts attention from the ambo, and replaces the human act of an assistant holding the book. All elements of furnishing and decoration have an effect, one way or another, on the liturgical action.

Chapter Nine

The Sanctuary

A Distinctive Design

The rooms used for the Eucharist in the earliest centuries were unified and open spaces. With the passing of time, a distinct sanctuary developed, separated from the nave by such architectural elements as choir screens and altar rails. With the reforms of the Second Vatican Council, and the restoration of the participation of the people, we have seen a return to a more unified worship space. The sanctuary is still clearly demarcated and designed, but the intent is no longer to keep the laity out. Rather, the distinction of the sanctuary area is intended to help focus the attention of the congregation, to allow enough open space for the rites, and to give a kind of breathing space around our holiest symbols, those central focal points of holy action. The *General Instruction of the Roman Missal* (294–295) highlights these values.

> The People of God which is gathered for Mass is coherently and hierarchically ordered, and this finds its expression in the variety of ministries and the variety of actions according to the different parts of the celebration. Hence the general arrangement of the sacred building must be such that in some way it conveys the image of the assembled

congregation and allows the appropriate ordering of all the participants, as well as facilitating each in the proper carrying out of his function. . . .

The sanctuary is the place where the altar stands, the Word of God is proclaimed, and the Priest, the Deacon, and the other ministers exercise their functions. It should be appropriately marked off from the body of the church either by its being somewhat elevated or by a particular structure and ornamentation. It should, moreover, be large enough to allow the Eucharist to be easily celebrated and seen.

In some buildings, the sanctuary is set off and made appropriately visible by risers or platforms. In others (for example, where the ambo and altar occupy different ends of the space for the congregation) they are distinguished by distinctive design and by floor space free from all other appointments. Decoration plays an important role here. A row of plants where an altar rail used to be may perpetuate division, separating people from their common table. On the other hand, flowers or candles at the foot of the four corners of the altar platform may help provide just the right marking. This balancing of distinct actions against the need for a unified congregation must be the foremost consideration in planning decorations.

Space for the Rites

The sanctuary area is designed and used for the celebration of Mass, but we should be attuned to the many other rites that are celebrated in this place besides the Eucharist—weddings, funerals, anointings and blessings, for example. The arrangement and decoration of the space should keep these various uses in mind. For example, a couple being married should be seated in the sanctuary, in positions that allow their participation in Word and Eucharist. At a funeral Mass, the coffin could be placed on the sanctuary floor, perhaps on a bed of flowers near the Paschal candle or other candles. The procession with the gifts should come to the chair of the Priest Celebrant or to the altar, not just to an old Communion rail (or an imagined one). Those being blessed or anointed do not need to stay outside of the sanctuary. This is not just "letting the laity in." It is using the ritual center for the holiest of actions.

Space for Few Decorations

The sanctuary should contain very few items other than the altar, ambo, chair of the Priest Celebrant, cross, and candles. Other things (statues, "seasonal theme" art, banners and their stands) should be in the sanctuary only in the rarest of circumstances—and should never impede sight lines and movement. The emphasis should be on simplicity, on the central furnishings. Chairs, kneelers, and candles not utilized for a rite should be stored out of sight. In other words, keep clutter out.

The United States Conference of Catholic Bishops discourages the placement of national flags in the sanctuary, but the local Bishop may determine the practice within the diocese. The *Order of Christian Funerals* (38, 132) expressly forbids them in the liturgy. Sacristans faced with a need to use flags on a special occasion should ideally place them in the vestibule or gathering space, perhaps with a book of remembrance or a place to record intentions, rather than in the sanctuary.

Chapter Ten

A Place for Instrumentalists and Leaders of Music

Liturgy and Music

Music is not an audience-pleasing embellishment, but an integral part of Catholic worship. The principal musicians of the liturgy are the members of the congregation and the Priest Celebrant. Through chant and acclamation we do not simply pray at Mass—we pray the Mass. It is not mere poetry, but the very heart of our belief, that the angels and the redeemed form a heavenly choir, that the Church on earth joins the Church in heaven in the praise of God. In the liturgy, we join in the unending Paschal hymn, "the canticle of victory over sin and death . . . the song of the saints" (*Sing to the Lord: Music in Divine Worship*, 7). To assist this singing body of Christ, we need instrumentalists and cantors, choirs and music directors. But we must resist the temptation to let the "experts" take care of the music, and claim our privilege— and responsibility—to sing the Church's liturgy.

The history of music at liturgy is a sad story of divorce. The shifting position of the choir in our church buildings gives evidence to the division of music and worship. As the participation of the faithful declined in the early Middle Ages, music was increasingly handled by clerics, grouped at the side of the altar. Over the later Middle Ages and through the Renaissance and Baroque eras, they moved to positions farther away from and above the sanctuary and congregation. By the time churches were built in the Americas, the choir and organ were usually in a back loft. Congregations understood their role to be one of listening to the music, which accompanied but was clearly distinct from the sacraments being celebrated.

These changes had a negative impact on sacred music; religious compositions were no longer rooted in the liturgy and in the prayer of assemblies voicing praise through liturgical times and feasts. Communal singing was impaired as the people lost their principal and most historic forum for becoming a vocalizing body. Liturgy was dramatically affected by the transfer of the people's acclamations and psalmody to small groups of servers or to the choir.

Today, we are newly aware of the importance of music in our worship. We have had a generation of experience with singing the Mass; we are finding our voices again. We are also finding out what works, and what doesn't, as contemporary settings of the Eucharistic acclamations and the other parts of the Mass come and go. With the implementation of the third edition of *The Roman Missal*, many priests are learning ancient chant tones and are introducing their assemblies to the beauty of sung liturgy. Music is here to stay.

Places for Musicians

Today, we recognize that distant galleries or lofts are not the ideal place for the choir, any more than they would be for readers, extraordinary ministers of Holy Communion, or other actively involved liturgical ministers. The choir, cantor, and psalmist are part of the congregation, though with a distinct role, and this should be reflected in the arrangements made for them. "Musicians and musical instruments should be located so as to enable proper interaction with the liturgical action, with the rest of the assembly, and among the various musicians. Ideally, ministers of music are located so as to enable their own full participation by being able to see and hear the Liturgy" (*Sing to the Lord*, 95).

The participation of the musicians in the liturgy is, however, not the only area to be considered in the placement of the choir or musical ensemble. Acoustics need to be taken into account as well. Whenever the choir is visible to the congregation, the music ministry space needs to be uncluttered, a clear reflection of "the sacredness of the music ministry," and the music ministers themselves are "attentive members of the gathered assembly and should never constitute a distraction" (*Sing to the Lord*, 100, 96).

Some members of the music ministry take on special roles as cantor, song leader, or psalmist. The Responsorial Psalm, as an integral part of the Liturgy of the Word, should ideally be sung from the ambo or another readily visible location. The cantor or song leader should be clearly visible to all when leading the singing of the people. When, however, the people are able to join fully in the singing without being led, there is no need for a cantor or song leader to be visible (see *Sing to the Lord*, 97).

The Pipe Organ and Other Instruments

Among musical instruments, the Roman Rite gives pride of place to the pipe organ. "Whether as an accompaniment for singing or as a solo instrument, this instrument adds splendor to sacred celebrations, offers praise to God, fosters a sense of prayer in the faithful, and raises their spirits to God" (*Book of Blessings*, 1325). The organ is so associated with festivity and joy that its use is reduced in the liturgical times of Advent and Lent, and it is not used at all from the Gloria on the Thursday of Holy Week until the Gloria at the Easter Vigil, when its reappearance helps to mark the return of Easter joy (see the *General Instruction of the Roman Missal*, 313). The documents do not specify where the organ should be placed, only that its placement be convenient for its primary purpose of accompanying the choir and the congregation.

The norms allow for and encourage the use of other instruments at liturgies. This can be particularly helpful when liturgical gatherings form in a part of the church complex far from organ or piano. Examples might include rites of reception in entryways, Baptisms in separate baptistries, outdoor blessings and processions, Eucharistic devotions in a separate chapel of reservation, and committals and other liturgical visits at cemeteries. Singing is normative in all such rites, so leaders of song are necessary, as are portable instruments.

In collaboration with the leaders of music and the instrumentalists themselves, sacristans should see to the safe maintenance and storage of instruments left in the church complex. This includes not only routine security procedures, but also careful attention to environmental factors such as temperature and humidity. Before temperature and humidity controls are set, local experts on the maintenance of the various musical instruments should be consulted.

Auxiliary Spaces

Ministers of music also need a storage place for sheet music, books, and other materials. And if choirs or individual ministers such as the cantor regularly vest in choir robes or albs (a highly recommended practice) then they also need a place to vest. Both of these needs might well be satisfied by a common vesting room for all ministers. In large parishes, particularly, a separate room might be used not only for storage and vesting, but for rehearsals as well.

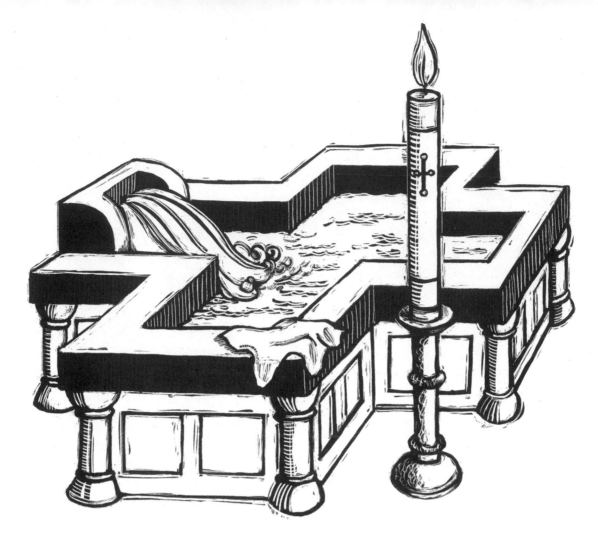

Chapter Eleven

The Baptistry

A Place Reserved for Baptism

SEPARATE BAPTISTRIES Early church complexes usually included a special place for Baptism. Though some romantics envision catechumens going down to the local river or sea, the event was too closely related to the Easter Vigil and Eucharist of the community for this to become normative. Besides, our earliest ancestors in faith understood Baptism as a dying and rising, or a bathing; the architecture and furnishings of tombs and baths expressed their belief better than an open body of water.

As cathedral complexes became public architecture, their urban planning often included a special separate building for Baptisms. These buildings often were quite large, and they drew on then-current forms of public baths or tombs. The exact shapes of the baptistries, their placement in relationship to the rest of the city center and cathedral complex, and local meanings differed from region to region, city to city. In several examples, the octagon shape is used, suggesting the Eighth Day of paradise after our current time of seven days. The hexagon, with its reference to the sixth day (Friday) and to death with Christ is also used; the baptistry is often placed by the entryway, because Baptism is entrance into the church; in other places it is placed north of the congregation, the archetypal shadowy or pagan side. So diverse were the local traditions, so complicated were the adaptations of one city's patterns by another, that generalizations about early baptistries are of little use. This is not to minimize the importance of history, but simply to highlight its immense variety and richness. The shape, design, and location of the place for Baptism were matters of great consequence for the early churches. They wanted the movement between parts of the complex to flow in good ritual order, and they wanted their baptistries to express certain truths of the faith.

THE SHRINKING OF BAPTISTRIES   As part of the general devolution of liturgical forms, noted in every aspect of liturgical history, with the rise of infant Baptism as the norm, the public catechumenate at the heart of the city died out. Separate baptistries still were built in many conservative regions, but the trend was toward merging a smaller font into a corner of the place of the congregation. Despite these changes, communities continued to believe that the shapes of the baptistry niche and of the font were important. They carried on their local traditions of circles or hexagons, squares or octagons, even though they had sometimes forgotten the original significance of these shapes.

The baptistry has continued to be an important focus in our churches. Official decrees and commentators have always warned those responsible for liturgical furnishings that the font is not just an object to put in some convenient empty space. It has always needed its own area, and this zone has been related to the other parts of the church complex. The space certainly shrank over the millennia, but the need for a special area was never totally forgotten.

CURRENT NORMS   The *General Introduction to Christian Initiation (25),* (printed before the rites for baptizing adults and the rites for baptizing children younger than catechetical age) reinforces this sense that a reserved place is necessary. It then notes the traditional options that still are operative:

> The baptistery or the area where the baptismal font is located should be reserved for the sacrament of baptism and should be worthy to serve as the place where Christians are reborn in water and the Holy Spirit. The baptistery may be situated in a chapel either inside or outside the church or in some other part of the church easily seen by the faithful; it should be large enough to accommodate a good number of people.

The *Book of Blessings* (1083–1084) summarizes these options while calling communities to see how the various parts of the church complex relate:

> In the case both of a baptistry that is erected apart from the main body of the church for the celebration of the entire baptismal rite and of a font that is set up within the church itself, everything must be arranged in such a way as to bring out the connection of baptism with the word of God and with the eucharist, the high point of Christian initiation.

A baptistry separated from the body of the church is to be worthy of the sacrament celebrated there and is to be set aside exclusively for baptism, as befits the place where, from the womb of the church, so to speak, Christians are reborn through water and the Holy Spirit.

DECORATING THE BAPTISTRY   Whether the baptistry is large or small, separated from the congregation area or visible from it, every parish church has one. We should see to its maintenance, provisioning, and decoration.

As in other parts of the church complex, the architectural surfaces should be studied. The colors and textures and materials of the walls, ceiling, and floor will help or hinder the action of Baptism. For example, the floor should not be covered with a carpet, because it will get wet; tile mosaics or fine patterns of stone are far more fitting. The ceiling, too, can be decorated, and the ancient practice of suspending a canopy over the area will be helpful for defining the space if it is near the main nave of the church building. Not every section of the church should be decorated at every liturgical time, but when higher festivity in the baptistry is suggested (Easter Time, especially), the walls, arches, windows, portals, and support systems can be fitting fields for decorations. Festooning the entrance portal or overhead canopy with greens or flowers is far more respectful of the font's power and far more visible than putting flower pots up against the font itself. As always, decorations should aid, not impede, the liturgical action, so careful consideration should be given to the movement of priests, deacons, candidates, sponsors, godparents, and parents in and out of the baptistry.

Font of Life

The font of living water is the heart of both the baptistry and of the community that is born there. One of the more obvious reforms of the twentieth century was the reemergence of large fonts. Set in the floor or resting on it, these pool-sized fonts are in many ways similar to the fonts preserved in early Christian complexes. The revived preference for large fonts does not spring from mere antiquarianism, but rather from a deliberate attempt to recover the fullness of the sacramental form by allowing those to be baptized actually to enter into the waters.

The witness of immersion Baptism was so strong during the first millennium, that throughout the second millennium the Roman Rite maintained the rubrics that allowed for immersion. Even as Baptisms were done almost universally by pouring a small amount of water, the ritual book maintained the historical record. As parishes have reexperienced this once almost-forgotten action of immersion, norms for larger fonts have been issued. They can help us appreciate this most sacred place.

> The baptismal font . . . should be spotlessly clean and of pleasing design. . . . As for the rite of baptizing, either immersion, which is more suitable as a symbol of participation in the death and resurrection of Christ, or pouring may lawfully be used. (*General Introduction to Christian Initiation*, 19, 22)

> Baptism by immersion is the fuller and more expressive sign of the sacrament and, therefore, provision should be made for its more frequent use in the baptism of

adults. The provision of the *Rite of Christian Initiation of Adults* for partial immersion, namely, immersion of the candidate's head, should be taken into account. (*National Statutes for the Catechumenate*, 17)

Living Water

Decorations in the baptistry should highlight the architecture of the space rather than crowding plants around the font, which may actually impede the celebration of the sacrament. Most importantly, we need to be zealous in our care for the water itself. Speaking of this primary element, current norms continue the best of Christian tradition:

> The water used in baptism should be true water and, both for the sake of authentic sacramental symbolism and for hygienic reasons, should be pure and clean. . . . If the climate requires, provision should be made for the water to be heated beforehand. (*General Introduction to Christian Initiation*, 18, 20)

> In order to enhance its force as a sign, the font should be designed in such a way that it functions as a fountain of running water. . . . (*Book of Blessings*, 1085)

The maintenance of clean water normally requires a filtered circulation system, but other tools need to be available; for example, nets or strainers on long poles. Similarly detailed plans need to be in place for the warming of water. On a regular schedule when the baptistry is not in use, the font needs to be emptied for a full cleaning.

Mesh guards, added for the safety of small children, drastically alter the clear, clean look of the water. Security provisions always should be a part of the initial design but, where re-fitting is necessary, these safeguards should be as inconspicuous as possible. The concern for safety actually points to a reason for keeping the font in a dedicated area, away from the traffic of gathering or sharing refreshment.

Running or living water obviously makes a sound. This should not be muffled as if it were intrusive; chutes or splash boards between levels of a font often weaken the design of the font in addition to silencing the water. Of course, a font too close to ambo or altar or chair of the Priest Celebrant can be distracting. This is precisely why our tradition calls for a distinct baptistry area by the entrance or in another separate place.

Paschal Candle

THE YEAR'S LIGHT This is the "pillar, / which glowing fire ignites for God's honor" (*Exsultet*). Casting its shifting light, the wax column leads the community into the church for the celebration of the Vigil. It is at the center of the year whose date is incised on it, at the center of the congregation that bears fire from its flame. It remains lit for all assemblies of the Fifty Days of Easter Time. And then it graces the baptistry and, throughout the rest of the year in many communities, the resting place of the coffin.

This always has been the largest candle of the community, made from the finest wax and decorated with great care. This heritage makes a sacristan's work easier. Parish members are often happy to work on its fabrication. If volunteers having the requisite skills and willingness cannot be found, then other options should be explored, such as engaging a professional artist or shopping carefully in church-goods stores and catalogs that have a reputation for quality merchandise.

Despite the availability of "perpetual Paschal candles" that are more plastic tube than candle (see page 29), a fresh candle must be used each year. Remaining parts of the former candle can be melted down as part of the preparation of the new one, or else they should be disposed of in a reverent manner. Two traditions suggest ways to recycle the wax and paraffin: Old candles in England used to be melted down and made into smaller tapers for parish use; at Rome, the remnants of the Paschal candle were used to make wax medallions impressed with the figure of a lamb. These discs, known as *agnusdei*, were kept through the year as a reminder of Easter.

DECORATIONS   There are equally rich traditions for decorating this pillar, all of them a decided improvement over the sticky decals issued by vendors. The rite suggests incisions in the wax: a cross, the first and last letters of the Greek alphabet (alpha and omega), and the numerals of the year. It also recommends the insertion of five pieces of incense.

The incisions can be made by the Priest Celebrant at the start of the Vigil, but certain preparations are advisable. Well before the Vigil, an artist can mark the design on the wax. Depending on the depth of the markings, made prior to Holy Saturday, the Priest Celebrant can simply trace or deepen these incisions at the beginning of the Vigil. If the incisions are to be accented with color, commercial decals should be bypassed in favor of engaging a professional artist to perform this work, as well as to add any other decorations.

Well in advance of the Vigil, the incense pieces also should be prepared. Most commercially produced paschal candles provide wax "nails" encasing a bit of incense, but another design using larger pieces of incense can also be prepared for insertion.

In addition to these traditional decorations, local artists can use subtle reliefs or colors to create a pillar of fire that is truly dignified. This form of liturgical art must be kept sublime so that the candle is not lost in the embellishments.

SIZE OF CANDLE AND STAND   Most vendors sell paschal candles that are just under or a little over two inches in diameter, with a height of three or three-and-a-half feet. In some places, this will be a fine size. Within the limits set by the ability of the deacon or another minister to carry it steadily, some communities may want a larger candle. In the interests of greater size, however, the ritual actions should not be omitted. This is, after all, a ritual object and not just a decoration. It is self-defeating for a parish to have a paschal candle so large that it cannot be carried in procession or used to spread its flame to other candles.

The size limit of the candle is more often set by the size of its stand, or of the fixture (called a sleeve) at the top of the stand. Existing stands sometimes can be fitted with new sleeves, or new stands might be procured over the years. Though there is only one candle each year, it could be located in different areas and in different stands throughout the year. For example:

- Through Easter to Pentecost, the candle is placed near the ambo or in the middle of the sanctuary. At the Vigil itself, the rite notes its movement from the place of fire to this stand, from the stand to the font and back again. It is lit throughout the Easter season, at least for the Sunday liturgies and other solemn occasions, though it may be lit for every Easter Mass, even on weekdays.

- From Pentecost night through the last baptisms before Lent or the Triduum, it is in a place of honor within the baptistry. Lit for every celebration there, it is the source of light for the candles of infants baptized through the year.

- The *Order of Christian Funerals* allows for the continuation of a custom popular in many regions. Taken from the baptistry or from its Easter Time position, the candle can be placed where the coffin will rest during the funeral rites. If the body will be received into the church for prayer vigils on the night before the funeral, the candle also can be in the place of vigil. During Easter Time, the coffin can be placed near the candle rather than moving the candle to the customary place for the coffin. There is no rubric restricting the coffin to a draped trolley in the center aisle.

Baptismal Candles

After his or her Baptism, each neophyte receives a baptismal candle as a remembrance. The candle is a symbol of the all-important Sacrament of Baptism, and it should stay with the baptized person until death, lit perhaps for Easter and on the baptismal anniversary if it falls at a time other than Easter. Even though the annual lighting of the baptismal candle may be rare in most communities, we can encourage its observance by providing the newly baptized with candles of sufficient size. Tiny candles won't do. Instead, choose large candles and have them decorated with Easter images by local artists. Prior to their use, baptismal candles should be kept in the sacristy or in an unobtrusive storage place within the baptistry.

Holy Oils

In many churches, the ambry, or place of the holy oils, is located near the baptistry. The oil of the sick and the oil of the catechumens bear names that denote their usage. The third, and the most important of the holy oils, is chrism. This mixture of oil and perfume is used at the holiest of moments that define Christian life—Baptism, Confirmation, Ordination, and the Dedication of Churches and Altars. Chrism also was used at the liturgies for coronations.

According to the Rite of Blessing for Holy Oils (#3–4), only olive oil should be used, or where circumstances warrant, other oil derived from plants. The perfume is unspecified, but most dioceses use one of the scents prepared and marketed as chrism fragrance.

On the morning of Thursday of Holy Week or at another time in late Lent, the Bishop presides at a Chrism Mass wherein these oils are blessed for the whole diocese. To show its importance in setting apart persons and buildings, chrism is said to be "consecrated." This setting apart, principally through the sacraments of initiation, is not a setting above or beyond. It is a consecration for service to and for the world and its transformation. Thus, the texts for the consecration rite speak of those marked by chrism as "radiant with the goodness of life," shining God's goodness throughout the world.

The Chrism Mass is a celebration of diocesan unity, a recognition of the various orders of liturgical service, of the ministries with the sick and with catechumens, of the way of life that makes those anointed with the chrism radiant. The Chrism Mass is complemented by a wonderful ritual in each parish at the beginning of the Evening Mass of the Lord's Supper on Thursday of Holy Week, when the oils to be used by the parish through the year, brought from the Chrism Mass by parish representatives (pastor, sacristan and/or others) are carried in the offertory procession and formally presented before the gifts of bread and wine. Texts for this rite are available from the United States Conference of Catholic Bishops.

Though most oils used during the year will come from this supply, additional oil of catechumens can be blessed by a priest (*Rite of Christian Initiation of Adults*, 101–102). Similarly, oil of the sick can be blessed in the context of the rite (*Pastoral Care of the Sick*, 21–22).

VESSELS FOR THE HOLY OILS   There are several kinds of vessels needed in every parish. First of all, every parish should have a set of three vessels for the year's supply of holy oils. These are called chrismatories, or a variant of that word, such as chrismals, or ampullae. The set of vessels used by the cathedral will probably be enormous—the size for a given parish much less so—depending on how much oil the parish uses. As described in the *Roman Ritual,* the vessels must be worthy of their function and closed in such a way to prevent spillage and maintain freshness. Many sacristans seem to prefer glass jars or decanters, but well-crafted ceramic or metal vessels can be used as well.

Second, parishes will need some smaller containers, especially for carrying the oil of the sick. Sometimes called "stocks," the small cylinders of metal, stuffed with cotton, are familiar to all sacristans, but other containers that not only will hold the oil, but permit generous pouring or rubbing, can be sought out as well.

Finally, vessels will sometimes be needed to hold portions of oil poured from the main vessels during liturgical actions. For example, when moving from one sick person to another at a communal anointing, the ministers will need smaller pitchers or bowls for the oil.

REPOSITORY FOR THE HOLY OILS   The *Roman Ritual* includes few notes about this place of reservation, but it should be secure, protected by a lock, and located in a public area of the church complex. Its case or door might be translucent, if this will not unduly minimize security. Other materials should be in keeping with the architectural surfaces. Vessels for the three oils may be kept in the same case or might be reserved in separate repositories. If kept together, the baptistry is the most obvious and popular place for them to reside. If they are not kept together, then at least the chrism should be stored in the baptistry; the oil of catechumens might be kept in the meeting place of the catechumens, the oil of the sick kept where intentions for the sick can be written nearby.

There is no universal practice here, but it seems quite clear that the oils, even in their smallest vessels, are not to be kept permanently in a priest's jacket, in the rectory, or in a safe or cabinet of the sacristy. The most popular custom, before the reforms of this past century, was to reserve the oils near the altar in a case affixed to the wall. The rite of anointing notes that priests should return the small vessel "to the place where it is kept with proper respect" (*Pastoral Care of the Sick*, 22). Reverence for the oils and for the church they serve necessitate the reservation of all of the parish's oils in one common repository or three individual repositories, one for each oil. Thus, the oil from the smaller vessels not used on a given visit to the sick is to be poured back into the larger vessel, or the several smaller vessels that are carried to the sick are to be reserved in the same repository.

Other Requisites for the Baptistry

PLACE FOR STORAGE   Unless the vesting room or sacristy is close by, a small, unobtrusive cabinet or credenza might be needed. In the cabinet or nearby sacristy or vesting room, the following items should be stored: the ritual for the Baptism of infants and any song sheets needed for the congregation; baptismal candles; matches; candle-lighter/extinguisher for the paschal candle and possibly for transferring light from it to baptismal candles; tapers for the lighter; receptacle for burnt matches; water vessels; towels; and perhaps baptismal robes.

WATER VESSELS   Several kinds of vessels and sprinklers will be needed, their size determined by the size of the font and local ceremonial customs. If fonts are large enough to accommodate the pouring of water over an adult standing in it (the traditional method of immersion), then a large pitcher, or amphora, will be needed. (The method familiar in Baptist communities, the plunging of the candidate into the water, is called "submersion" to distinguish it from the more traditional immersion form.) If Baptism still is celebrated by pouring the water over the forehead of the individual into a small font, the baptizing minister may use his hand, a shell, or another small vessel or pitcher. Some seashells work very well. What's more, they come directly from nature, which makes them highly desirable in terms of the value that the liturgy places on natural materials. Metal shells are available from church goods catalogs.

Baptismal water is used regularly for the Rite for the Blessing and Sprinkling of Water on Sundays and after the renewal of baptismal promises at the Easter Vigil and on Easter Sunday. It is also a part of many "occasional rites"—Marriage, funeral, and various orders of blessing. The traditional bucket (situla) or a beautiful bowl with a complementary sprinkler are better symbols than the combined-unit sprinklers with reservoirs that look like microphones. The terms *aspersorium* and *aspergillum* in contemporary usage have come to mean either the bucket or the sprinkler, or both. The sprinkler can be metal, a brush, or branches. Traditionally, branches of hyssop, laurel, palm, and boxwood were favored. Wisps of straw and the tail of a fox have been used, although the latter would probably distract people from the liturgical gesture.

If the laudable practice of bringing baptismal water home continues in the local community, additional vessels might be made available (small bottles with twist tops) for those who do not bring their own container. The water for this, as for the other rites described here, should not be drawn from the ugly vats seen in so many sacristies over the first half of the past century. The font should be large enough to provide this water. If it is too small, then the community should use a more dignified tank in which to store baptismal water. This should be near the baptistry, not hidden in the sacristy.

Towels   For the Baptism of adults by immersion, very large or bath-size towels should be used. They can be held by godparents, then wrapped about the neophytes to catch the dripping water as they step out of the font. Much smaller towels will be needed for the immersion of infants, and still smaller ones for the pouring of water over infants. Ideally, a parish should have plenty of towels in all sizes. The middle sizes also can be used for the washing of the feet on Thursday of Holy Week. The smaller ones can double as hand towels for the washing of hands at the preparation of the altar. All towels should be very absorbent; the traditional material is linen.

Baptismal Garments   Local customs will determine what robe (called "chrisom" in some liturgical traditions) is provided for adult neophytes and for children of catechetical age. Parishes should give priority to the alb. It is the basic garment of all liturgical ministers, as well as the traditional baptismal garment. Albs are readily available from many suppliers. (See pages 121–24 for a fuller description of albs.) If the neophytes keep their robes after taking them off at the end of the Vigil, the expense might be borne by special donors.

For the Baptism of infants, most parents dress their infants for the occasion in wonderful christening dresses sometimes passed on from generation to generation. If there will be immersion Baptism, then the baby can be wrapped "in swaddling clothes" (a towel is usually adequate) until the Baptism, and vested in the gown after. If families are unable to provide white garments like this, then a special group of parish members might be able to provide gowns that carry on the wonderfully full tradition of flowing, white vesture.

Place for Drying and Vesting   With immersion Baptism, a side room will be necessary. If none presently exists, it should be a part of any renovation or new construction plans, perhaps with the vesting room and the baptistry near one another and the entrance. For the immersion of infants, at least a drying table with soft towels is needed.

Chapter Twelve

Catechumeneon: Gathering Place for Catechesis and Prayer

The Catechumens

The *Rite of Christian Initiation of Adults* presumes that catechumens will be dismissed from the congregation near the conclusion of the Liturgy of the Word, before the intercessions and Profession of Faith (see *Rite of Christian Initiation of Adults*, 67). Buildings and rooms designed for the gathering of the catechumens and located near the church are by no means a new concept. Archaeological and historical evidence can trace them back to the earliest centuries of Christianity. Scholars have termed this part of the church complex the "catechumeneon."

Today, the place of this sharing most often is called the "center for the catechumenate" (*Rite of Christian Initiation of Adults*, 92). This meeting after the Liturgy of the Word of the Sunday Mass also may include a minor exorcism, a blessing, or a rite of anointing (fn., *Rite of Christian Initiation of Adults*, 89).

Whatever term is employed, there needs to be a special place for this Sunday gathering. It also could be used by the catechumens during the week for prayer and catechesis. The celebrations of the word (and exorcisms, blessings, or anointings) that may accompany these catechetical sessions also can take place in the same center or room, or in another nearby part of the church complex. The center also should accommodate any uncatechized adults who may be preparing for Confirmation and Eucharist and who may be participating with the catechumens in catechetical sessions or celebrations of the word (*Rite of Christian Initiation of Adults*, 402, 407). The same should apply to baptized, catechized Christians preparing for entrance into full communion (*Rite of Christian Initiation of Adults*, 478). And the room could be used by "inquirers" as well (*Rite of Christian Initiation of Adults*, 39). If a reception has been planned for inquirers (as envisioned in *Rite of Christian Initiation of Adults*, 39), the room should meet the standards set by the rite of being fitting for friendly conversation.

In keeping with the history of such spaces and their intimate connection with the sacrament of Baptism, they might well be located near the baptistry or entrance in new church buildings or as renovations of older buildings are prepared.

Other Gatherings for Catechesis or Prayer

Depending on the frequency of sessions for inquirers and catechumens, and on the number of catechumens and candidates, a parish community may feel quite comfortable designating an entire room, center, or series of rooms to this purpose. But the catechumeneon, or center for the catechumenate, can justly and appropriately be used for these other gatherings of a prayerful or catechetical nature:

- Gatherings for the ongoing catechesis of adults or, if the furniture is appropriate, of children.

- The separate Liturgy of the Word with children at Sunday Mass envisioned in the *Directory for Masses with Children* (17). The furniture would have to be appropriate for young children, or rugs could be provided to allow the children to sit on the floor. If the children's Liturgy of the Word uses this space at the same Mass from which the catechumens are dismissed, then careful timing of the dismissal can allow both groups to use the space without a "traffic jam" developing.

- Another possible use for this space is for child care of infants and toddlers during the Mass.

- If the community receives the bodies of its deceased on the day before the funeral Mass, then this room might well be fitting for the vigil of prayer and visiting normally associated with this part of the funeral process.

Furnishings and Decoration

The multiple uses envisioned here (for catechumens, those engaged in catechesis, children at their Liturgy of the Word, infants, and even the bereaved with their beloved's remains) will not work in every parish. But the many possible uses of such a space help us to consider the kinds of furniture and decor appropriate for such a room. The catechumeneon, or whatever it is called in the local setting, is neither classroom, corporate conference room, nor group therapy site. Chairs and desks should not be set up as in a parochial school or continuing education center. Instead, seating for various ages should be provided; there may even be a movable chalkboard or media center. The ambience should be that of an ecclesial gathering—with chairs more in a circle than in the straight lines of an auditorium; with decor that speaks of the Paschal Mystery; with the liturgical times expressed in flowers or decorations; with a well-bound Lectionary as a focal point.

Catechesis always should be enriched by local traditions, stories, and art. Because the persons meeting here are either seeking entrance into the Church or are pursuing a deeper commitment to the life of the Church, the decor might well include historic displays or images of parish life. If the room or another part of the catechetical center is used for toddlers or children, then their colorful art of the liturgical time might grace certain areas.

Chapter Thirteen
Reconciliation Chapel

Community of Reconciliation

The Sacrament of Penance has probably been through more major transformations than any other rite. Even the name given to the action has shifted, and today several different terms are used—confession, reconciliation, penance. All of them refer to the same sacrament, which the *Catechism of the Catholic Church* pairs with the Sacrament of the Anointing of the Sick as one of the two sacraments of healing.

In the early years of the Church, rituals for the reconciliation of penitents were far more demanding and public than in our own time. Scholars still debate the actual forms used, but it seems clear that the rites often took place with the participation of the congregation, in the entryway, and before the Bishop or priest. The penitent would be dressed in a penitential garment, sometimes sackcloth, and would be ritually expelled from the congregation to do penance, usually taking the traditional form of prayer, fasting, and almsgiving. Upon completion of the prescribed penance, the penitent would be restored to communion with the Church. It was not until the thirteenth century that sacramental penance began to take the shape we know today, with private confession in a separate room or chapel.

The Council of Trent, and the decrees associated with its implementation after 1600, did away with the prominent chair in the sanctuary for the priest, but his chair for reconciliation remained. It was usually in the place where the Eucharist was celebrated, in order to highlight the relationship between reconciliation and Eucharist. (Hence, the long-standing custom of praying before the altar or the Blessed Sacrament after receiving absolution.) Over the years, this chair became more and more enclosed, with an enclosure later provided for the penitent as well.

The liturgical movement of the early twentieth century brought new trends. Even as architects and designers of church interiors were perfecting the isolation of penitents in completely sound-proof chambers, liturgists were insisting that the area of confession be related to Baptism and the Eucharist; for example, by positioning the action off the baptistry. Liturgists began calling for more light and square footage for this action, more ability for the priest and penitent to see each other or at least so that the penitent could see the priest making the gesture of reconciliation— the laying on of hands. Some even called for the elimination of all or most of the enclosure, allowing the action to be seen but not heard by those in the church complex, fostering an appreciation of the communal nature of all reconciliation. These early voices helped to guide the Council's reforms.

A Place for Reconciliation

Church guidelines provide for considerable flexibility in the place for this sacrament. The *Code of Canon Law* simply states that a church or oratory is the proper place for the sacrament, and that a screen or grille be placed between the penitent and the confessor to ensure anonymity for those who wish it. The United States Conference of Catholic Bishops has clarified the guidelines further, directing "that the place for sacramental confession be visible and accessible, that it contain a fixed grille, and that it allow for confession face-to-face for those who wish to do so" (*Built of Living Stones*, 103). The choice of whether to confess behind a screen or face-to-face is left not to the confessor, but to the penitent.

Given the demands of the sacrament and our increased awareness due to the abuse crisis, a balance between public and private is needed in the arrangement of the place of the sacrament. Confessionals that are too isolated from the liturgical space, or too private, convey a weak theology of the sacrament, which is about restoring the penitent to his or her place in the Christian community. No sin is totally private: sin separates us from each other, and thus weakens the community. While it is of the utmost importance that the confessions not be audible, there is no requirement that they be unseen. Open confessionals, perhaps placed in relation to the baptistry in the body of the church, can serve as visual reminders of the importance of the sacrament.

Furnishings and Decor of the Place

Within the reserved area, room, or chapel, the furnishings and decor should be simple and well chosen. They should include seating for priest and penitent; a screen and kneeler for penitents who want to retain a measure of anonymity; cards or books with the order of the ritual for both priest and penitent; and a Lectionary or Bible. All these should be placed so that the penitent, after entering, can freely choose anonymous or face-to-face sitting before being seen by the priest. There is no need for rugs or comfortable armchairs. The look should not be that of a living room or therapist's office, but of a liturgical place of prayer.

The art used in these areas should express the fullness of the Eucharistic community to which the Sacrament of Reconciliation restores us. Depending on the size of the area, there may be no space for representational art. A lit candle, live plants, and open scriptures are suitable.

Chapter Fourteen

Chapel for the Reservation of the Most Holy Eucharist

Serving the Sick and Fostering Adoration

From the earliest times onward, the Blessed Sacrament has been reserved after the Mass. The places for that reservation, though, have changed in every era. They have included Christians' homes or priests' residences; side rooms, sacristies, and sanctuaries; a vessel on the altar or suspended over the sanctuary; a castle-like tower away from the altar or a simpler case near the altar. The Blessed Sacrament has even been reserved in a dove made of metal and enamel, flying over the altar. In the years before and after the Council of Trent, the most popular container for the reserved Blessed Sacrament was a tabernacle case fixed at the center of the altar. Until the Second Vatican Council, this was the normative way of reserving the Eucharist.

The *Book of Blessings* (1192) gives two purposes for the tabernacle:

> The tabernacle for eucharistic reservation is a reminder of Christ's presence that comes about in the sacrifice of the Mass. But it is also a reminder of the brothers and sisters we must cherish in charity, since it was in fulfillment of the sacramental ministry received from Christ that the Church first began to reserve the eucharist for the sake of the sick and the dying.

> In our churches adoration has always been offered to the reserved sacrament, the bread which came down from heaven.

The Reforms after Vatican II

During the first part of the twentieth century, liturgists and leaders like Pope Pius XII became more conscious of problems arising from the reservation of the Blessed Sacrament on the altar. The reception of Communion by the congregation became more and more frequent, but the connection between celebration and Communion was weakened. While the Priest Celebrant always received from the host consecrated at the Mass, the people often received from the ciborium, taken out of the tabernacle. At the same time, the *Ceremonial of Bishops* noted that Bishops were not to celebrate the Eucharist at an altar with a tabernacle containing the reserved Blessed Sacrament; any tabernacle there was to be emptied before Mass began. The common practice was in conflict with the tradition and values expressed in such norms.

These problems were addressed in the years following the Second Vatican Council. In the first of the instructions for implementing the *Constitution on the Sacred Liturgy* (*Inter Oecumenici*, 95), the placement of the tabernacle was considered, and two new options were given. Thenceforth, the Blessed Sacrament could be reserved on the main altar, on a side altar, or in "another, special, and properly adorned part of the church." Within a year, clarifications from the Vatican congregations noted that these were not equal choices. When altars were facing the people, then a place apart from the altar was far better for the reservation.

In 1967, an official instruction (*Eucharisticum Mysterium*, 53–55) repeated the same choices for tabernacle placement, but made an even more forceful case for the preferred option:

> The place in a church or oratory where the Blessed Sacrament is reserved in the tabernacle should be truly prominent. It ought to be suitable for private prayer so that the faithful may easily and fruitfully, by private devotion also, continue to honor our Lord in this sacrament. It is therefore recommended that, as far as possible, the tabernacle be placed in a chapel distinct from the middle or central part of the church, above all in those churches where marriages and funerals take place frequently and in places which are much visited for their artistic or historical treasures.

> The Blessed Sacrament should be reserved in a solid, inviolable tabernacle in the middle of the main altar or on a secondary altar, but in a truly prominent place. Alternatively, according to legitimate customs and in individual cases to be decided by the local Ordinary, it may be placed in some other part of the church which is really worthy and properly equipped.

Mass may be celebrated facing the people even though there is a tabernacle on the altar, provided this is small yet adequate.

In the celebration of Mass the principal modes of worship by which Christ is present to His Church are gradually revealed. First of all, Christ is seen to be present among the faithful gathered in His name; then in his Word, as the Scriptures are read and explained; in the person of the minister; finally and in a unique way (*modo singular*) under the species of the Eucharist. Consequently, because of the sign, it is more in keeping with the nature of the celebration that the Eucharistic presence of Christ, which is the fruit of the consecration and should be seen as such, should not be on the altar from the very beginning of Mass through the reservation of the sacred species in the tabernacle.

Today, our liturgical books and our own national documents reinforce this directive. The *General Instruction of the Roman Missal* (315) notes that "It is more appropriate as a sign that on an altar on which Mass is celebrated there not be a tabernacle in which the Most Holy Eucharist is reserved." The Blessed Sacrament should instead be reserved, at the discretion of the local Bishop, "either in the sanctuary, apart from the altar of celebration, . . . or even in some chapel suitable for the private adoration and prayer of the faithful and organically connected to the church and readily noticeable by the Christian faithful" (315).

Today, both these options are frequently seen. In some churches, separate chapels have been established for Eucharistic adoration, while in other places the tabernacle is positioned in the sanctuary, behind the altar or on one side. Whether the tabernacle is in the sanctuary or in a separate chapel, it should be clearly visible and accessible to the faithful for adoration, at the same time that it is not so prominent as to form a distraction during the celebration of the Mass. Additional guidelines can be found in *Built of Living Stones*, 74–80, which suggests the use of special lighting as a way of differentiating the place of reservation from the place of celebration, and which also points to accessibility as a value in new church buildings or in renovations.

Forms of the Reserved Sacrament

EUCHARISTIC BREAD   The documents stress the importance of receiving Holy Communion from hosts consecrated at the same Mass (see *General Instruction of the Roman Missal,* 85). Thus, sacristans need to be alert to patterns of attendance and participation in Holy Communion and plan for the right number of fresh hosts at each Mass. Adjustments can be made to this amount when all are assembled, right up until the presentation of the gifts. If the estimate is found to be incorrect during the Communion Rite, hosts can be broken by ministers. In general, the hosts from the tabernacle should be used in cases of real necessity, not simply for the convenience of the ministers.

On Sunday, the sacristan should ensure that there are enough consecrated hosts in the tabernacle for Communion to be taken to the sick and homebound during the coming week, as well as for a Communion service outside of Mass in case of an emergency during the week.

EUCHARISTIC WINE   The restoration of Eucharistic cup-sharing has given rise to questions of reservation. The *Norms for the Distribution and Reception of Holy Communion under Both Kinds in the Dioceses of the United States of America* (54) allow such reservation only in this circumstance:

> The Precious Blood may not be reserved, except for giving Communion to someone who is sick. Only sick people who are unable to receive Communion under the form of bread may receive it under the form of wine alone at the discretion of the priest. If not consecrated at a Mass in the presence of the sick person, the Blood of the Lord is kept in a properly covered vessel and is placed in the tabernacle after Communion. The Precious Blood should be carried to the sick in a vessel that is closed in such a way as to eliminate all danger of spilling. If some of the Precious Blood remains after the sick person has received Communion, it should be consumed by the minister, who should also see to it that the vessel is properly purified.

The Tabernacle

The word *tabernacle*, with all of its rich religious history, long ago came to designate the locked container or safe in which the Blessed Sacrament is reserved. There is to be only one in each church.

The various documents describe the tabernacle as solid, unbreakable, made of non-transparent or opaque material, dignified, and properly ornamented. It is to be locked, and its key is to be kept carefully. None of the current rites gives further specification to the design and materials. In some places, the tabernacle is covered with an opaque veil of white or of the color of the day.

If the tabernacle is lined with linen or some other fabric, this should be removable for periodic cleaning, perhaps during the period when the tabernacle is empty, from the Communion Rite on Friday of Holy Week to the Easter Vigil. If there is no lining in the tabernacle, and depending on local climate, the tabernacle might well benefit from a lining of wood that protects against moisture.

In the case of older tabernacles, the sacristan should be aware that tabernacles with doors that revolve inside on ball bearings (instead of opening outward) were normally constructed with an asbestos lining between metal plates. Given the justifiable concern about asbestos, the sacristan should consult with a local expert to confirm whether the tabernacle has asbestos lining.

Lamp before the Tabernacle

As a mark of reverence and as an indication of the presence of the Blessed Sacrament in the tabernacle, it has long been required to have a lamp burning perpetually before it. While all other liturgical illumination in the church complex is by candles, here there is a choice—a candle (preferably of wax) in a lamp, or an oil lamp. (See page 29 regarding strictures against tubes and other inappropriate substitutes for lamps.) There is no set place for the lamp other than near the tabernacle, but local codes for open flames should be respected. A suspended lamp, or multiple suspended lamps, is most traditional, but the "tabernacle light" or "sanctuary lamp" can be mounted on floor stands or on wall brackets. The continual vigilance necessary to keep an oil lamp burning is an ancient and biblical symbol of human preparedness for the Lord's coming, and has always been one of the more symbolic acts performed by sacristans.

Other Materials for the Chapel of Reservation

FURNITURE   The chapel should not be crowded with furniture, but chairs and kneelers should be provided for the adoration and prayer. These should harmonize well with the overall design of the space. Pastoral ministers may want to provide suitable prayer texts or biblical passages in racks.

WATER AND TOWEL   In some churches there is a small cup of water, called an "ablution cup," and a towel stand near the tabernacle so that ministers may cleanse their thumb and forefinger after Communion. These cups might more fittingly be placed at the credence table, where the ministers bring the vessels following Communion, or in the sacristy.

DECORATIONS   Flowers and decorations, in addition to the lamp, can grace the chapel. But they should not overwhelm the tabernacle. This room should be as carefully supervised by sacristans as any other part of the church. The decoration should be carefully considered, and needless to say, the place where the Blessed Sacrament is reserved should never be used for storage, even temporarily.

Chapter Fifteen

Shrines and Other Areas for Private Devotions

Representations of Christ and of the saints grace our church buildings so that we might interact with them, tracing in our hearts the patterns of their holiness. This activity is not to be equated with liturgical celebrations of Christ and the saints, celebrated by the whole local Church in communion with other churches. Instead, these devotions, as they have come to be called, are undertaken by the faithful outside of the set liturgical forms. Such shrines should invite the devotion of the faithful without distracting from the primary purpose of the space: the celebration of the Mass.

Norms for Shrines

Shrines can be outdoors, off the entryway or vestibule, in alcoves in the nave, or in other corners of the church complex. They should allow space for the interaction of people and images, but they should not impede the core actions of liturgy.

According to a long-standing tradition, the church complex should contain no more than one image of any one saint. Exceptions always have been made for images of Jesus and of Mary; one image for any given title can be placed for adoration. This rule does not apply to narratives of a given saint played out in windows, mosaics, or frescoes.

Not all the images in the parish's collection need be displayed at the same time, particularly if the parish has limited space. If a parish has images of many saints, or many images of the same saint, the images can be moved back and forth between shrine and storage areas according to the liturgical times of the year or some other logical scheme.

Those who prepare the liturgy might also consider the old custom of covering images and crosses during the last days of Lent. *The Roman Missal* includes the following rubric for the Fifth Sunday of Lent: "In the Dioceses of the United States, the practice of covering crosses and images throughout the church from this Sunday may be observed. Crosses remain covered until the end of the Celebration of the Lord's Passion on Good Friday, but images remain covered until the beginning of the Easter Vigil." The optional veiling of the cross and images can help focus our attention during the last week of Lent and Holy Week (the days formerly known as "Passiontide"). It is a fast for the eyes, not unlike the fast from food we observe during Lent, and the fast of the ears in the reduction of the use of the organ.

Image of the Church's Titular

Every parish should have an image of its titular, either inside or outside the building. The image of this saint or of this aspect of Christ should be of such a scale, of such dignity, and so positioned that it invites interaction. Examples of interaction include placing flowers and, on occasion, other festal decorations, lighting votive candles, and simple touching. Obviously this will not work for parishes entitled Holy Spirit or Holy Trinity or Transfiguration. Yet even in those parishes, consideration should be given to the decorative program related to the titular of the parish or chapel.

Stations of the Cross

The Stations of the Cross are not required, and yet these beloved images are found in almost every church. The list of 14 traditional stations has only been codified for a few hundred years, and Blessed Pope John Paul II introduced a new set of 14 scriptural stations, replacing such traditional features as the three falls and the encounter with Veronica with scripturally based stations, like the agony in the garden, the denial of Peter, and the exchange with the good thief on the cross. Except on Friday of Holy Week, a fifteenth station of the Resurrection is usually added, and when new Stations of the Cross are installed in a church this fifteenth station should be included. The stations should be placed in such a way that the faithful have a sense of journeying with Christ in his Passion and Death. They should not be so close together that the sense of movement is lost. The art should invite meditation and reflection.

In most cases, the 15 stations need only cleaning and regular maintenance, though some more elaborate stations have special candles or lights that will need maintenance as well.

Images of Mary and of Other Saints

Virtually every Catholic church has a Marian shrine or image. As in the case of all shrines, any statue of Mary should be of dignified design. If possible, it would be appropriate for the shrine for Mary to be large enough to accommodate groups that want to pray the Rosary in common. It can be decorated with extra candles and flowers for Marian feasts and memorials.

Decorations should be selected in keeping with the liturgical year. In Advent, when the Solemnity of the Immaculate Conception of the Blessed Virgin Mary and the Feast of Our Lady of Guadalupe occur, and the scriptures describe Mary's preparations for the great coming of the Lord, the shrine might be decorated in keeping with the rest of the church building; Mary's shrine might even be an appropriate place for the Advent wreath. In Easter Time, to show the unity of the Fifty Days and to honor Mary as *Regina Caeli* (Queen of Heaven), the shrine might be decorated from the Easter Vigil until Pentecost, days normally including most of May.

After Mary, the most frequently enshrined images are those of the Sacred Heart of Jesus and of Saint Joseph. Other favorite saints worldwide are Saint Thérèse of the Child Jesus and Saint Anthony of Padua. In preparing permanent and "seasonal" images, sacristans should consider the devotions favored by the specific community they serve. *Built of Living Stones*, 122–139, provides much wisdom about balancing the needs of the community in decorating the church for the liturgical times and preparing the shrines and other images of the saints.

Chapter Sixteen

Entrance Area

The wondrous vision of the new Jerusalem, described at the end of the book of Revelation, has inspired every generation of Christian believers: "the city has no need of sun or moon to shine on it, for the glory of God is its light, and its lamp is the Lamb. . . . Its gates will never be shut by day—and there will be no night there" (Revelation 21:23, 25). Our medieval ancestors were holding to that same vision when they pictured the entrance of the church as a sign of paradise, surrounding the doors with images of the ranks of the blessed, praising God in heaven. All were welcomed to a place of nightless glory.

The architectural prominence and decor of ancient church entryways attest to their importance. The communities wanted all who passed by to feel the pull of the open doors, to be drawn into sacramental brilliance. The entrance halls were as large as they were beautiful. They provided both a transition to ecclesial space and shelter for many of the rites. Indeed, in some places the whole congregation would gather in the entrance hall, so that all could enter the congregation together in solemn procession.

Depending upon the region and upon architectural form, the entrance area might have been called the atrium, narthex, or vestibule. Closer to our own times, terms like lobby, foyer, commons, and concourse have been added to the mix. Whatever the term used, there still is a need for an entrance hall distinct from the main body of the church. As in the past, this space provides a transition from the world without to the sacred space within.

Exterior

Every part of the church building has its importance in revealing the Gospel, in drawing the people into liturgical action. The exterior areas associated with parish churches are no exception. Parking areas, walkways, yards, and outdoor shrines need to be clean, hospitable, and well suited to their gathering function. They not only draw all into the buildings, they often serve as gathering places for devotions and receptions, blessings, and processions.

BELLS The use of sound to summon a congregation is very ancient. The First Reading on Ash Wednesday contains one of the classic references: "Blow the trumpet in Zion! / proclaim a fast, / call an assembly" (Joel 2:15). The shofar still heralds the new year in Jewish congregations everywhere. Eastern Churches from the very first centuries often used a simandron, a hanging percussion instrument which was sounded by being struck with a mallet.

The use of bells for summoning the congregation can be traced to the fourth or fifth century. Many sources indicate that they were introduced by Paulinus of Nola (in Campania), the Bishop who said that he really wanted to be a sacristan. Yet this association may have arisen from a similarity between terms like *campanile* (a free-standing bell tower) and *Campania*, or from the Latin term *nola* for bells, or from the fact that the pealing of bells was traditionally a duty of sacristans.

Over the centuries, bells took on other functions. In addition to calling the congregation, they were used to draw those absent from the congregation into prayerful union. For example, the exterior bells would be rung at the words of consecration in the Eucharistic Prayer or during special hymns of praise. Through the Middle Ages, they also were utilized as civic clocks, as invitations to non-liturgical private prayer (the times of the Angelus prayer), and as heralds of extraordinary events. In its blessing of bells, the *Book of Blessings* (#1305) notes that bells express the sentiments of the people of God "as they rejoice or grieve, offer thanks or petition, gather together and show outwardly the mystery of their oneness in Christ." Thus they both signal and enhance the unity of the congregation.

The tradition of silencing all bells from the start of the Paschal Triduum (the Gloria during the Evening Mass of the Lord's Supper on Thursday of Holy Week) to the Gloria at the Easter Vigil should be respected. Their stillness is a powerful symbol of the importance of these days. Working with music ministers, sacristans and bell-ringers can establish other customs, with bells especially enhancing outdoor processions.

DECORATIONS Exterior ornaments should, of course, respect both the local landscape and the architectural forms of the church complex. Perhaps the most obvious item needed by every facility is a sign naming the church and giving pertinent data about services. Sacristans, other decorators, and pastoral staff members should give careful consideration to this simple but powerful element. The wording, the use of lettering that can be read from afar, the updating of festal information, and the possibility of embellishments for the various liturgical times are all important and should be periodically reviewed.

Other obvious possibilities for the outdoor area flow from this basic sign. If the church's name is that of a saint, there might well be an outdoor statue in his or her honor, specially decorated for the annual feasts of title and dedication. During the great liturgical times, colorful hangings on the building or arrangements of flowers announce a festive time. At Christmas Time, it's hard to beat a large evergreen decorated with lights. The manger scene might be placed outdoors as well, and there are many other possibilities. All should suit the liturgical time well, so that they don't have to be explained, and they should be attractive and durable, so that parishioners will look forward to seeing them year after year. And of course, outdoor decorations should respect the liturgical times; for example, no creche in Advent, no lilies in Lent.

If national, state or territory, city or Vatican flags are to be used at the church complex, their positions should be carefully considered. They should not be placed in the sanctuary (see page 54), nor in other areas such as the baptistry. They might well find an appropriate place in a yard or plaza area, or in a memorial area of the parish cemetery. Here assemblies can gather for any civil ceremonies on holidays, while maintaining the distinction between the national and the liturgical, and allowing non-Christian neighbors or relatives to feel comfortable.

DOORS In their materials and surface decorations, their handles and lintels, doors can be a powerful expression of the community. Reviewing the texts associated with their blessing (Ch. 34 of the *Book of Blessings*) is a way to be reminded of the liturgical importance of doors. They are the place for receiving bridal couples and infants to be baptized, for welcoming mourners bearing their deceased, and for greeting catechumens. They are the passageway for formal processions and for the gathering of the faithful. For all of these actions, the doors can provide dignified decoration, invitations to the liturgical time and feast.

There are many possibilities for decorating the doors for the various liturgical times. As with other "seasonal" elements, they should be simple and repeatable on an annual basis. During Christmas Time and Easter Time, wreaths might hang from the doors; near the end of Lent, olive branches. At Pentecost, and for the final days of Easter Time leading up to this solemnity, the door casing could be decorated with greens, similar to the way the Jewish people traditionally decorate their synagogues. Or one could copy the old European custom of observing all major festivals by framing the main doorway of the church with well-made draperies. Such draperies should be of the utmost dignity and durable enough to be used year after year at Christmas Time, Easter Time, the parish anniversary of dedication, and at other major feasts.

Entrance Hall

Whether called the narthex, vestibule, commons, foyer, or lobby, this area should be given careful attention by ushers and sacristans. Here people make the transition from the outside to the liturgical action, from the world as experienced every day to the transformed world promised in the sacraments. Over the centuries, when congregations understood themselves to be spectators or an audience for the priest's words, the transition was commonly described as one from the hustle and bustle of the street to the reverent silence before the Blessed Sacrament. The liturgical movement and the subsequent reforms have helped us to appreciate a different kind of transition—from private or household preoccupations to action with a broader body of people; from all manner of worthwhile pursuits in the world to a dedicated participation in sacramental action. Thus, the entrance hall does not have to be a decompression chamber, but rather a re-focusing place, a place to be equipped for community action, for singing, for the feast.

VESTURE   The old name "vestibule" can remind us that vesture needs are not restricted to the priest and deacon. On any day when members of the congregation enter with coats or umbrellas, special foot gear or hats, provisions must be made for their transition to an indoor action that presumes their full participation. The vestibule should have a place to hang coats, and there should be special mats or grates for absorbing moisture from foot gear. For many parishes, coat rooms are a wish that is listed with other renovation needs. In the meantime, perhaps an unused space off the vestibule can be turned into a coat room (with systems and ministers that assure convenient and secure drop-off and pick-up). Portable coat racks might fit in the vestibule itself—a somewhat ugly, but extraordinarily important, compromise until a new coat room is built. If no possibilities present themselves at the entryway, then we should allow enough space for a coat pile in every row of seats.

HOLY WATER STOUPS   Since at least the early medieval period, these vessels or basins with baptismal or holy water have been placed in the entryway. They are related to earlier precedents (vessels of water in early Christian atria) and to the ritual action of sprinkling that takes place at the start of many Masses, especially in Easter Time. In a sense, they are a reminder of the baptismal font that is located elsewhere in the church. When we enter the building before Mass begins, dip our fingers in the water and cross ourselves, we are being reminded of our Baptism, and are performing the first of a series of liturgical acts that will follow.

In places where the font is at or near the entrance hall, this primordial vessel of blessed water can be the source for signing those entering and for sprinkling coffins being received. In church communities where the font is housed separately from the entrance, one or more fitting stoups or vessels can be positioned for those entering. Sacristans should keep the stoups free of litter and sponges, and filled with fresh, clean, blessed water taken from the font.

PARTICIPATION MATERIALS   Besides taking off our coats and signing ourselves with baptismal water, we also need to receive the hymnals or song sheets, as well as any other items we may need to use at a given liturgy (for example, candles or palm branches). These might be placed in advance on all of the seats, but it is often more efficient, and more hospitable, for designated greeters to distribute them in the entrance hall. For times when greeters are not available, racks or tables may need to be purchased for the distribution of these worship aids. These should be simple and unobtrusive, but sizable enough to perform their function. Their position should be a factor in preparing decorations for particular feasts or liturgical times.

THE GIFTS Also called the oblations table in some liturgical traditions, this stand or table should be in the entryway or near the entrance of the church. The rite that provides for the presentation of bread and wine is meant to be a procession through the congregation, not just a quick passing from front pew to sanctuary. This table can be the place for "seasonal" decoration or a feast day image that beckons all to the feast.

The close relationship between this presentation of bread and wine and gifts for the poor is expressed in the general norm, printed after the presentation of bread and wine in the *General Instruction of the Roman Missal* (73), "Even money or other gifts for the poor or for the Church, brought by the faithful or collected in the church, are acceptable; given their purpose, they are to be put in a suitable place away from the Eucharistic table."

After the collection, the procession of bread and wine and monetary donations can leave from the gifts table and proceed to the altar area, where the collection is placed off to the side. This ceremonial action is seen most forcefully on Thursday of Holy Week evening, when the rubrics read, "At the beginning of the Liturgy of the Eucharist, there may be a procession of the faithful in which gifts for the poor may be presented with the bread and wine." Yet, on regular Sundays and feast days, these offerings might better be collected at a position related to the gifts table in the entryway, especially when the gifts are of various sorts—canned goods or used clothing. Thus, the bread and wine are visually related to the gifts of the people. In keeping with this relationship, any "poor boxes" or containers for the collection of parish-related funds can be positioned near the gifts table and the reception area for canned goods.

COMMUNICATIONS The church entryways are usually the best places to post notices and photographs of parish activities. A board or appropriately covered wall can provide space for all of the posters and sign-up sheets necessitated by an active community. A particularly important facet of this intercommunication is the recruitment of volunteers for all of the parish's ministries. A "wall of opportunity" can be set up with brief job descriptions, requirements, and opportunities to sign up; this can be done as an annual campaign for volunteers or as an opportunity to promote more involvement before Christmas Time and Easter Time. Pamphlet and book racks also can be positioned in relationship to these displays.

Certain displays will occur with regularity each year (biographies of parish pastoral council candidates, background on the group that will receive Lenten alms, pictures of those elected for Easter initiation, prayer requests), and these should be remembered in the preparations for each liturgical time. When approaching each liturgical time, consider decorations for this area of the entrance, as well as the areas for the gifts and for the hymnals or song sheets.

OTHER DECORATIONS The entrance hall might be an appropriate place for certain decorations for each liturgical time, such as the Advent wreath or a Jesse tree, the Christmas manger or tree, flowers and candles before the statue of the saint of the day.

STORAGE Most churches have at least a small closet off the entrance hall—and for good reason. Besides the obvious tools necessary for ushers, collection baskets, and mops for wet entrance floors, some of the items listed under security and health (page 155) might be stored here. When selecting any of these materials, the sacristan should consult the ministers who are most involved. Their opinions should be weighed along with applicable liturgical principles. For example, when selecting collection baskets or plates, the interaction of the congregation and the dignity of the collection process should be considered. From a liturgical point of view, baskets that can be passed from hand to hand are better in most cases. Here again, the selection of an object relates to a style of action.

OTHER FACILITIES Though rest rooms are best positioned off the entrance hall or "commons," there are many other arrangements that are possible or even necessary in older buildings. Both men and woman should have access to changing tables for infants. Halls or rooms for cooking and for other forms of hospitality, offices and conference rooms, and other parish spaces can be related to the liturgical spaces. All of these spaces should be considered in a comprehensive way when decorators, sacristans, educators, and pastoral staff meet for joint preparation.

Chapter Seventeen

Gathering Place or Narthex

Gathering

The entrance hall or, in a warm climate, an exterior space might well be large enough to allow for many members of the congregation to gather before and after liturgical celebrations. As noted in *Built of Living Stones*, "the narthex is a place of welcome—a threshold space between the congregation's space and the outside environment. . . . [I]t serves as gathering space as well as the entrance and exit to the building. The gathering space helps believers to make the transition from everyday life to the celebration of the liturgy, and after the liturgy, it helps them return to daily life to live out the mystery that has been celebrated" (95).

Rituals

The narthex, or gathering space, is different from the parish hall where parishioners can gather for social time after Mass. The Roman Rite presumes the existence of another kind of gathering place that is used for various rituals throughout the liturgical year:

1. Rites of blessing that precede Eucharistic gatherings. Each of these is described in *The Roman Missal* as starting in a place that is separate from the church building:

   - the blessing of candles for the Feast of the Presentation of the Lord

   - the blessing of palms on Palm Sunday of the Lord's Passion

   - the blessing of fire at the Easter Vigil

2. Rites of preparation and the gathering of all for solemn processions:

   - the penitential procession recommended for the First Sunday of Lent (*Ceremonial of Bishops*, 261; recommended for all parishes in *Paschale Solemnitatis*, 23)

   - any procession that will later move to the area for the congregation

3. Rites of reception at the beginning of certain sacramental celebrations:

   - receiving children at the beginning of the Rite of Baptism for Children

   - receiving the candidates at the start of the Rite of Acceptance into the Order of Catechumens

   - the Introductory Rites in the Rite of Marriage

   - the reception of the body at the vigil for the deceased or at the beginning of the funeral Mass.

Location and Decoration

In the *Ceremonial of Bishops* (#54), these rites are envisioned as unfolding in "another church, a suitable hall, a square, or a cloister." Some rites might ideally take place at an outdoor gathering place somewhat removed from the entryway of the church—particularly the blessing of the fire at the beginning of the Easter Vigil. The rites of gathering for processions, indoors or out, should also be somewhat removed to allow for a full movement of the procession. The rites of reception of new members are better held at the doors of the church, just inside or outside the narthex.

Local specifications depend on the floor plan of the complex and on the climate. Each community should fully utilize the available spaces. Looking at the forthcoming rites, those who prepare the liturgy should evaluate all lawn areas and parish center halls, entrance halls, and porticos. The place most fitting for the occasion should be equipped for use. Then, local traditions for such preparatory gatherings can be established. There is no need to find a new starting place for Palm Sunday every year, or a new place for the Easter fire. Once a good place is found, it should be used every year. Not every one of these special rites needs to happen in the same place. The blessing of fire, for example, is certainly different from the rite of receiving mourners and their loved one's remains.

In parishes where the movement of whole assemblies presumed in such rites is deemed impossible because of limited space, sacristans and those who prepare the liturgy should try to review this question on a periodic basis. Sometimes a creative approach becomes clear only after several reviews of options—use of the street out front for one or two annual occasions, a procession arranged with neighboring churches, the removal of rear pews to create space for fitting receptions of infants and bridal couples. Usually it is not space that hinders the full and beautiful celebration of these rites; it's the imagination of leaders.

All of these preparatory gatherings will need some equipment from the sacristy: a podium or platform, a microphone, certain vessels or elements. The gatherings also will benefit from decorations on occasion. These will differ according to the event. Please refer to the descriptions under the lists for February 2 (page 211), First Sunday of Lent (pages 185 and 188), Palm Sunday (page 192), Easter Vigil (page 204), Baptism (pages 226 and 228), acceptance of catechumens (page 223), Marriage (pages 234 and 236), and funerals (page 231).

Chapter Eighteen
Cemetery

In various periods of our history, the cemetery was a treasured part of the parish church complex. The bereaved often wanted their loved ones buried near the place of worship or near the graves of important martyrs and saints. Even today, parish cemeteries surround the church buildings in some dioceses, providing a wonderful context of memory around the holy congregation. Sacristans in parishes with a cemetery or crypt have received a great gift; they should include these spaces when decorating for the liturgical times.

At other times in our history, especially for the first few centuries, Christians were buried away from the places of regular Eucharistic gatherings. This was generally true in urban communities, where there were strictures against burying the dead within the city walls. The famous catacombs outside Rome are examples of this practice. In the same centuries, Christians also used both above-ground cemeteries and covered, hall-like cemeteries. Rites of memorial, perhaps even an occasional Eucharist, were celebrated in some of these settings, especially on days of special remembrance for the dead. Even through persecutions, Christians gathered for worship in the city. Then, as is often the case now, cemeteries were occasional places.

A Liturgical Space

Whether near or far from the place of the funeral Mass, the cemetery is the hallowed place where the liturgical rites surrounding committal take place. These are not just hurried prayers murmured before the family returns home again. The rite is a public action of the local Church, involving set prayers and scripture, music, and the lowering of the body into the ground for burial. In the United States of America, the coffin often is not lowered into the grave until all mourners have departed. Despite this truncation of the action, the Rite of Committal is always a powerful, even wrenching, event. When it occurs within the church complex at a parish cemetery, it flows from the procession of the entire congregation. When it is more detached by time and distance, the congregation, unfortunately, will be smaller.

Other actions also occur at the cemetery. Family members visit plots at cemeteries throughout the year. One can always see people making their way through the grounds on the anniversary of the death of a spouse or loved one. On days such as Memorial Day, the numbers increase. Special groups, particularly of military veterans, converge upon the grounds for annual memorial programs.

Pastoral leaders should do everything possible to encourage such interactions. Whether a civic or parish-owned cemetery, they should see that hours are extended and conditions are congenial for the regular visitation of the grounds. These efforts can be reinforced by occasional catechetical sessions at the tombs (reading inscriptions or drawing some of the found symbols) or by parish-sponsored memorial picnics. Even when the antiquity of a cemetery decreases the number of personally bereaved, such communal events link all to their local history and provide irreplaceable formation in faith.

In addition to these private and civic prayers, the church has a wonderful Order for Visiting a Cemetery (Ch. 57, *Book of Blessings*). Meant for use on days like All Souls' Day and Memorial Day, it is a public liturgy for the whole parish, often occurring after a Mass in the church building or at the cemetery.

Decoration

The prayer for blessing a cemetery (*Book of Blessings*, 1432) alerts us to the ambience befitting such a liturgical place. These places of rest and hope are "a comfort to the living, / a sign of their hope for unending life." The prayers offered here are "in supplication for those who sleep in Christ / and in constant praise of your [God's] mercy."

The principal decoration of a church cemetery, whether part of the parish building complex or separated from it, continues to be a large cross erected in a prominent place. Placed under this sign, the cemetery becomes a more powerful place of hope in the Resurrection. Where such a central cross exists, it can be decorated for liturgical times such as Easter, for such festival days as Christmas, All Saints, and the Commemoration of All the Faithful Departed (All Souls' Day), and perhaps even for the whole month of November (a month typically celebrated as the Month of All Souls).

When arranging other permanent or temporary decorations, parish ministers might consider supplementing the cross with improved plantings (if permitted) in common areas of the grounds. Roses and lilies can join the more somber cypress and willow. Obviously, the sacristan and any trustees of the cemetery can be joined in this by many parish members with knowledge of local planting cycles.

Besides such care for the garden areas, those who prepare the liturgy should recall the primitive use of candles in early Christian cemeteries. In cemeteries surrounding church edifices, luminaria might burn by each tomb or along walkways before and after evening Mass on such days as All Souls' Day (November 2). In those same communities blessed with an on-site cemetery, this might be the gathering place for blessings such as the fire at the Easter Vigil. Candlelight vigils in cemeteries are an old and still worthy custom, perhaps on the eve of All Saints or of the parish's dedication anniversary. Eternal flames can also be arranged to great benefit.

Whether near or far, cemeteries should be a factor in every liturgical time's decoration program. The community will be enormously grateful to every sacristan and those who prepare the liturgy who allow Advent and Christmas Time, Lent, the Paschal Triduum, and Easter Time to shine in this place of hope and prayer.

Part Three
Equipping the Sacristy

Chapter Nineteen

Sacristy Furnishings

Two Rooms

Many parishes have two sacristies, which should be differentiated by their function. One room, called the vesting room, can serve all who vest for liturgy, priests as well as all others. If possible, this room should be located close to the entryway so that processions can be formed with greater ease (see, for example, *Built of Living Stones*, 234). The other room, called here the "sacristy," can be closer to the sanctuary, providing preparation areas for all liturgical requisites. While this two-room arrangement is presented as an ideal, every parish and church setting is different. The use of space should be evaluated on a regular basis so that preparations for Mass can be made as prayerfully and efficiently as possible.

The vesting room should contain the following items or equivalents:

- cabinets for books and for vesture

- cabinets for the storage of chasubles and dalmatics

- closets with high rods for albs, cassocks, surplices, and other vesture

- countertops or tables for the laying out of vestments and the preparation of texts

- sink and materials for washing of hands (unless rest rooms are nearby)

- appointments appropriate to this room's function: clock, bulletin board, full-length mirror, and perhaps a floor-mounted shoe polisher, and an umbrella stand

- a cross and a sign with local information like the Bishop's name so that visiting priests can insert into the Eucharistic Prayer

The sacristy will be most functional if it has these furnishings:

- a sacrarium for the reverent disposal of sacred substances (see below)

- cases, cabinets, perhaps a metal safe for historic items, and/or closets with flexible shelving for vessels, linens, candles and holders, incense materials, floral equipment, decorations, and tools

- tables or countertops for the preparation of materials

- a sink with hot water for the washing of vessels after they have been purified, with a drain board and drying rack (equipped with vertical pegs for holding the cruets, flagons, cups), paper towels or cloth towels and rack

- a janitorial sink if necessary

- other basic appointments: bulletin board, stool or ladder, cart with shelves for moving many vessels at once, dolly for cartons of supplies or larger objects, and hooks for candle-lighters.

The Sacrarium

The most unusual sink in the church complex is the sacrarium. It is a basin, usually covered, with a drain pipe that leads directly into the earth. This allows the reverent cleaning of chalices and patens after they have been purified, and the disposal of baptismal water, water used in ritual purifications, holy oils from a previous year, or ashes made from burning liturgical items for reverent disposal (for example, cotton balls from oil stocks). A sacrarium has been required in Roman Rite churches since the early Middle Ages, and most churches have one. The usual location for the sacrarium is in the sacristy.

The long history of the sacrarium testifies to the careful attention that Catholics have given to Eucharistic particles over the centuries, a witness to our belief in the real presence of Christ in the Sacrament of his Body and Blood. (See *Built of Living Stones*, 236–237, for more information on the use of the sacrarium.)

Drinking Water

These sinks and their sources of water may be sufficient for drinking water as well. Yet, depending upon the quality of local water, and recognizing the proclivity of most Americans to drink very cold water, a separate source of cold drinking water might be necessary or at least hospitable. Small or large, portable or permanent, water coolers and cup dispensers can be installed in both vesting room and sacristy. Better yet, in order to be usable by the whole community, they might be located in more common areas of the complex: near the rest rooms, cloakroom, or entrance hall.

The Portable Sacristy

Liturgical events on occasion take place away from the church building—Mass in a nursing home, Anointing of the Sick and Holy Communion, and the blessing of homes, for example. The small vessels and packing cases marketed for these functions often contain unnecessary items of trivial size (but not insignificant cost). Though doll house-sized items may be easier to transport, the need for mobility is better met by packing only those items needed for the rite. In the case of *Viaticum*, those items would be the pyx containing the Blessed Sacrament, the oil of the sick, the ritual book, song sheets or prayer cards, and vesture for the priest. For Mass the list includes cups, purificators, paten, bread and wine, water vessel (and towel), vesture, *The Roman Missal* and *Lectionary for Mass*, participation materials, table cover, candles, and cross. Several of these items may already be at the site. By knowing what is already available at the site, the sacristan can outfit small or large cases with only those items that are necessary.

Chapter Twenty
Liturgical Books

Collections of Texts

From the very earliest years, the various texts of Christian liturgies were transcribed and collected. As the centuries unfolded, the sharing of these text collections among churches was determined by their communion with a particular patriarchate or metropolitan see, by trade routes and river valleys, as well as by theological convictions. The texts themselves have been passed down over the centuries in many forms.

For the first several centuries, texts were written on a rotulus, a papyrus roll set on spindles at each end. This first format for liturgical collections still can be seen in many synagogues.

As Christianity spread and was legalized, the second phase began. The codex, folded sheets of animal skin gathered into a book, came into use. It facilitated the fast and broad spread of liturgical and biblical texts. Codices were copied laboriously by hand, but this new format used more durable material, and, unlike the scroll, it allowed random access to a text at any page.

The mechanical printing of codices or books on paper developed just as the prayer texts and Lectionary lists were being standardized for all Roman Rite churches. This third stage of formats facilitated, and in some respects even brought about, the demise of local variants and the acceptance of conformity to universal models. By this time, the collections of texts came to be grouped as sacramentaries or missals (for *missa* or Mass), containing the readings and prayers for the Mass, pontificals (for rites led by Bishops), breviaries (the Liturgy of the Hours), and rituals (for all of the other rites).

Today we find ourselves in a fourth phase of text retrieval: the digital age. Computers now have an enormous effect on liturgical text compositions. The conformity of published texts to the mandated "typical editions" has always been a concern of ecclesial authorities. Current technology now guarantees conformity, and in the case of the third edition of *The Roman Missal* seven publishers were given the option to use the same digital files in order to achieve an amazing level of consistency among editions of the text. But in this digital age, we still reverence our books, particularly the *Book of the Gospels*, carrying it in procession, surrounding it with candles, incensing it, kissing it. The parish should purchase the highest quality *Lectionary for Mass*, *The Roman Missal*, *Book of the Gospels*, and hymnals it can afford. It is an investment in a great tradition—and one that will last for many years into the future.

Worthy and Beautiful Symbols

In each successive format, the official books of rites have been a significant part of the liturgical environment. Our tradition describes them as signs and symbols of the sacred, expressive of our belief that God speaks through these texts, that the community is shaped by these words. Thus, we should treat them as we do all of the artifacts and works of art in the sacristy: with great care and reverence. When selecting new volumes, we should be guided by the qualities noted in the *General Instruction of the Roman Missal*: "Special care must be taken to ensure that the liturgical books, particularly the *Book of the Gospels* and the Lectionary, which are intended for the proclamation of the Word of God and hence receive special veneration, are to be in a liturgical action truly signs and symbols of higher realities and hence should be truly worthy, dignified, and beautiful" (349).

The importance of these books rules out the substitution of disposable missals, study text editions, or loose sheets for ritual use (see the *Introduction to the Lectionary for Mass*, 37). Visually attractive and impressive books play a formative role in public congregation; flimsy pamphlets convey a disposable or trivial message, as if the texts or the "things" in general do not matter. The forms of our material objects really matter. They are at the center of the sacristan's ministry because we believe that communities find holiness in sacramental interaction with material elements.

The Books of the Roman Rite in the United States of America

OFFICIAL BOOKS   The books that we use in the liturgy are issued first by the Vatican for the universal Church. Then the Bishops' conferences of each language grouping and of each nation see to their translation and adaptation. In the official English-language books, many of the texts are translated by the International Commission on English in the Liturgy Corporation (ICEL). Scriptural texts are taken from one of the translations approved for liturgical usage. Publishers of Bibles, ICEL, and others maintain copyright ownership to the texts, as delimited on the acknowledgments page of each ritual book. All of these texts and ceremonial adaptations are approved by the Bishops' conference and then confirmed by the Vatican before they are published.

In the United States, several publishers provide distinct editions of the liturgical books—all with the same texts, but differing in artistic quality. The parish should review various editions before selecting one that provides the most worthy symbol.

The following titles are the official English-language books for the Roman Rite dioceses of our country. Every sacristy in a parish church should have all of them, with the possible exceptions of the *Rite of Religious Profession* and the full Pontifical. Chapels where a given rite is never celebrated would not, of course, need the corresponding ritual book. When reviewing this list periodically, you should purchase sufficient copies to cover normal use. Several copies of some rites will need to be available for ministers other than the celebrant. For example, the *Order for Christian Funerals* includes texts used at the same rite by priests, deacons, and lectors and readers.

As this second edition of *The Sacristy Manual* is being prepared, many of these ritual books are being revised in light of *Liturgiam Authenticam*, the 2001 Vatican instruction on liturgical translation. Pastoral leaders will want to stay abreast of changes in this area as new editions are published.

1. *The Roman Missal* (formerly known as *The Sacramentary*), Third Edition, 2011

   Complementary volumes:

   - The *Collection of Masses of the Blessed Virgin Mary: Sacramentary*: 1992. (In parishes, this can be used on those Saturdays in Ordinary Time that do not have an obligatory memorial or feast. In Marian shrines, its use can be frequent.)

2. *Lectionary for Mass*: 2001

   Complementary volumes:

   - *The Lectionary for Masses with Children* (in use beginning Advent 1993).

   - *Book of the Gospels*. The *Order of Christian Funerals* suggests this as one of the possible symbols to rest on the coffin during a funeral.

   - *The Collection of Masses of the Blessed Virgin Mary: Lectionary*: 1992 (can be used on those Saturdays in Ordinary Time when the accompanying

Sacramentary is utilized, but it is always better to waive this option and use the semicontinuous readings of the weekday Lectionary).

3. *Roman Calendar:* The 1969 universal calendar and the particular calendar of the dioceses of the United States of America form our proper calendar. These lists and the *Universal Norms on the Liturgical Year and the General Roman Calendar* are reprinted at the front of every edition of *The Roman Missal.* As new saints and the blessed are added to either the universal or national calendars, these lists will continue to evolve and be noted in annual ordos. They always should be complemented by particular feasts of the diocese and parish (diocesan patron, anniversaries of dedication of the cathedral and of the parish church, local church title).

> Complementary volume: Dioceses are mandated to issue annual calendars, with local feasts and norms. Many publishers issue annual ordos, often in local editions that incorporate these observances.

4. *The Liturgy of the Hours*: 1975 (4 volumes).

> Complementary volumes:
>
> - *Christian Prayer*, a one-volume excerpt.
> - *Shorter Christian Prayer*, a simplified edition.
> - Supplements with texts for new memorials.

5. *The Roman Ritual*, published in one volume before Vatican II, is now in several volumes, one for each sacrament or rite:

a. *Rite of Christian Initiation of Adults*: 1988. This includes the Rite for the Reception of Baptized Christians.

b. *Rite of Baptism for Children*: 1970.

c. *Rite of Marriage*: 1970.

d. *Order of Christian Funerals*: 1989.

> Complementary volumes: Various parts of this order (for example, the committal rites) have been published in separate volumes. An appendix, added in 1997, addresses cremation and is an essential insert in any edition of the *Order of Christian Funerals.*

e. *Rite of Penance*: 1975, reprinted in 2010.

f. *Pastoral Care of the Sick: Rites of Anointing and Viaticum*: 1983.

g. *Holy Communion and Worship of the Eucharist outside Mass*: 1976.

h. *Rite of Religious Profession*: 1988.

i. *Book of Blessings*: 1989.

> Complementary volumes:
>
> - *Catholic Household Blessings & Prayers, Revised Edition*: 2007.
> - *Shorter Book of Blessings:* 1990.

5. *The Roman Pontifical* includes those rites normally celebrated by a Bishop. The rites for Confirmation and for a church dedication, at least, should be in every liturgical library:

   a. *Roman Pontifical, Part* I: 1978.

   b. Complementary volume: *Confirmation*: 1973 (excerpted from the fuller Pontifical).

   c. *Dedication of a Church and an Altar*: 1989 (an important resource for parishes undergoing renovation or construction; useful for parishes preparing for each year's anniversary).

   d. *Rite of Ordination of Deacons, Priests and Bishops: 1975*

6. Other Official Books:

   a. *Ceremonial of Bishops*: 1989. (Though not a book of liturgical texts, it is an official compilation of rubrics and of emendations made since the various ritual books were published. The notes are useful for charting parish celebrations.)

   b. *The Roman Martyrology*: (This is a special kind of calendar, cataloging all the saints according to their date of observance. This includes not only the scores of saints who are on the current universal [Roman] calendar, but the thousands of others who might be part of national, diocesan, or religious community calendars).

OTHER BOOKS   In addition to these books, sacristies should have the following:

- copies of the hymnal or other materials used by the congregation

- a book or folder with locally prepared intercessions or with copies of the intercessions contained in a particular rite

- special books for Priest Celebrants and other ministers at complicated or combined rites (Using removable tape, copies of varied rites' texts can be collated with local ceremonial directives into a nicely bound book. This might well be more dignified than juggling two or three ritual books during the same event.)

- official liturgical books in other approved languages of the United States (The list of books in Spanish-language editions for the dioceses of the United States continues to expand.)

- official liturgical books in other languages, from the respective nations of those tongues when they are unavailable in United States editions—to be used for multi-lingual rites.

The Care and Storage of Liturgical Books

Older editions of any of these texts that are no longer used in the liturgy should not be stored in the sacristy. Every parish, particularly older and larger ones with many of these books, should find a place in its library or parish center to house them. Liturgists, historians, and other researchers might utilize them; their block prints are often useful for "seasonal" or feast day clip art, if the copyrights have expired. Some outdated books, particularly those with leather binding, gold leaf edges, and high quality artwork, may be quite valuable.

Current books should be kept in the vesting room. If there is no vesting room, the books should be kept in the sacristy. If individual priests want any books for their own shelves, these should be separate copies. Most of these books are available in study or chapel editions at reasonable prices.

In some logical order understood by all, these thirty or more volumes should be available to ministers and those who prepare the liturgy. The basics of book-shelving should be observed: sturdy bookends, avoidance of horizontal piles that make the bottom books inconvenient to withdraw, and the removal of clips and extraneous papers after each use of a particular book.

Preparing Books for Use

COVERS   While reviewing the available editions of a liturgical book, we also can consider the use of special covers. A special cover might be commissioned or purchased, for example, in the case of a book that has beautiful art and typography, but a very plain binding. Certain outfitters can provide covers fitted for the Lectionary and the *Book of the Gospels* (in brass or in silver or gold plate). Local artists and some suppliers can fashion covers of leather or metal for any book. Durable, long-lasting covers convey the sense of "book" better than soft, pliable covers.

SELECTING TEXTS   At a meeting for liturgy preparation, or after such a meeting, the overall terms for a liturgy can be set, and texts of prayers and scriptures can be selected for particular rites. (See notes on pages 170–172.) Most often, the readings and prayers of the day are used, but at times when other choices are available, the sacristan may not know which readings the homilist or Priest Celebrant wishes to use until shortly before Mass. But ideally, the text selection process will take place before the day on which the rite takes place, so that musicians, homilists, and other ministers can prepare well in advance for the service. In addition to selecting texts, the preparation of them might include some local composition.

MARKING TEXTS   As the liturgy nears, the selected texts should be marked in the appropriate books. In the vesting room or sacristy, rather than in the full view of the congregation, the ministers can preview the texts and set the ribbons in the right places. If markers other than ribbons are used, they should be made of a material that will not fall out during the rite. All ribbons or markers should be in place well before the rite begins; there should be no searching for readings or prayers during the liturgy itself.

For Mass on weekdays and many Sundays, the ribbons or other markers need to be set at these pages of *The Roman Missal*:

- the Presidential Prayers — Collect, Prayer over the Gifts, and Prayer after Communion (On certain weekdays it will be necessary to set two ribbons because the Collect is at the day — proper — and the other two are in the general sections — commons.)

- the Universal Prayer (Prayer of the Faithful) is sometimes taken from the appendix in *The Roman Missal*, sometimes led by the Priest Celebrant or deacon without text, and sometimes prepared in advance. The sacristan needs to know what the custom is in the parish and mark the necessary pages in *The Roman Missal*, or prepare a separate binder.

- the Profession of Faith or the texts for the Preparation of the Gifts

- the Preface of the Eucharistic Prayer, unless this is already printed with the selected Eucharistic Prayer (Preface common to the liturgical time, or specific to a day, or related to a type of saint). Several of the Eucharistic Prayers, including II and IV, Eucharistic Prayers for Reconciliation I and II, and the Eucharistic Prayers for Masses for Use in Various Needs and Occasions I, II, III, and IV have their own Prefaces.

- a Solemn Blessing or Prayer over the People, if used and if not already positioned with the presidential prayers

- other texts (Introductory Rite and Eucharistic Prayers are usually marked with permanent tabs set by the publisher)

In addition, text marking might include small, self-stick removable notes (or tiny, removable, colored dot-labels) positioned at the appointed text (e. g., at funerals when there are many options spread on the pages). Small, removable stickers can also be used to note texts for concelebrating priests.

To accomplish these tasks, the vesting room will need an "editorial" or "lay-out" supply drawer by the liturgical books. It should have an ever-replenished supply of removable tape and a dispenser, self-stick removable notes or labels, loose writing paper of various sizes, scissors, pencils (and pencil sharpener) or pens, and paper clips. This list may appear to be unduly long, but the task of selecting and preparing texts is important, far too important to be left to chance or to be done at the last minute. All these items, trivial as they may appear to be individually, combine to help us reach our goal: equipping our ministers to perform their assigned actions with competence and confidence so that the entire congregation enters into the full action of praise.

Chapter Twenty-one
Liturgical Vessels

Sacred and Artistic Containers

Reverence through the Ages   The vessels used at Christian liturgy always have reflected the importance of our sacramental actions. As with our Jewish ancestors and neighbors, and with adherents to most other religions of the world, we set aside vessels for liturgical use that are distinguished by their size, form, nobility, and decoration. Some reformers and fundamentalists today, as in past centuries, are uneasy when art and religion meet. Some say that Christians are at their most "spiritual" when they have no need of art. Yet both Jewish and Christian history demonstrates that such iconoclasm has never prevailed for long. The history of art shows us that all the arts (architecture, sculpture, painting, and a myriad of others) reach the greatest heights when they seek to give expression to the sacred truths of religion. And we know from our own experience that the beauty of our church buildings, their adornments, and the sacred vessels dedicated to liturgical use can help inspire our devotion and form our faith.

The sanctuary artisan Bezalel is praised in Exodus 35:30–33, as so filled with divine spirit that he was able to devise artistic designs, to cut stones, to carve wood, and to work in gold, silver, and bronze. Later, in the eleven hundred years of the period of the Temples (ending in our apostolic period), all Jews, including the disciples of Jesus, revered their holy place in Jerusalem, a building complex of the finest materials that was filled with precious vessels and artifacts. In later centuries, domestic and synagogue gatherings of Jews utilized wonderful plates and cups, lamp stands, and spice boxes. Christians, too, in domestic prayer and in public assemblies of liturgy, always used splendid liturgical vessels made by artists and artisans—their own Bezalels.

The *General Instruction of the Roman Missal* (327–334) employs the term *sacred* to describe liturgical vessels, especially chalices and patens. Because of their centrality at Mass, and because they are used to hold the Body and Blood of the Lord, Christian communities rightly esteem these vessels and treat them with reverence. It is only natural that the most central vessels, the chalices and the patens, should be created with more artistry than others. Yet all of the vessels used in the liturgy should be considered beautiful and holy and be handled accordingly, for they invite us to interaction with the divine.

CURRENT MATERIALS AND FORMS　The chalice and paten placed on the altar before the Eucharistic Prayer should each be large enough to be seen by all and to be the clear sign of the "one bread and one chalice" of Christ (Eucharistic Prayer IV). *Norms for the Distribution and Reception of Holy Communion under Both Kinds* emphasizes the sign value of having just one paten and one chalice of sufficient size for the communion of the entire congregation, but notes that this will not always be possible, especially in large gatherings. When additional vessels are used, "care should be taken that the number of vessels should not exceed the need" (*Norms for the Distribution and Reception of Holy Communion under Both Kinds*, 32).

The *General Instruction of the Roman Missal* provides a number of details about the materials that may be used for chalices and patens (328–330):

> Sacred vessels should be made from precious metal. If they are made from metal that rusts or from a metal less precious than gold, they should generally be gilded on the inside.

> In the Dioceses of the United States of America, sacred vessels may also be made from other solid materials which in the common estimation in each region are considered precious or noble, for example, ebony or other harder woods, provided that such materials are suitable for sacred use. In this case, preference is always to be given to materials that do not easily break or deteriorate. This applies to all vessels that are intended to hold the hosts, such as the paten, the ciborium, the pyx, the monstrance, and others of this kind.

> As regards chalices and other vessels that are intended to serve as receptacles for the Blood of the Lord, they are to have a bowl of material that does not absorb liquids. The base, on the other hand, may be made of other solid and worthy materials.

So long as the vessels used function appropriately in the liturgy, they can be made by artists in whatever shapes express the local community's faith. This suggests that local artists—not catalogs of mass-produced items—be consulted when vessels are needed.

Wine and Vessels for Wine

THE MEANINGS OF CUP-SHARING   Eucharistic cup-sharing was so essential to the act of sharing Communion that, for early Christians, Communion under both kinds was the norm. Communion from the cup was the sharing that formed ecclesial unity and reconciliation (1 Corinthians 10:16). It was wine mixed with a little water, like the mixtures shared even today in Mediterranean cultures, but more importantly like the Sabbath cup of the Jews, a beverage of blessing and praising God. Sharing the cup was perceived by communicants as a sharing of life and immortality. To drink of the cup was to express commitment to God's will.

In the Middle Ages, as part of the overall clericalization of liturgical forms during that period, the Eucharistic wine became reserved to the Priest Celebrant. Theologians maintained the rich meanings associated with Eucharistic wine and the chalice, but the vitality of these meanings was compromised as the practice was curtailed. When reformers pressed for the restoration of cup-sharing to the congregation, the Bishops of the Roman Catholic Church responded with the doctrine of concomitance—the belief that the whole Christ is received under either form of the Eucharist, that the sharing of the chalice was not necessary for additional grace.

Through the decades leading to Vatican II, pastoral liturgists recognized the deficiency of this perspective; to receive Holy Communion under one form only was seen to weaken the integrity of the sacramental sign, for the Lord commanded, "take this, all of you, and drink from it." The *Constitution on the Sacred Liturgy* (#55) began the reforms which were implemented several years later, with the instruction *Eucharisticum Mysterium* (#32):

> Holy communion has a more complete form as a sign when it is received under both kinds. For in this manner of reception (without prejudice to the principles laid down by the Council of Trent, that under each element Christ whole and entire and the true sacrament are received), a fuller light shines on the sign of the eucharistic banquet. Moreover there is a clearer expression of that will by which the new and everlasting covenant is ratified in the blood of the Lord and of the relationship of the eucharistic banquet to the eschatological banquet in the Father's kingdom.

This perspective later found its way into the *General Instruction of the Roman Missal* (#281). As more and more assemblies receive Holy Communion under both kinds, as catechists and pastors fearlessly face the doubts about hygiene, the Christian vision of covenant and banquet will more and more become part of our common consciousness.

WINE   From time to time, reformers have undertaken to eliminate wine from the celebration of the Eucharist. From the second to the fifth centuries, ascetical groups (termed "Aquarians") refused to acknowledge that the messianic era symbolized by wine had been inaugurated with Jesus. They used water instead of wine and were vigorously opposed by church leaders. Church councils confronted another aberration, the substitution of milk for wine in seventh-century Spain. Even today, certain Baptists and other Protestants use grape juice instead of wine. Despite all this, Catholic liturgical tradition has prevailed. Wine has survived as a vital sacramental sign, proclaiming the covenant, the messianic era, and the "spiritual inebriation" of conversion.

The *General Instruction of the Roman Missal* (#322–323) sets the requirement for wine in brief terms:

> The wine for the celebration of the Eucharist must be from the fruit of the vine (cf. Lk 22:18), natural, and unadulterated, that is, without admixture of extraneous substances.

> Diligent care should be taken to ensure that the bread and wine intended for the Eucharist are kept in a perfect state of conservation: that is, that the wine does not turn to vinegar nor the bread spoil or become too hard to be broken easily.

Sacristans might periodically review their methods of storing and replenishing wine supplies. A good reserve is always appropriate, especially when large funerals can come at a moment's notice. However, the supply should not be so great that any given bottle is kept for more than six months. For open bottles of wine, a small refrigerator helps preserve the wine's taste.

The wine can be made by parish members (in those few geographic regions where this ideal is possible), donated by members, or purchased from any reputable supplier. Church goods stores and "sacramental wine" distributors can be used, but general wine merchants can provide equally appealing—perhaps better—wine that is natural, pure, and without additives. Aside from these canonical requirements, each community should evaluate these characteristics of wine:

- type of grape—some wines are labeled in a more generic way, but the varietal wines are often finer
- color—red is a clearer symbol, but both red and white wines are permitted
- body—often the lighter-bodied reds taste better in the morning
- sweet or dry—most communities find some middle ground taste.

For health reasons, a priest may substitute mustum, a special, unprocessed grape juice, for wine. The mustum should be kept in a separate location. When the priest uses mustum, the rest of the congregation still shares the Eucharistic wine (placed on the altar in separate chalices before the Eucharistic Prayer). In rare cases, for a person with severe allergies to both gluten and properties of wine, the Bishop may grant permission for a lay person to receive Holy Communion in the form of mustum.

CHALICES Our English word *chalice* comes from the Latin word *calix,* meaning "cup." In many places, we have grown used to calling the main vessel used through the Eucharistic Prayer the "chalice," and the smaller vessels used for Communion distribution the "cups." *The Roman Missal* uses the term *chalice* to describe all the vessels used to contain and distribute the Precious Blood.

In selecting chalices for use, the church should have enough to accommodate the most crowded congregation of the year. We should evaluate their functionality, their nobility of form, their expressiveness of festivity and messianic fullness, and their congruence with other visible objects at the celebration.

VESSELS FOR THE EUCHARISTIC ACTION Wine and a small amount of water are placed in the primary chalice during the Preparation of the Gifts just before the Eucharistic Prayer. This simple action implies the presence of other containers.

VESSELS FOR PRESENTING WINE The wine must be in a bottle or container when prepared before the celebration until it is presented to the Priest Celebrant and poured into the chalice. Few if any examples of these containers exist from the first millennium, and there does not seem to have been a great deal of distinction made between, on the one hand, the bottles of wine brought to the church by members, and on the other hand, the vessels used to pour this wine into the chalice. In the Middle Ages, though, there is evidence of the existence of special bottles for the presentation and pouring of wine. Some of these bottles were, for a brief time, quite large; they quickly gave way to small bottles when receiving from the chalice was reserved to the priest. Many names were used for these bottles — ampullae (there were also ampullae of oils), phials or vials, vinaria and aquaria, even the general term "vessel." By the time of the Renaissance, the term cruet was universally used in English-language areas. At roughly the same time, glass became standardized as the preferred material, because it was the easiest to clean and because it was transparent. The latter property made it easy to tell whether the cruet contained wine or water. Stoppers also became normative.

Since the Second Vatican Council, the return of Eucharistic cup-sharing by entire assemblies has resulted in the use of much larger bottles for the presentation of the wine. These sometimes look like large cruets, but might also appear as carafes, decanters, or flagons. All of these terms connote large, ornamental vessels, but the term *flagon* is most appropriate if the vessel has a handle, spout, and cover. Decanters and carafes often appear noble when carried in procession and presented to the deacon or priest. Because they usually lack spouts, however, they tend to be less suited for pouring.

Every parish needs a variety of vessels for the presentation and pouring of wine—small cruets for weekday Masses and much larger cruets or flagons for larger assemblies. While metals of various kinds may be used for these containers as well as for the chalices, the norms about the use of materials do not apply to these vessels, because the wine is poured from it into the cups before the Eucharistic Prayer begins. In keeping with tradition, these might be glass. They also could be of the same nonabsorbent material as the chalice—precious metal or ceramic. Some writers have suggested that glass is better, since it allows all to see the sacramental sign. The job of the sacristan is to choose vessels that are made of the worthiest materials.

1. *Vessels for the Altar Table.* In some cases, the one chalice will contain sufficient wine for Holy Communion. If it cannot, then the rest of the wine is poured into additional chalices and placed with the chalice and paten on the altar for the eucharistic action. Parishes should have as many of these additional chalices as are needed for the largest Eucharistic congregation of the year.

2. *Vessel for the Water that Will Be Added.* The mixture of wine with water, rooted in ancient Jewish custom, presumes a vessel of water prepared before Mass and given to the Priest Celebrant at the Preparation of the Gifts. This was always a small amount of water. Except at small gatherings, they should not match the scale of the wine vessel. It is best if this pouring of the water is kept quite distinct from the washing of the hands, with a separate ewer or pitcher reserved for that later action.

VESSELS FOR EUCHARISTIC RESERVATION As described on page 73, the Precious Blood may be reserved in the tabernacle for those sick members who are either allergic to gluten or unable to swallow with ease. This is an admirable practice of our reform era but seldom utilized because of the danger of spoiling. Bottles or flasks or pyxes should be found or commissioned. They should exhibit the following characteristics:

- a secure lid

- a worthy design

- a neck or opening that allows the Eucharistic wine to be poured from flagon or chalice into it

- a lip or spout that allows pouring into a spoon or cup

- a material that can be cleansed easily

In addition, they should have cases that will permit them to be carried safely. Because of the rubrics against the pouring of the wine after it has been consecrated, if Holy Communion under this form is to be taken to the sick, the already filled vessel should be placed on the altar at the preparation of the gifts.

OTHER REQUISITES FOR THE WINE Two other types of functional equipment assist in the dignified use of the vessels for use in the celebration of the Eucharist. They are funnels and trays. Funnels are helpful in pouring wine from a bottle or other container into most cruets and into some flagons. They should be large enough at the top so that liquids can be poured into them easily without spilling, and small enough at the bottom to fit into the mouth of the receiving vessel. They should be made of a material that can be easily cleaned.

Parishes also should have a variety of dignified-looking trays. Some communities have begun using larger trays for carrying the Communion cups from the sacristy to the credence table. When the wine is poured into these cups at the altar table, the same trays might bear them from credence to altar. They should be of a noble or formal design, and not resemble the trays used in self-serve restaurants.

Bread and Vessels for Bread

THE RESTORATION OF HOLY COMMUNION   For many centuries, the priest was the only one eating at the Eucharistic banquet at many Masses, and he was mandated to do so. The congregation waited for special feasts, for a Sunday made special by their group's sharing in Communion before a "Communion breakfast," or for the mandated reception in Easter Time. Meanwhile, they engaged in "spiritual communion." This act of mental prayer was complemented by other favored practices: silence and devotional prayers at the consecration, participation in Eucharistic benediction, and private visits to the blessed sacrament—prayer before the tabernacle.

Though such Eucharistic adoration is a praiseworthy practice, it gradually became more important for many than participation in the sacraments themselves. Spiritual communion and worship of the Eucharist outside of Mass were put back into perspective by the many reforms that have unfolded throughout the entire twentieth century. Pope Pius X lowered the age for first Holy Communion. Both he and later Popes urged all Catholics to receive Communion more often. And with the Council's reforms in the 1960s, the return to active participation was pronounced at the Sunday celebrations of the Eucharist.

BREAD   While the bread for Eucharist may have been leavened through large parts of the first millennium, churches of the Roman Rite have now been using unleavened bread for many centuries. We in the Roman Rite have long been accustomed to round breads, called hosts, sometimes with monograms or designs printed on them. Current norms are found in the *General Instruction of the Roman Missal:*

> It is most desirable that the faithful, just as the Priest himself is bound to do, receive the Lord's Body from hosts consecrated at the same Mass and that, in the cases where this is foreseen, they partake of the chalice (see 283), so that even by means of the signs Communion may stand out more clearly as a participation in the sacrifice actually being celebrated. (85)

> The bread for celebrating the Eucharist must be made only from wheat, must be recently made, and, according to the ancient tradition of the Latin Church, must be unleavened. (320)

> By reason of the sign, it is required that the material for the Eucharistic Celebration truly have the appearance of food. Therefore, it is desirable that the Eucharistic bread, even though unleavened and made in the traditional form, be fashioned in such a way that the Priest at Mass with the people is truly able to break it into parts and distribute these to at least some of the faithful. However, small hosts are not at all excluded when the large number of those receiving Holy Communion or other pastoral reasons call for them. Moreover, the gesture of the fraction (or breaking of bread, which was quite simply the term by which the Eucharist was known in apostolic times) will bring out more clearly the force and importance of the sign of the unity of all in the one bread, and of the sign of charity by the fact that the one bread is distributed among the brothers and sisters. (321)

> Diligent care should be taken to ensure that the bread and wine intended for the Eucharist are kept in a perfect state of conservation: that is, that the wine does not turn to vinegar nor the bread spoil or become too hard to be broken easily. (323)

The Church's ideal is for the Eucharistic bread to be large enough, allowing all to share from the same loaf or host. As with all the reforms, this ideal is imbued with an appreciation of sacramental signs. The sacristan must make sure that hosts are delivered regularly and on time and should be stored in canisters or other containers.

Patens or Plates for the Eucharistic Action In the first millennium, the Eucharist was distributed from the same paten or plate that contained the elements on the altar table. These were quite large and circular, holding bread for the entire congregation. With the introduction of wafer-breads, these patens could be much smaller. When the reception of Holy Communion declined so radically in the Middle Ages, the single paten often held only the one host for the priest. As the paten became smaller, it came to be made of the same material as the chalice and in proportion to it. From this flowed the practice of placing the paten on top of the chalice before and after the Eucharist.

As with other liturgical artifacts, the norms for patens are quite simple. In addition to the general norms for all vessels (solid and noble materials, in shapes appreciated by the local culture), the *General Instruction of the Roman Missal* says:

> In the Dioceses of the United States of America, sacred vessels may also be made from other solid materials which in the common estimation in each region are considered precious or noble, for example, ebony or other harder woods, provided that such materials are suitable for sacred use. In this case, preference is always to be given to materials that do not easily break or deteriorate. This applies to all vessels that are intended to hold the hosts, such as the paten, the ciborium, the pyx, the monstrance, and others of this kind. (#329)

> For the Consecration of hosts, a large paten may fittingly be used, on which is placed the bread both for the Priest and the Deacon and also for the other ministers and for the faithful. (#331)

This large paten can take one of many different shapes; for example, concave plates, shallow bowls, larger vessels shaped like pie plates (but of fine materials), and traditional ciboria. Additional patens are brought from the credence table during the breaking of the bread. They are filled with pieces as the loaves are broken. These patens may or may not form a matched set with the various chalices. The terms *plate* and *paten* can be used interchangeably, but the latter term is specific to the Mass.

Vessels for Eucharistic Reservation The term *pyx* can signify any one of the many containers that hold Eucharistic bread for reservation. They keep the Eucharistic banquet fresh and available for the absent, the sick, and the dying, and provide for safe storage of the consecrated hosts in the tabernacle for the Prayer of the Faithful. In the early centuries, many Christians used these vessels to bring the Eucharist to their homes. In the Middle Ages, before tabernacles were regularly installed in sanctuaries, the pyx often was shaped as a dove or veiled with beautiful fabric and then suspended by the altar. On occasion, pyxes were made with base and stem.

In the fourteenth century the term *ciborium* (the plural is *ciboria*) came to be used for one variant of the pyx. Originally, this term had been used to describe the architectural canopies or roofs above altars. These new ciboria differed from many other pyxes in that their covers were loose, rather than attached by hinges. In shape, they resembled the chalice. The ciborium is still used in most parishes to reserve the hosts in the tabernacle and, in some places, to distribute Holy Communion during Mass as well.

Each parish should own as many pyxes as are needed by the extraordinary ministers of Holy Communion who visit the sick. They should generally be of a smaller size, owing to the fact that long itineraries of "Communion calls" rarely exist outside hospitals. There should also be a ciborium of appropriate size, so that enough consecrated hosts can be kept in the tabernacle during the week.

VESSELS FOR EUCHARISTIC EXPOSITION   Beginning in the twelfth century, the desire of the people to see the consecrated host resulted in various developments in the liturgy. The elevations of the consecrated elements were added at the Mass, and processions with the Blessed Sacrament became common. To accommodate the desire for visibility, monstrances or ostensoria designed to show the consecrated host to the faithful became part of the regular furnishing of the church. These were often designed in the shape of the sun, with rays extending out on all sides, but other forms were used as well. The host is placed in a holder called a lunette, which fits in the window of the monstrance. When exposition is over, the lunette is removed and kept in a special pyx sometimes called a custodia.

Exposition of the Blessed Sacrament remains a well-loved part of our Catholic tradition today. On those occasions when lunettes, custodia, and monstrances are used, the sacristan needs to be sure that the lunette fits into the given monstrance and that the host fits into the lunette. Sacristans should also be aware that whenever exposition takes place following Mass, a new host is to be consecrated. The previous host can be consumed or broken into smaller pieces for distribution to the homebound.

Vessels for Liturgical Washings

The orders for Christian liturgies were first developed and shared between communities that were quite familiar with ceremonial washings. Many civic, religious, and domestic settings called for fountains or basins of water. The scriptures and the annals of early churches contain many stories of washing the ceremonial place, the whole body, the head, hair, feet, hands, or fingers. Such ceremonial washings often were done after cures.

FEET   Stories of the Last Supper and traditions that called for foot-washing (on Thursday of Holy Week and at other ritual moments) have provided our current ritual with its only ceremony of washing feet—at the Evening Mass of the Lord's Supper on Thursday of Holy Week. For this we need towels for each of those whose feet will be washed, one or more large pitchers of warm water, and several basins large enough to hold both feet of those chosen. These vessels should be quite a bit larger than those used for washing hands. And even though they are used only once a year, they should be made of materials that are both serviceable and worthy.

HANDS   The Order of Mass continues to include the minor but long-standing tradition of washing the hands of the Priest Celebrant before the Eucharistic Prayer. The first word of Psalm 26 formerly said during this action, *lavabo* ("I wash"), is still frequently used to describe both the action itself and the equipment used in it. Through the centuries, this washing has been considered both a practical and a symbolic act. It is practical, because after receiving the gifts and handling the incense, the Priest Celebrant may well need to wash his hands. It is symbolic as well, a prayer for forgiveness as he prepares for the Eucharistic Prayer. The accompanying prayer, said silently, is from Psalm 51:2 "wash me, O Lord, from my iniquity, / and cleanse me from my sin."

Before the reforms, pitchers and basins for this action often were reserved to special and episcopal liturgies (where they often were called "ewer" and "bacile"). At other Masses, the water cruet and even the cruet dish were used not only for their traditional purpose, but for washing the hands, too. The current liturgical books clearly define two containers that are used for very different purposes. One is the cruet that is used in conjunction with the chalice; the other is the container of water used for the washing of hands. All parishes should have pitchers and basins (of metal, glass, or other dignified material) that are used only for the washing of hands, and they should not resemble the vessels that are used for wine and water meant for drinking.

In addition to this washing of hands at Mass, there are a number of other times when the Priest Celebrant will need to wash his hands. For washings after anointings, the traditional addition of lemon wedge slices is helpful. For washing after the distribution of ashes, small bars of soap will be helpful. These may rest in the basin itself, or perhaps in a side dish. In general, it is better if the priest stays within the ritual areas (generally at the credence table where the equipment rests) and performs these washings with the assistance of other ministers. This is more dignified than disappearing into the sacristy to wash.

Hand-washing supplies usually are most needed:

- for the one who washes feet on Thursday of Holy Week, right after that action (possibly with a small bar of soap)

- for the various ministers who impose ashes, right after that act (with small bars of soap); several vessels can help

- for those performing anointings with oil at liturgies, if the oil is not absorbed, while the songs accompanying the anointings continue and before the liturgy proceeds (communal anointings of the sick, Confirmation, rites of the catechumenate).

Lemon wedges are traditionally helpful here. If several ministers are performing the anointings, several basins and pitchers are helpful.

FINGERS   A covered "ablution cup" with water is used in some parishes to allow those who have distributed Communion to cleanse their thumbs and forefingers in it. Ministers may also simply wipe their fingers on a purificator or use a designated basin and pitcher.

FLOOR   The *General Instruction of the Roman Missal* (#280) explains: "If a host or any particle should fall, it is to be picked up reverently; and if any of the Precious Blood is spilled, the area where the spill occurred should be washed with water, and this water should then be poured into the sacrarium in the sacristy." The water for this washing can come from the basin at the credence table, and the cloths used with it can be extra purificators from the sacristy. This should be handled as quickly and simply as possible, and no blame, alarm, or drama should be conveyed by sacristans and ministers of Communion.

Other Vessels

This chapter has focused on Eucharistic vessels. There are many other containers or receptacles used for rites and feasts. Many are described elsewhere in this manual, especially in the chapter on the baptistry. In every case, they are to be both worthy (beautiful in design and in materials) and suited to their particular purpose in the liturgical action. Plates for the rings at Marriage should express the importance of this jewelry and the festivity of the rite, but they should be made in such a way that the rings won't slip off easily. Bowls for ashes at the start of Lent should be deep enough to contain the ashes securely, but not so deep and narrow as to complicate the repeated insertion of the minister's fingers. Stands for the reverent display of saints' relics (reliquaries) should be large enough and attractive enough to perform that function efficiently and nobly, but neither relics nor stands should compete for attention with the primary liturgical vessels. They should be positioned away from the altar and ambo, then securely stored away after the period of veneration ends.

Care and Storage of Vessels

Not many general rules can be set for such a wide variety of vessels. Each community should establish its own procedures for the regular care of its objects, depending on what kinds of vessels it uses. One general rule is that metal vessels should not be cleaned with paper towels or steel wool pads; these scratch the surface of the metal. Commercially produced polishes and chemicals also may do damage to metal or clay vessels. Periodically, regilding or polishing may need to be done.

Each community also will decide on the best way to store all of these vessels. A metal safe is traditionally useful for the most treasured ones. In any event, every sacristy needs cabinets with flexible shelving and countertops for preparation. A review of the contents of these vessel cabinets should give an idea of their size to those planning to furnish a new or renovated sacristy:

- the current store of bread and wine
- enough Communion cups for the largest Mass
- cruets and flagons for wine
- cruets for water
- funnel and saucer

- trays (especially for multiple cups)
- pyxes for consecrated wine and for consecrated bread (some of these might be ciboria, others might be lunettes)
- enough patens/plates/ciboria for all Communion stations
- a monstrance
- basins and pitchers for water
- any reliquaries
- occasional dishes for symbols like rings and ashes.

Chapter Twenty-two

Liturgical Vestments

Vesture of the Congregation

Few norms ever have been universally issued for the vesture of the congregation. Such instructions have arisen from concerns about modesty and reverence. At one time there was a long-standing prohibition against wearing gloves at liturgy, for both men and women, founded on a conviction that bare hands conveyed the proper humility when receiving a blessed candle or palm, when serving as a godparent, and when receiving Holy Communion. Catholics of middle age or older will have no trouble remembering other rules that governed the covering—or uncovering—of the head. Through the 1960s, women had to wear hats; men had to take theirs off. The rule requiring hats for women was grounded in hellenistic or Jewish history, and especially in the classic articulation by Paul (1 Corinthians 11:–16). Veils for women, the special sign of consecrated virgins, sprang from similar origins. If there are rules about proper attire in the local diocese, the sacristan should be aware of these and should also be aware of the action to be taken (if any) when someone comes who may not be properly attired.

Special Vesture for Certain Ministries

Liturgical commentators often repeat the story that early Christian leaders of liturgy wore no distinctive vesture, just the "Sunday best" of the late antique Mediterranean culture. Images of that culture's vesture and of Christian vestments are too strikingly similar to dismiss their ancient bonds. This does not mean that Christians adopted imperial costume for their events; the vesture communicated more a message of "public act" and of "important act" than of imperial homage.

Once these links are acknowledged, it also must be noted that at a very early date, the robes for priest and deacon and other ministers were distinct from civic dress and from the vesture of others in the congregation. The wearing of special clothes for festivals and to designate special roles is pervasive in every century and in every social grouping. This was not just an abstract, cultural idea or rule. The earliest Christians knew that leaders in Jewish prayer, leaders and members of many different assemblies, wore specific vesture. As the centuries have passed, liturgical vesture has evolved slowly, though always revealing its roots in late antique, Mediterranean culture. As one new style of secular dress has replaced another, the gulf between liturgical garments and street dress has widened. This difference is to be welcomed, not bemoaned. A diversity of vesture expresses a rich diversity of ministries. Secondly, the beauty of the vestments makes a contribution to the celebration of the liturgy, enhancing the expression of festivity and helping to sharpen visual focus. The *General Instruction of the Roman Missal* (#335) articulates these reasons for distinctive vesture:

> In the Church, which is the Body of Christ, not all members have the same function. This diversity of offices is shown outwardly in the celebration of the Eucharist by the diversity of sacred vestments, which must therefore be a sign of the function proper to each minister. Moreover, these same sacred vestments should also contribute to the decoration of the sacred action itself. . . .

There is a third reason for our distinctive vesture: These are not just any old "dress up" costumes; they are the robes of our earliest ancestors in the faith. We continue to perform our liturgical actions with ministers dressed more or less like they were in ancient Rome and Gaul and Carthage. Vesture is living art and acts as a historical link between us and all of the Christians who have gone before us.

While maintaining a high level of continuity, the Roman vestments have undergone a number of modifications over the centuries. There were periods when many attempted to reject the use of vestments altogether; for example, sixteenth-century Calvinists. During certain periods, factions for and against vestments were active simultaneously. In the tumultuous 1960s, for example, some of those who were experimenting with home Masses did away with vestments. But during that same decade, the brothers of the ecumenical community at Taizé adopted the alb. Changes in rites and communal life also have affected vesture, resulting in elements being added and subtracted. For example, the restoration of the permanent diaconate following the Second Vatican Council has given fresh prominence to dalmatics and diaconal stoles. Available materials and shifting technologies also have played a role, as in the regrettable flooding of markets with mass-produced vestments in recent generations.

Whatever garb is worn, it should be evaluated in terms of its ability to serve and enhance the liturgy to the benefit of both the ministers and the people gathered.

The Use of Liturgical Colors

For the first millennium, little attention was paid to creating fixed cycles of colors for the vestments that were related to particular liturgical times and feasts, though white was always central. Through the Middle Ages, most dioceses and local communities of western and central Europe began developing and sharing customs that associated certain days and certain colors. Until 1570, when Roman authorities issued universal rules as part of the Tridentine reforms, these patterns differed from region to region and from parish to parish.

This system, now 400 years old, has been accepted by each generation and was retained in the recent reforms. It has been an enduring and popular part of the Tridentine heritage because Western Christians see it as assisting their progress through the liturgical year, as lending a "seasonal" unity and as expressing the shifting moods of the congregation.

Here is the list of vestment colors for Masses and for all other liturgies found in the *General Instruction of the Roman Missal* (345–347).

White:

- festive times such as Christmas Time and Easter Time
- days of the Lord—except days related to the Passion
- days of saints—except the anniversary of death of martyrs, apostles, evangelists
- Conversion of Paul, Chair of Peter, Nativity of John the Baptist, All Saints, John the Evangelist—days associated with martyrs or apostles, but not anniversaries of martyrdom

Red:

- Passion/Palm Sunday and Friday of Holy Week
- Pentecost
- days of the Lord related to the Passion
- days of martyrs, apostles, evangelists
  (If only a few red vestments are owned by a community, they should not be so specifically decorated for the Passion, for Pentecost, or for martyrs, that they cannot be used on all of these days.)

Green:

- Ordinary Time

Violet:

- Advent

- Lent
  (If only a few violet vestments are available, Lenten and penitential motifs should not be so prevalent as to disallow their use in Advent.)

Rose:

- Third Sunday of Advent (Gaudete Sunday)

- Fourth Sunday of Lent (Laetare Sunday)
  (When there are limited resources, this tradition need not be kept, and violet can be worn.)

Gold or silver:

- solemn occasions

Funerals and liturgies held on the Commemoration of All the Faithful Departed (All Souls' Day, which falls on November 2) can utilize white, violet, or even black vesture. Each community should review its policy on choosing vesture for funerals. In the context of existing pastoral practice and other decorations, a case might be made for one color over another. Perhaps the liturgical times and colors already in the church complex should be respected. Violet could be used at funerals through Advent and Lent; white, during the weeks of Christmas Time and Easter Time; black, during Ordinary Time. If the community has a truly worthy chasuble in any one of these colors, then this might be the best choice. The chasuble does not need to match the coffin pall, which is always white in color since it recalls the white baptismal garment.

There is no need to memorize any of these lists, to worry about whether to give priority to a color for a particular liturgical time or to the color of a particular day. The annual ordo in every sacristy lists the correct colors for each day (as does LTP's *Sourcebook for Sundays, Seasons, and Weekdays*). When optional memorials are selected for a given parish (see pages 170–172), they determine the color for that day; these, too, are in the ordo. When votive or other special Masses are celebrated, their colors are of the given day (unless there is an obvious association like red with Masses of the Holy Spirit). As we become ever more aware of our local resources, of the emotional power of varied colors, and of visual relationships, we can breathe fresh life into this enduring system of linking liturgical times and affections.

Materials and Design of Vestments

Between the fourteenth and the twentieth centuries, the flowing robes of the late antique Mediterranean, adapted to distinguish liturgical ministries and passed down through the centuries, came upon hard times. In that period, when assemblies were called to look at rather than interact with the liturgy, antique simplicity was replaced by complex layers of flamboyant embroidery and lace.

As ornamentation increased, the length and width of most vesture forms were cut back. As in other forms of liturgical art (see page 23), private emotions and pieties prevailed. The images and shapes no longer served a public action; instead they bore inspirational messages or dramatic displays. Where once the symbol had been the robe itself, now the attached symbol pictures became the focus.

The *General Instruction of the Roman Missal* (343–344) expresses the ideals of the Church regarding materials and design for vesture:

> For making sacred vestments, in addition to traditional materials, natural fabrics proper to each region may be used, and also artificial fabrics that are in keeping with the dignity of the sacred action and the sacred person. The Conference of Bishops will be the judge of this matter.

> It is fitting that the beauty and nobility of each vestment not be sought in an abundance of overlaid ornamentation, but rather in the material used and in the design. Ornamentation on vestments should, moreover, consist of figures, that is, of images or symbols, that denote sacred use, avoiding anything unbecoming to this.

Materials The traditional material for albs was linen. For all other vesture, silk and fabrics related to it (satin, damask, or silk interwoven with gold or silver threads) were preferred. Cloth woven from real gold threads was also allowed, but for obvious reasons was rare.

Though the new rules continue to stress the need for dignity in vestments, they also now permit great freedom regarding the materials used in their manufacture. The traditional materials no longer dominate. New technology has encouraged the nearly universal spread of other materials, often blends of natural and artificial fibers.

Despite the freedom we now enjoy to choose vestments made from a much wider range of materials, we should nevertheless stay clear of cheap materials or those that impede the liturgical action. Inexpensive cotton and polyester that doesn't breathe can be just as distracting and undignified as excessive lace and heavy brocade.

Design A glance through the catalogs of liturgical suppliers reveals a vast range of designs and of quality in vesture. Some ground rules, however, remain. The material and design that bring beauty and functionality to liturgical clothes presume a pliancy of material, a flowing form and plentiful folds that allow the fabric to hang well. Such fullness is most fitting for the movements and gestures demanded of ministers. Within each height and girth range, there are ways for vesture to be richly draped.

Ornamentation on the fabric can be justified only if it is well-executed, congruent with the other elements of design and color, and fitting for liturgical action. Any that fails to meet these standards should not be purchased, commissioned, accepted, or used. Because albs are to be simple baptismal garments of white, decorations are even less likely to be appropriate here. Some terms associated with the ornamentation of vestments other than the alb, and utilized by many catalogs and artists, are listed below.

- Appliqués (often of silk, or of gold metallic threads) of crosses or other small symbols are traditionally applied to the vestment by stitching (with gold metallic cord or with floss of a contrasting color).

- Cording is a trimming used to add detail to other ornamentation.

- Fringes (of varying materials and colors) are often used on antependia, but were and are rare on vestments.

- Galloons are colorful and narrow borders, often used along either side of orphreys. They can sometimes highlight the main lines of the vestment.

- Gems and pearls and ornamental glass are sometimes used with restraint (and some success) on miters. They are rarely appropriate elsewhere, but they might be considered because of their allusions to the new Jerusalem in the book of Revelation.

- Inscriptions of text are rarely appropriate on ministers' clothes.

- Medallions (see vesicas).

- Monograms (see symbols).

- Orphrey bandings are strips of fabric that contrast with the vestment on which they are sewn. They are often multi-colored brocades (tapestries) or are embroidered with symbols. They are often edged with galloon borders. If they are used with restraint and are properly positioned, they can highlight the main shapes and movements of the vesture.

- Protectors, by whatever name their proponents call them, are needless and intrusive strips of linen or other cloth, often edged with lace. They are affixed to stoles in hopes of protecting them from sweat and dirt. This is disrespectful to the design of the stole. It is an exaggerated concern as well, because the stole rarely rides above the alb to the bare neck.

- Symbols in this context mean small images of the cross, lamb, dove, or other such devices sewn onto vestments. At their worst, they provide sentimental or stylized pictures of saints or other creatures. They were the principal villains in the devolution of vestments from clothing to billboards. They are rarely appropriate.

- Tassels can be used at the bottom of stoles or cope hoods. The extra weight sometimes helps the garment hang correctly, but their positioning, size, and color should not be obtrusive.

- Vesicas (often shaped liked medallions) are pieces of colorful fabric (often velvet) that provide background frames for applied symbols. Like the symbols themselves, they are rarely helpful.

Vestment for All Ministers: The Alb and Its Accessories

ROBE OF GLORY At the Transfiguration, Jesus' clothes became "dazzling white." The angelic herald of the Resurrection was arrayed in white. The books of Daniel and of Revelation describe the Ancient One in white; the singing multitudes in the new Jerusalem are similarly seen in white robes.

It is no wonder that both early and later Christians wore an equivalent of the basic robe of classical Rome, the tunica alba, at Baptism and at virtually every other liturgy. In an unbroken tradition, the billowing christening dress of infants, the long white robe of adult neophytes, and the basic vestment of Catholic liturgy all express our baptismal destiny in the new Jerusalem. When first Holy Communion was separated from the other initiatory sacraments, it is no mere coincidence that white became the preferred color for the vesture of communicants. This meaning is not some later invention of catechists, for long and flowing white robes are rather archetypal. They have a primal ability to express and enhance the purity of new life.

The unbroken heritage has been periodically diverted. Shorter versions of the alb, with wider sleeves, eventually became "surplices," worn over a cassock. Yet the full, unembellished white robe survives and continues to be the basic vestment for all. The *General Instruction of the Roman Missal* (#336, 339) states:

> The sacred garment common to all ordained and instituted ministers of any rank is the alb, to be tied at the waist with a cincture unless it is made so as to fit even without such. Before the alb is put on, should this not completely cover the ordinary clothing at the neck, an amice should be used. . . .

> In the Dioceses of the United States of America, acolytes, altar servers, readers, and other lay ministers may wear the alb or other appropriate and dignified clothing.

CURRENT ALBS   Today, all those who minister in the liturgy have the option to wear the albs. In some regions, many parish ministers—choir members, lectors and readers, extraordinary ministers of Holy Communion and acolytes—all may wear the baptismal garment, the alb. This possibility, once realized, obviously presents new challenges for sacristans, because sufficient albs in many sizes will need to be acquired and maintained.

For most, the alb is not an undergarment, and it should be dignified in appearance and of good material. For the same reasons that linen was used for altar cloths (see page 45), our ancestors usually preferred albs made of linen. This is still a wonderful fabric, though wrinkle-resistant blends requiring less care are more regularly used today. As is the case with all vestments, there should be plenty of albs on hand, in various sizes for the wearers. The collar should be such that undergarments are covered, making amices unnecessary. The sleeves should be wide enough to accommodate many different-sized arms and to allow for gracious gestures with the amply vested arm, and the alb itself should be long enough to cover the legs. Cinctures should be used only if required by the design of the alb (many albs are designed to fit and hang properly without a cincture). Newly appointed ministers may need a few pointers on how to walk up stairs—for the sake of a dignified liturgy, offering such advice is superior to giving them hiked-up robes.

THE CINCTURE   The first embellishment to the alb mentioned in the *General Instruction of the Roman Missal* is the cincture, to be used only if necessary. This will depend on the design and fit of the alb. When a cincture is used, for example to raise up the hem for a person who is too short for an available robe, then it should be white and as simply made as possible. Colored cinctures and those with elaborate tassels or fringe should be avoided. The alb is what is important, and no ornamental accessory should detract from it.

THE AMICE   Another embellishment is the amice. It is to be worn by all ministers, male and female, young and old, whose albs do not adequately cover their street clothes. If the right kind of albs have been aquired, then amices should seldom be necessary.

Amices are square or preferably oblong pieces of white linen, large enough to be stretched around the shoulders and to be tucked inside the neck of the underlying street clothes. From two corners of the fabric, long strings extend for three feet or more—long enough to be crossed on the breast, carried round to the back, crossed there, and brought around again to the front to be tied. Whether the amice originated as a head covering or as a protection around the neck is debated by historians. Even though it is a minor vestment, it nonetheless gives witness to the first purpose of liturgical vestments—to envelop the minister in distinct garb, to put aside the dress of Main Street and wear the white of the new Jerusalem.

Vestments Proper to the Ordained: Stole, Dalmatic, Chasuble

THE STOLE   This long, scarf-like vestment is the mark of ordination. Deacons wear it over the left shoulder, drawn across the chest and back toward the lower right side. Other ordained ministers wear it around the neck, hanging down in front. On many occasions, deacons, priests, and Bishops wear just a stole of the day's color over the alb. The dalmatic or chasuble is worn over the alb and stole only for certain liturgies, principally the Mass. When the stole is used with these or with a cope, it usually matches them in material and design.

Many theories have been advanced, none of them conclusive, on the historical origins of the stole, as well as its etymology. Plausible theories hold that it is related to the Jewish prayer mantle, to a Roman neck-cloth, to a ceremonial garland, or to another surviving vestment, the pallium (see page 129). This last theory is based on the fact that civil and ecclesial officials in late antiquity wore scarfs as badges of office. A Bishop's scarf was called a pallium; the scarf worn by priests and deacons was called an orarium. Meanwhile the term stola or stole was used in the scriptures to denote a long, flowing robe. Around the ninth century, there was a confusing change of designations, and the orarium scarf began to be called a stole.

Aside from such confusing changes in name, the stole has changed remarkably little throughout its long history. Its shape is much the same; so is the silken material used to make it. Like the chasuble, it was sometimes over-decorated.

We need to have many stoles in our sacristies: for priests and deacons; in various colors to complement all of the chasubles, dalmatics, and copes (usually purchased or commissioned with them); in shapes and colors to be worn independently;

for wearers of different heights; sufficient in numbers to accommodate all local rites, including concelebrated Masses. While many ordained ministers have stoles of their own, they may not have them in all colors. The community should have its own sets, so that the departures of individual clergy do not strip sacristies of the necessary variety.

There are many variants on the basic shape of the stole, all named differently by individual artists, all to be examined before acquisition. The differences to be reviewed include width, length, finish at the ends (and how well this holds them down evenly), shape at the back of the neck (or over the shoulder of the deacon), and how well the stole rests without riding up onto the neck. Obviously, a lot depends on whether the given stole will be worn alone with an alb, under a chasuble, or over a plain chasuble. With so many variables, those charged with the selection of stoles should inspect and try on as many as possible.

The Dalmatic   The *General Instruction of the Roman Missal (#338)* has just a few laconic references to this ancient robe: "The vestment proper to the Deacon is the dalmatic, worn over the alb and stole; however, the dalmatic may be omitted out of necessity or on account of a lesser degree of solemnity."

The alb began as the tunica alba, a long white robe with strips of ornamentation. The dalmatic began perhaps in Dalmatia (later Croatia) as another tunica alba, with similar bands of decoration, worn over the first. As both forms of the tunica alba passed into strictly liturgical usage, the lower tunica alba lost its stripes and became the alb. The upper tunica alba was reduced in length, given broader sleeves and slit open at the sides, becoming the dalmatic.

Dalmatics usually come with matching stoles. They regularly match a chasuble as well, because of the ministerial role that deacons fill beside the Priest Celebrant at Mass. This pairing of proper vestments is never necessary. Indeed, it is sometimes undesirable, owing to the fact that at a number of rites deacons can preside on their own. Even when together, ministers needn't be vested as a matched set.

Dalmatics come in all the liturgical colors. Though white always can be worn whenever a community does not have the color for the feast or liturgical time, deacons should wear the colors designated whenever possible. In other respects, the materials and design of dalmatics follow the same general rules as other vestments. They should be made of dignified material, and they should envelop the ministers in color, with ample folds and flowing lines.

As with all vestments, we should establish procedures for the ongoing acquisition of dalmatics in sufficient numbers and colors for all the liturgical times. In deciding how many dalmatics will be needed, keep the following in mind:

- Deacons should not be expected to own their own

- On certain occasions (for example, at his ordination) a Bishop can wear a dalmatic between his stole and chasuble.

This latter custom is both ancient and curious, and speaks to the fullness of the priesthood the Bishop receives in his ordination. On the few solemn occasions when the extra robe is added, it is the only time that Bishops wear different liturgical vestments than priests. At such solemn events, with multiple deacons or a Bishop, parishes can borrow dalmatics from neighboring communities, a diocesan liturgy office, or the cathedral.

THE CHASUBLE The *General Instruction of the Roman Missal* (#337) is similarly brief about this most visible vestment: "The vestment proper to the Priest Celebrant at Mass and during other sacred actions directly connected with Mass is the chasuble worn, unless otherwise indicated, over the alb and stole."

The word *chasuble* is related to the terms that other languages use to denote "cottage" or "hut," such as the Spanish *casa* for house, and *casita* for small house. Several ancient sources, indeed, describe it as a "little house" enveloping the Priest Celebrant. Small hut or large robe, the original shape of the vestment was the *paenula* or *planeta* of classical Rome, a sort of poncho or circular garment with an opening in the center for the head. With or without a hood, this eminently practical and ample robe passed into strictly liturgical usage as the proper garb of priests at the celebration of the Eucharist.

We should supply the sacristy with more than one chasuble in each of the four major liturgical colors (white, red, violet, green). In addition, the sacristy should have as many of the lesser colors (gold, silver, black, and rose) as ritual customs and finances will permit. As with other vestments, if the community owns more than one chasuble in a single color, then these should be in different sizes to accommodate the maximum amount of variation in the heights of the Priest Celebrants. All should be amply cut to hang loosely. As stated before, the beauty of vesture comes from colorful materials and full forms enveloping the ministers and enhancing ministerial gestures, not from form-fitting panels of polyester emblazoned with pretty pictures.

Vestments of Special Festivity: Cope, Humeral Veil

THE COPE The Roman *paenula*, which later became the chasuble, was a circular garment extending to the ground. It had a center opening for the head and often a hood. This same poncho-type garment was slit completely up the front and equipped with a clasp (called a morse) to become a great cloak or cape. It was our ancestors' favorite protection against rain. Thus, the word for *cope* in various modern languages is related either to cape or to rain-cloak (*pluvial* or *piviale*). This raincoat evolved slightly in the early medieval period for use at liturgy: Often orphrey bands or other decorations were added. Some decorative materials, stiffer than silk, made the cape somewhat too heavy for easy wearing. The original hood often was transformed into a decorative, apron-like flap. On occasion, this flap was sometimes attached at a lower point unrelated to the neckline.

Despite these changes, the cope was passed on to us fairly intact. Old copes often are eloquently full cloaks of splendid material and restrained decoration. The cope is used outside of Mass, including but not limited to the following times:

- At celebrations of the Liturgy of Hours

- At Eucharistic adoration

- At outdoor processions, for example on Palm Sunday of the Passion of the Lord and on the Solemnity of the Most Holy Body and Blood of Christ (*Corpus Christi*)

- At certain solemn moments like the reception of a Bishop.

Given the beauty of copes, it's unfortunate that many communities use them only for priests and then only on rare occasions. This vestment was passed down to us not only with its original form intact, but with its originally broad access unchanged by liturgical law. The cope was never reserved to priests, although in the twelfth century some local churches restricted its use to cantors. Though many cantors were tonsured clerics, rubrics ensured the use of copes by untonsured cantors as well. In other areas before and during the Middle Ages, monastic communities used such ceremonial cloaks to vest all monks except the Priest Celebrant, who wore a chasuble. Another prevalent and still current custom is for assisting ministers, especially masters of ceremonies and servers (even children) who hold the episcopal insignia (miter, pastoral staff), to wear liturgical capes or copes. These were not aberrations, but fully appreciated ancient customs acknowledged by various liturgical books (especially successive editions of the *Ceremonial of Bishops*). In keeping with this broad usage, copes were never given allegorical meanings, blessed, or otherwise set aside for the exclusive use of the ordained.

If copes have been an unfamiliar part of our experience in the twentieth century, or were thought to be reserved to priests, it was because they had generally fallen from favor, not because their use was restricted by law. The reformed rites have changed neither their low level of usage nor their great potential. They are hardly mentioned at all.

Most sacristans and priests know that chasubles are reserved to the Eucharist, that when other rites are scheduled a cope can be added over the Priest Celebrant's stole and alb. Yet copes also are mentioned in these settings:

- for presiding deacons or priests at liturgies other than Mass (for example, eucharistic benediction, the Baptism of infants, orders of blessing)

- for as many priests as are assisting in solemn liturgies other than Mass (for example, celebrations of the Liturgy of the Hours, Eucharistic exposition, public processions)

- for the deacon or cantor at the solemn proclamation of the year's feasts on Epiphany (see *Ceremonial of Bishops*, 240).

These occasions provide parishes with extraordinary opportunities. On particularly important occasions, we can provide truly festive vesture for ministers to wear over their albs. The continued use of copes by priests, deacons, monks, cantors, masters of ceremonies, and ministers assisting with episcopal insignia has prevented the use of copes from dying out, as have the brief notes in today's liturgical books. Resistance might come from some who see no point to liturgical vesture of any kind. Others might think that copes are just too good looking! This is not a call to confront those who hold this belief, nor to unduly increase the use of these festive cloaks. Yet, if we agree that the leadership of Priest Celebrants and the aesthetic environment are enhanced by proper robes, then other leaders of our most solemn moments should don copes. In addition to being used by the cantor at the Epiphany proclamation, the cope can be worn by other non-ordained persons on a variety of other occasions, such as by

- the cantor of the *Exsultet* (Easter Proclamation)

- the psalmist-cantor at the most solemn liturgies

- the leader of a large congregation for an order of blessing

- the Priest Celebrant or lay presider at the Liturgy of the Hours.

Such possibilities and current usage can determine how many copes, and of what color, are needed. White or gold, of course, would fit with usage on the most festive occasions. The other colors used on Sundays should be available if copes are regularly used for presiding at Evening Prayer. Keeping to the standards applicable to good vesture of all kinds, new copes for different ministers do not have to be heavily ornamented. But plain, ample, colorful cloaks for ministerial leadership do have to be available in sizes for all ministers.

HUMERAL VEIL   This is another vestment of high festivity, but it is more restricted to certain occasions and ministers. The term *humeral* comes from the Latin word for shoulder, around which this large, scarf-like veil is worn. It is usually equipped with a chain clasp to hold it on; this is far easier for the minister than strings. The best humeral veils do not display applied symbols; thus, they are better able to continue doing what they have done for centuries—give particular prominence to some of our holiest elements.

In various lands and periods of history, some of them marked by fully participatory liturgies, many liturgical elements were not handled in public by bare human hands, but by hands covered with a vestment. This was a way of showing profound respect in a nonverbal way to such things as Lectionaries and other liturgical books, Eucharistic vessels and other objects.

Humeral veils are currently worn

- by the deacon or priest at Eucharistic exposition, benediction, or in Eucharistic processions, while holding the monstrance at the blessing and while carrying the Blessed Sacrament from (or back to) the chapel of reservation

- by priest or deacon bearing the Eucharistic vessel for the transfer at the end of the Evening Mass of the Lord's Supper on Thursday of Holy Week and at the Holy Communion of the Celebration of the Lord's Passion on Friday of Holy Week; if there are multiple vessels, more than one minister might be so vested

- by ministers bearing relics in solemn processions

- by ministers assisting with episcopal insignia (in some dioceses, where they are not already wearing copes)

White is the normative color for the humeral veil in all liturgical times, though veils that match the cope in liturgical color may certainly be used.

Final Vestment: The Funeral Pall

Bereaved communities always have honored the remains of their deceased. From the earliest periods of Christian liturgy, cemeteries were an important place for memorial gatherings and for decorations; gardens were the favored setting, and lamps were the normal decoration. In later centuries, the coffins or corpses of Christians in many lands were embellished with rich fabric covers or "palls." When these customs spread and became regulated, black became the normative color for covers. These would be large enough to cover the coffin, extending down over the bier or trestle as well. The pall could be ornamented with cross, galloons, or fringes. White palls were forbidden, except for young children. In the mid-nineteenth century, communities in many areas discontinued the use of palls.

In the late 1960s, during extensive experimentation and preparation for the reformed funeral rite, liturgical leaders in several American dioceses played a strong role in helping communities to rediscover the funeral pall. White was now used to express the Paschal nature of the rite, to remember the white garment worn at Baptism, and to express hope that the deceased be clothed in glory with all in the new Jerusalem.

The pall is not the only symbol that can be placed on the coffin as part of the reception of the body before the vigil or Mass. Alternatives include the *Book of the Gospels*, the Bible, or a cross. Yet the pall remains as one of the most successful renovations of the late twentieth century. To satisfy the various circumstances encountered over the course of the year, our local places of worship should have a sufficient number of palls on hand. Dimensions of palls depend on the size of coffin for children and adults, the method of carrying the coffin after the pall has been positioned, and the resting place of the coffin before the altar (bier, funeral-trolley cart, or floor of the sanctuary). The fabric and its lining should hang well and present a dignified appearance. The pall should be white even if the chasuble is black or violet. Decorations should be kept to a minimum. As with all vesture, the material and design are more important. The symbol is a coffin enveloped in white, not an appliquéed "symbol" on that symbol.

Other Special Clothing in Church Communities

INSIGNIA OF BISHOPS   At any liturgical celebration, the vestments worn by a Bishop are the same as those worn by priests—alb (with cincture and amice only if necessary) and stole, with a chasuble or cope if the rite calls for this. At Eucharistic celebrations on certain very solemn occasions, Bishops may wear a simple dalmatic between the stole and chasuble.

In addition to these liturgical vestments, certain articles of clothing or insignia are often worn by Bishops. They are not, strictly speaking, vestments, but they are nonetheless part of the rites and thus part of the sacristy's provisions. Sacristans in cathedrals are often concerned with these items, and periodically they are called upon to care for, procure, or store them. For an episcopal visitation or liturgy in other parishes, the Bishop normally brings everything he will need, which may include any or all of the following items:

- the ring, which expresses the Bishop's fidelity to the local church, always worn by him.

- the pastoral staff (crosier or crozier), a symbol of pastoral office, used at many (but not all) liturgies. The pastoral staff is typically used only by the Bishop of the diocese, not by visiting or auxiliary Bishops. If it is brought to the sacristy unassembled in a carrying case, the sacristan or the minister who will hold the staff during the liturgy must assemble it and place it by the area where the Bishop will vest.

- the miter, a traditional hat and a mark of liturgical presidency, worn at most liturgies when the Bishop presides. Sacristans need merely place it on the vesting table. After many stages of development, its current form is two pieces forming a circle at the bottom and rising to two peaks, with two lappets (fannons) extending down off the back.

- the skull cap (zucchetto), worn by the Bishop at almost all liturgies. It began as a practical covering worn by all tonsured clerics over their bald spot. In most countries, Bishops are the only ones who have kept the custom, even though tonsure long ago fell into disuse. Thus, it is perceived by many to be an important episcopal sign. If the Bishop is not already wearing a skull cap when he arrives, the sacristan or an assistant should set it out. An old custom, still in force in some dioceses, is to put a small tray or dish on the credence table before Mass, so the skull cap can be placed there when it is removed during the celebration. But it is much simpler, and more in keeping with the minor import of the skull cap, to have it rest between uses directly on the Priest Celebrant's chair or the *cathedra*.

- the pectoral cross, which the Bishop will be wearing when he arrives, placed under the liturgical vestments, not over them.

- the pallium, worn only at Eucharistic celebrations of great solemnity and only by residential Archbishops, that is, Bishops of dioceses designated as the metropolitan centers with certain jurisdiction over neighboring dioceses. The pallium is a narrow band of white wool. It forms a circle around the neck with strips extending down the front and back and is worn over and pinned to the chasuble. Each pallium is given by the Pope as a sign of the metropolitan's communion with Rome. This sign is made all the more potent by the traditional manufacture of a pallium. It is made from the wool of sheep blessed in Rome on the memorial of Saint Agnes, an early Roman martyr (with a name that sounds like *agnus*, the Latin word for *lamb*). On the night before the Feast of Saint Peter, the pallium is placed on his tomb, and it remains there until the next day. It is then blessed and presented personally by the Pope to the Archbishop.

CHOIR DRESS   The various items of "choir dress" for Bishops include clothing such as colored cassocks that can be worn at a liturgy when choir members are not wearing liturgical vestments. Choir dress is described in the *Ceremonial of Bishops* (#63–64, 1199–1202, 1205).

DISTINCTIVE DRESS OF OTHER ORDERS AND SOCIETIES   At certain liturgies, especially pilgrimage gatherings, stational Masses, and diocesan convocations, sacristans will see many other special costumes and habits, insignia and symbols. When pontifical knights and ladies, representative of special orders and societies, are scheduled to vest in their respective garb and participate in the procession, we do not have to provide their robes or even know what these items are. We do, however, need to know the amount of space that each group will need for vesting. We also need to provide tables or racks and hangers; ensure the delivery of hymnals, song sheets or orders of service into their hands; and organize vesting areas so that the clusters or groups end up in the right processional order.

At some nonliturgical events in the church complex, Bishops or priests might wear special garments. Their traditional ensembles are described in the *Ceremonial of Bishops* (1203–1204, bishops; 1205, cardinals; 1207–1209, other prelates).

Care and Storage of Vestments

PREPARATION FOR USE   Most lay ministers neither need nor expect their vestments to be laid out. Because closets are used far more than drawers, the various colors and sizes are readily accessible to all. Still, if the preferences and sizes of the ministers are known, their vestments could be laid out as a courtesy. The vestments can be placed on the vesting table, positioned on a garment stand, or hung on racks with ministers' names pinned on.

Before any major liturgy involving many ministers, sacristans should have a list of those who need to be vested. With this information, they can prepare a set-up list.

To assist in vesting, you should always have (in addition to the regular furnishings of the vesting room described on page 95) the following items:

- lint brush or roller
- comb, hair brush
- a variety of pins (safety, straight, hat)
- shoe horn
- eye-glass cleaning sheets
- facial tissue
- drawers for the storage of personal items

PRIEST CELEBRANT FOR MASS

- chasuble of day's color
- complementary stole

- cincture (only if necessary)
- alb
- amice (rarely needed)

The traditional way to lay these items out is to put them down in that exact order, so that the items to be put on first are found on top. Here, then, is how the items would be arranged, bottom to top:

- chasuble, front-side down, with the bottom of the back folded up a bit so that it can be lifted
- stole splayed out with the middle of the stole resting in the middle
- cincture, unknotted
- alb, front side down, with the bottom of the back folded up a bit, and the bottom opening facing the minister
- amice, opened out and with the strings untangled.

PRESIDING BISHOP FOR MASS

- the same as above;
- the miter (if used)
- skull cap (if not already on)
- pastoral staff (and pallium, if used) placed nearby
- a dalmatic, which may be set between the chasuble and stole (used on rare occasions)

PRESIDING PRIEST FOR LITURGIES OTHER THAN MASS

- cope of the day's color or rite's color (if used)
- stole complementing the cope
- cincture (if necessary)
- alb
- amice (if necessary)

PRESIDING BISHOP FOR LITURGIES OTHER THAN MASS

- the same as above
- the miter
- skull cap
- pastoral staff placed nearby

PRESIDING DEACON FOR LITURGIES OTHER THAN MASS

- cope or dalmatic of the day's color (if used)
- stole complementing the cope or dalmatic

- cincture (if necessary)

- alb

- amice (if necessary)

CONCELEBRATING PRIESTS AT MASS

- chasuble of the color of the day, or in white if these are worn in local practice

- stole in color of the day or white

- alb

- amice and/or cincture (if necessary)

OTHER MINISTERS AT ANY LITURGY

- alb

- cincture and/or amice (if necessary)

REGULAR MAINTENANCE   Sacristans obviously need to establish and follow some standard procedures for the regular maintenance of vestments. Thus, most vestments will be ready for use at any time. Set procedures are especially necessary when there are multiple volunteers in the sacristy. Procedures should include washing or cleaning instructions for each kind of vestment, whether it is to be washed by hand, washed by machine or dry-cleaned. Arrangements may need to be made with a variety of companies and individuals, such as dry-cleaning establishments that have the experience and know-how necessary to clean vestments; parishioners with expertise in the cleaning and laundering of vestments; commercial laundry operations that have large washing machines; volunteers who are expert at mending fine textiles; and local tailors.

STORAGE   Vestments can be hung in closets or stretched out in drawers. If the local vesting room is provided with wide, shallow drawers, then they certainly should be utilized. Chasubles, dalmatics, copes, stoles, humeral veils, and coffin palls should be in the drawers if at all possible. Here they are protected from light, dust, and the stress of their weight. If this is not convenient, then at least they should be stored in these drawers during the liturgical times when their particular color is less used. Old drawer linings or acid-free tissue should be used. Folds should be padded with acid-free tissue to avoid creases and damage. The alb's accessories (amices and cinctures) can be kept in smaller drawers, along with the textile items described in the following chapter.

Vestments hanging in closets (those taken out of the drawers for use that week, albs, or all of the vestments if no drawers are at hand) should never be put on wire or bendable plastic hangers. They need to be on the widest possible wooden hangers, hung from very high rods. Garment bags of plastic should never be used; natural fibers must breathe. Opaque doors on the closets, or cloth bags, provide better protection against light, and thus reduce fading.

Chapter Twenty-three

Linens and Textiles Other Than Vesture

In the rich variety of rituals and liturgical movement, many small textiles have their place. Cloth is used not only to make clothes and wall decoration; it is also used to cover tables, clean vessels, and to dry people after ritual washings including Baptism, the washing of feet on Thursday of Holy Week, and hand-washing during the Mass and at other times as well.

Linen

The plagues of Egypt included the destruction by hail of its flax (Exodus 9:31), an important part of the country's economy. From the stalks of their flax plants, Egyptians fabricated the most highly prized linen of the ancient world. It was specified for use in the Temple at Jerusalem, and was used to wrap the dead and to make clothing, bed sheets, curtains, sails for ships, and wrappers for scrolls.

In Christian communities, linen was used for the first altar covers (page 45). It was the preferred fabric for public rites and for burial, for vesting the symbols of the body of Christ (altar and people). For two millennia, Christian churches prescribed linen for a wide variety of purposes. It was the fabric used for albs and altar cloths, as well as for the smaller textiles at church. These items as a group came to be called "church linens" or "altar linens." Even as communities lost the historical sense of the way linen linked them to the ancient people of Israel and to early Christians, the natural properties of linen continued to make it the fabric of choice for church use.

The use of linen is no longer mandated, and other fabrics are now often used, chiefly cotton or polyester blended with either cotton or linen. Still, the beauty and functionality of linen continue to make it the ideal material for many of the smaller textile items discussed in this chapter. Pure linen may be more expensive, but it functions better and lasts much longer than the alternatives. It wrinkles more readily, but most of the items described in this chapter should be laundered and pressed after every use anyway. Whatever material is chosen, be sure it launders well. Bear in mind that white fabric without polyester in the blend probably will come out cleanest after laundering because higher water temperatures can be used. Whenever it comes time to order new textiles, we should always evaluate all the available fabrics with an eye to their past performance.

The vestments, along with corporals, purificators, palls, veils, gremials, and towels were often decorated with symbols. Added symbols and decoration, especially lace, are not required, and can be distracting.

Linens or Other Textiles for Church Furnishings

Altar Cloths and Corporals at the Eucharist   Altar cloths are described on page 45. They are closely linked to the cloth we call the "corporal." The corporal is a smaller cloth, placed over the primary altar cloth immediately under the Eucharistic vessels. Over the centuries, it has shrunk in size and taken on its own distinct identity, although in a few groups, the Carthusians, for example, it continues to resemble an altar cloth. The corporal is a small square, spread out just before the Eucharistic Prayer, and folded in on itself just after communion, thereby gathering any Eucharistic particles—hence its name, from the Latin word for "body," because the Body of Christ rests on it during the Mass. In its late medieval form, it was carried to and from the altar in a fabric-covered case or envelope called a "burse."

The size for today's corporals should relate to their ritual use and the dimensions of the local altar. The *General Instruction of the Roman Missal* indicates that a corporal is spread out as part of the preparation of the altar, as a second altar cover to rest under the Eucharistic vessels (see #73, 139). Thus, the corporal should be measured in feet or yards, not in inches. It should be rolled or folded as befits the size of the altar and the number of Eucharistic vessels. No burse or specific rubrics about ironing the corporals are mentioned in any of the ritual books of the reformed rites. Corporals should be seen as altar covers, not as accessories of the chalice.

OTHER COVERS FOR FURNISHINGS The credence table, the table holding the bread and wine before a procession of the gifts, and various other occasional tables might benefit from cloth covers. In each case, the need for a cover is to be based on the table's design, use, and placement.

Those who prepare the liturgy might also consider the old custom of covering images and crosses during the last days of Lent. *The Roman Missal* includes the following rubric for the Fifth Sunday of Lent: "In the Dioceses of the United States, the practice of covering crosses and images throughout the church from this Sunday may be observed. Crosses remain covered until the end of the Celebration of the Lord's Passion on Good Friday, but images remain covered until the beginning of the Easter Vigil." The optional veiling of the cross and images can help focus our attention during the last week of Lent and Holy Week (the days formerly known as "Passiontide"). It is a fast for the eyes, not unlike the fast from food we observe during Lent, and the fast of the ears in the reduction of the use of the organ.

Local decisions should be made about the best ways to express austerity. Images can be removed or covered, and the processional cross (or other sanctuary cross) can be veiled from the start of Lent or only for the final, more intense, Passion-oriented weeks of the liturgical time. If any of these veils have been passed on from earlier generations, they are probably violet. New ones may be made of other colors.

A unified approach to stripping the space may help restore a unity to the room as a sacred space. The stripped-down environment allows us to focus on what is most important: the congregation, the penitents, the catechumens.

Linens or Other Textiles for Use with the Chalice

PURIFICATOR This cloth functions as a liturgical napkin. It is used to wipe the lip of the chalice after each communicant partakes of the Precious Blood of Christ; it is used again for drying vessels after they have been cleansed. The expansion of Eucharistic cup-sharing has necessitated an increase of purificators. Before the current age of reform, the general practice was for a priest to keep his purificator for several Masses, even for a whole week. Now they are more clearly seen as textiles at service to the whole community, one purificator per chalice per Mass, to be laundered and pressed after each use. Sacristans should make sure that extra purificators are on hand at Christmas Time and Easter Time.

Like the other cloths described in this chapter, purificators should be made of white linen. The absorbent qualities of linen (always unstarched) are particularly important for this textile object. Perhaps some types of cotton will be durable and absorbent, but probably no synthetic fabric will perform very well as a purificator. Its traditional size is still fitting, as is the traditional folding in thirds. White is the traditional color, and a small red cross, stitched at the center of the corporal, is customary but not required. The purpose of the purificator is not to add additional symbolism, but simply to serve of the cup of salvation.

CHALICE PALL The word *pall* means "cover," and this word might be used in various ways in the sacristy, denoting the coffin pall, the altar cloth, any other covering over ambo or other furniture during Lent or at other times. The word can also be used for the cover for the chalice. The chalice pall is completely optional, but it was formerly seen at every Mass, a stiff square of linen protecting the contents of the chalice from dust and insects. A purificator or corporal can also be used for this purpose, reflecting ancient usage, when part of the top altar cloth was folded up over the cup for such protection.

Following the Council of Trent, the chalice pall took on different uses and meanings. The chalice and paten were prepared before Mass, with the empty chalice draped with the purificator, a small paten resting over this, and then the pall over the paten. Placed over all this was the chalice veil, followed by the burse containing the corporal. To hold this all together, the pall needed to be more than just a bug-deterring cover for the cup. It became quite thick and starched, or a piece of cardboard was added into a linen pocket to provide a firm base and shape to veil and burse. Now that this arrangement is not required, palls need not be as large or as stiff as they once were.

CHALICE VEILS In some catechetical traditions of a generation or more ago, we were taught that if you came into Mass after the priest took the chalice veil off, then you had come too late to have that Mass "count." Fortunately, we have now laid aside such minimalistic attitudes about liturgical participation. But chalice veils can still be used, though they are optional and are seldom seen in many areas. The veil covers the chalice as it stands on the credence table during the Liturgy of the Word and is removed by the priest or deacon at the preparation of the altar:

- It is a praiseworthy practice for the chalice to be covered with a veil, which may be either of the color of the day or white. (GIRM, 118)

- It is . . . permitted to leave vessels needing to be purified, especially if there are several, on a corporal, suitably covered, either on the altar or on the credence table, and to purify them immediately after Mass, after the Dismissal of the people. (GIRM, 163)

A veil that is large enough may be used to cover the vessels as indicated here; another cloth can also be used (for example, a purificator opened and placed over the vessels). A larger corporal, perhaps the one taken from the altar, would be fitting as well.

Towels

Most liturgical towels of earlier years were of fine linen. They were both absorbent and unobtrusive. New towels can be made either of linen or of the other materials now acceptable for liturgical textiles. Close attention should be paid to the absorbency of any material selected. Also, there should be some system to keep purificators separate from any similarly sized towels as they are laundered and are put back into their drawers. You need to have at least the following towels at hand:

- towels of a large size for each of the persons involved in the washing of the feet on Thursday of Holy Week. If towels from rectories or other homes are used, they should be plain and of a subdued color so they do not distract anyone from the ongoing rite.

- towels for washing of the hands at Mass (at the Preparation of the Gifts or after Holy Communion). White is traditional; other colors used should be plain and unobtrusive. The vessels and towels should presume the washing of hands, not fingertips.

- towels for drying neophytes—babies, children, and adults. Obviously the number will vary from year to year, and the size will be determined by the method of Baptism. As adults step from an immersion font, they are best enshrouded in a huge towel.

- a liturgical apron (gremial) is used by a Bishop or his delegate at certain rites to protect vestments from drops of chrism. When called for in the rites, this large linen square or rectangle with strings is supplied by the Bishop's office. If not, a large amice can be used.

Care and Storage of Linens and Other Textiles

LAUNDRY The more linens used, the larger the group of laundry volunteers is needed. The setting up of this system, the monitoring of it, and the continuous flow of gratitude should be high priorities for every sacristan. One or more hampers or laundry bags need to be provided in every sacristy, often by the sink where the chalices are washed after Mass. The ideal time for washing these linens is Sunday night or first thing Monday, so that stains do not set. There are several traditional procedures for laundry. The simplest is to spray simple stains like lipstick with pre-wash spray and then wash the item in very hot water (an argument for natural fibers of white). Wine stains can be sprinkled with salt, doused with boiling water, then washed with very hot water containing chlorine bleach. (Once again, white, natural fiber is preferred because hotter water can be used.)

Though the impulse is to remove stains as soon as we see them, candle wax must harden before being removed from textiles. With an instrument that will not cut the fabric, excess wax can be removed after hardening. Then the wax spot should be ironed either with a plain brown paper bag, paper towels, or absorbent brown wrapping paper under and on top of the fabric. Once this process has removed the wax, the item should be washed in hot water with bleach added.

Linens that have begun to turn yellow may regain their whiteness by being washed in water and bleach. But some traditionalists insist that fine linens are incompatible with chemical bleaches. The alternative methods they suggest include bleaching the fabric in the sun or boiling it for 30 minutes in water that contains baking soda and mild soap.

IRONING Starch must never be used. It retards the pliancy and draping ability of veils and altar cloths (including the corporal) and diminishes the absorbency of purificators and towels. The best way to iron a linen item is with a steam iron while the linen is damp, although some insist that linens are best stretched out in the sun for drying (and for whitening). According to many experienced volunteers, both of these methods are preferable to using automatic dryers or rolling the wet linens in towels before ironing.

STORAGE   Altar cloths and very large corporals are best rolled on acid-free tubes and stored in sacristy drawers. This eliminates the stress of hanging. Smaller corporals, purificators, chalice veils, towels, and any remaining chalice palls should all be in readily -accessible drawers near the Eucharistic vessels in the sacristy.

Chapter Twenty-four

Candles and Their Equipment

Interaction with Light

The candles and oil lamps in our churches are never just pretty decorations or minimal props required by liturgical law. They are signs of the light of Christ, a light we share through Baptism. Interacting with these symbols of his light can shape and direct our devotion. Candles should be natural and beautiful elements in our liturgical celebrations, and should never be substituted with tubes of polyethylene or electric bulbs. (For a fuller description of illumination and natural materials, see pages 27–28.)

CANDLES IN PARTICULAR PLACES   We do not just look at candles in church. We share flames from them, we follow their lead in procession, and use them to delimit certain reserved areas. Every parish needs candles for at least these actions:

1. The large Paschal candle leads us in procession and continues to share its light with the newly baptized and the bereaved all year (page 61).

2. Baptismal candles are held by neophytes or by infants' parents and godparents, to be cherished and used for many years afterward (page 63).

3. Altar candles (two, four, six, or even seven) are carried in processions and positioned near the altar to bring beauty and festivity to our celebrations of the feasts of the liturgical year (page 47).

4. Dedication candles (12 or 4) mounted on the walls about the congregation place provide an embracing light on the anniversary of dedication, and can be lit at other great solemnities as well (page 220).

5. The lamp or candle in the chapel for the Blessed Sacrament is the nonverbal signal of that very reservation (page 76).

6. Votive candles continue to be, as they always were, popular lights that encourage interactions: choosing a candle, transferring light, and pausing in prayer.

These principal candles do not restrict the use of still others, positioned as the community's actions and spaces suggest: defining the open space about the ambo, marking processional routes, gracing the catechumeneon, flickering in the chapel of reconciliation, burning before an image of the day's saint, grouped about the coffin (especially if the Paschal candle is not used), or bringing light to a cemetery during communal gatherings.

Candles for the Entire Congregation   At the Easter Vigil, each member of the congregation must receive a candle for the service of light and the renewal of baptismal promises. Though these sometimes are called "congregational tapers," they are always more than the wick-sized strings of wax used as candle-lighting tapers. Small shields to protect the hands from dripping wax, called "bobeches," should be distributed as well; these look like paper disks, paper cups, or plastic cups with a hole in the center. The best candles and holders often are marketed by the suppliers to Orthodox and other Eastern churches.

Smaller assemblies on other occasions also will need individual lights. If Evening Prayer on Sunday includes the offering of light and candle-lighting (*Lucernarium*), then everyone can hold a lit candle, especially on great feasts. Except in cases of real necessity, the blessing of candles and procession on February 2 should not be replaced by the more minimalist "solemn entrance." On this one special day of the year, the candles for use throughout the year should be blessed, and everyone — even when the Feast of the Presentation of the Lord (Candlemas) on February 2 is a weekday — should experience the joy of participating in this wondrous celebration of light and candles. Especially when Candlemas falls on Sunday (2014, 2020, 2025, 2031), the entire community should be given candles and invited into the full experience of illumination called for in *The Roman Missal*.

Candle Stands

The proper stands and auxiliary equipment for all of these candles, as well as for the candle or oil lamp near the tabernacle, should be determined by the overall decor of the church. Candles should be chosen and placed based on sight lines, congruence with other furnishings in the sanctuary, and the number needed (two, four, six, or even seven are possible for Mass, depending on the degree of festivity and the scale of the room).

Stands and candles normally should not be in the view unless they will be lit and used as part of a rite. If candles and stand will not be used, they should be put away. There are two exceptions to this. When not in use during Easter Time the Paschal candle remains in the baptistry, bearing the name of our year and waiting for the next celebration of eternal light — Baptism or a Christian funeral. The dedication candles on the walls are the other exception to this general rule.

Advent Wreath

For good reason, this domestic custom made its way into many churches in the twentieth century. The Advent wreath hints at the greens and light of Christmas Time, the light of Christ, the brilliance of the end time, and the progression of this liturgical time of preparation. It is always made from real greens. The natural smell and honesty of form are very important; it would be better to use no wreath at all than one made of artificial branches. The *Book of Blessings* gives the current norms for the wreath. Note the mention of scale if the Advent wreath is to be used in church:

> Customarily the Advent Wreath is constructed of a circle of evergreen branches into which are inserted four candles. According to tradition, three of the candles are violet and the fourth is rose. However, four violet or white candles may also be used. If the Advent wreath is to be used in church, it should be of sufficient size to be visible to the congregation. It may be suspended from the ceiling or placed on a stand. If it is placed in the presbyterium [sanctuary], it should not interfere with the celebration of the liturgy, nor should it obscure the altar, lectern or chair. (*Book of Blessings*, 1510, 1512).

Maintenance of Candles and Accessories

LIGHTING   Before any ritual, we should check the wicks, whether in the oil lamp by the tabernacle or on any candles to be lit. It is far better to extract wicks from dried wax well before the sacristy and the congregation area begin filling up with people. New candles should be lit for a minute in the sacristy before they are set up for a liturgy. In lighting candles, at least four methods are prevalent, each with its own drawbacks and potential:

1. The use of matches or long-reach butane lighters may be convenient, but it is never graceful, and disposing of several burned matches is awkward when more than one candle must be lit. Burnt matches should never be left in candle stands.

2. The use of long, wax tapers without holders is very dangerous. The person lighting the candles could lose control of the taper and drop it; wax could drip on the altar or floor. Unless handled by a true veteran who knows how to hold, shield, and restrain these wicks, they should never be used without being inserted in a pole.

3. The most traditional method (candle-lighting poles or "lucifers" with wax tapers inserted) is also the most graceful way to transfer light to multiple candles. But it should be used only if the minister can follow the proper procedures:

- Use a holder that allows for the bottom of the taper to be inserted in a metal hole, not a wire spring.

- Know how to trim the taper to remove a frayed end.

- Walk slowly and shield flame from drafts.

- Expose only a little taper at a time for burning, watching that just enough is always being pressed up.

- Hold the pole as vertically as possible to keep the flame a manageable size.

- Extinguish the taper after lighting candles by drawing it into the tube and immediately pushing it out again so that the tube doesn't get clogged.

EXTINGUISHING AND CLEANING   For extinguishing candles, the same candle-lighting poles usually have snuffers on them. They must never be pressed down onto the wick; if the wick tips into the molten wax, it should be fished out immediately. Snuffers on poles are far preferable to blowing out a candle (and spraying wax), but they must be cleaned periodically to prevent black soot from accumulating and then dropping out of them onto people, vestments and candle-holders.

FOLLOWERS AND BOBECHES   So that candles burn evenly and don't spill wax—especially in drafty sanctuaries—caps, called "followers," and shallow dishes or holders, called "bobeches," should be used. Many sacristies of older churches have a wide array of these in differing materials: brass, chrome, or glass. If brass is used, it should be unlacquered for easier cleaning. Both followers and bobeches (glass or unlacquered metal) should be cleaned by using hot water in a basin, not by scraping and scratching the item. Candle implements should be cleaned in a basin other than the sink, so that particles of wax will not clog the drain.

OTHER EQUIPMENT   In addition to the many candles sized for their respective uses, and their accessories (holders, stands, followers, bobeches), these items are also needed in a sacristy's candle-care section:

- candle-lighting devices (preferably the traditional poles with taper tube and snuffing cup)

- tapers for use in candle-lighting tubes

- a blunt knife for trimming candles

- long matches in a container that retards moisture

- a basin for cleaning accessories

- paper towels

- a receptacle for used matches

- a stylus for the Easter Vigil

- at least one fire extinguisher, its use understood by all sacristans and ministers (page 156)

All of these materials might best be kept in an area of the sacristy related to the incense materials. Candles, matches, and charcoal are best stored in metal cabinets with many adjustable shelves. The traditional cases include useful hooks for candle-lighting poles and thuribles. If possible, the temperature and humidity of the entire sacristy should be carefully controlled, in deference to the many items that can melt, warp, or become useless when damp. The candle and incense areas should be as far as possible from sources of heat and sunshine.

Chapter Twenty-five

Incense and Its Implements

History of Incensation

Scent is an essential part of human interactions. In a unique way, the nose helps to form memory. The frequent use of scents in worship has ancient precedents.

Incense (bark, wood shavings, or resins, capable of producing fragrance when heated or burned) has been used in worship for thousands of years. In ancient times it was available in its truest, pure form—frankincense. This is the solidified resin from certain trees belonging to a certain species (boswellia or terebinth) found in Arabia and India. Exodus 30:34–38 contains a recipe for mixing frankincense with other elements to make an incense specially blended for fuller aroma and thicker smoke at ritual.

Incense was not given high religious significance in and of itself, but the smoke and aroma was. Psalm 141:2 sees the use of incense as an expression of prayer: "Let my prayer be counted as incense before you." Many other literary sources attest to incensations in Jewish prayer through the time of John the Baptist's father, Zechariah (Luke 1:10). The book of Revelation 8:3–5, which envisions incense being used by angels in heavenly worship, attests to the continuing significance of incense for early Christians.

Despite this history, it seems that early Christians were reluctant to use incense at their liturgies. The writings of many Bishops and commentators of the earliest centuries warn of incensation as an action of alien rites and of imperial idolatry. Once introduced into Christian liturgies, in the fourth century or earlier, the practices associated with incensation differed from region to region. Through the centuries, Churches united to Rome took on more and more of that city's liturgical customs. After the Council of Trent, almost all of these Churches followed strict rules governing the use of incense at funerals, Masses, and Eucharistic benediction.

Current Norms for Incensation

The reforms of the late twentieth century removed both obligations and restrictions governing the use of incense. At all of the points in the Eucharistic celebration where incense was required for solemn Masses, it can now be used at any Mass (see the *General Instruction of the Roman Missal*, 276). It also may be used in other liturgical celebrations, particularly in orders of blessings and the Liturgy of the Hours. Sacristans need to know the services at which incensations will occur, as well as when the lit charcoal should be ready. The use of incense usually depends upon the solemnity of the event. For example, some parishes use incense at all Sunday Masses, while others restrict the use of incense to funerals and solemnities such as Christmas and Easter.

An important task for the sacristan is to ascertain the proper times for lighting the charcoal. Usually this will be about ten minutes before it will be needed. Given the properties of most coals and most incense used these days, the coals lit before Mass may burn out too quickly to be used later in the same liturgy. In most cases, we need to use multiple coals, lit at different times when incensations take place at various points of the liturgy. The traditional times when incense can be used at Mass are listed here:

- at the head of the procession from the vesting room to the altar, with charcoal lit ten minutes before Mass begins.

- at the altar as the procession ends and the Entrance Chant (or hymn or song) continues, with the same charcoal that was used in procession.

- at the head of the Gospel Procession and at the ambo before the proclamation of the Gospel, with new charcoal lit after the Entrance Procession to replace or supplement the original charcoals.

- during the Preparation of the Gifts, when the altar and congregation can be incensed. Charcoal for this is best lit after the Gospel, before or during the homily.

- during the elevation of the host and chalice during the Eucharistic Prayer. Usually, the coals and incense from the incensation of the people are used for this since there is no opportunity for the Priest Celebrant to add additional incense to the thurible.

The closing procession or recessional is not listed in the *General Instruction of the Roman Missal*, but it is often led by incense. If additional coals are needed, they can be lit during Communion.

Communal celebrations of Morning Prayer and Evening Prayer can also be enhanced by the use of incense during the Gospel canticle. Incense is also customary in Eucharistic exposition and benediction, and at funerals. When incense will be used as a sign of farewell during the final commendation of a funeral Mass, coals are best lit at the start of Holy Communion.

The same simplification of rules that made incensations possible at any Mass also simplified the rules for the thurifer, the minister who carries the thurible with what the old official books called a "grave and graceful mien." The number of times the thurible should be swung also has been simplified. The details can be found in the *Ceremonial of Bishops*, 91–97.

Benefits of Incensation

Throughout history, various communities have seen a variety of benefits arising from the use of incense. From the dawn of recorded history, peoples of the Mediterranean basin and further to the southeast used the burning of incense as an antidote to the lassitude caused by tropical heat. Ancient Hebrews and early Christians burned incense as an intense expression of reverence during prayer. Like their neighbors, they used charcoal pans or other ceremonial braziers to mark important places and shrines. As the use of scent became formalized in medieval Christian rites, and as perfume burners were put on chains, the persons or objects toward whom the smoke was directed were seen as being honored. Chains also facilitated the use of fragrant smoke in leading processions on feast days.

Contemporary commentators have a more scientific understanding of these and other human emotions and responses. We know, for example, that the release of certain smells and the sight of clouds of incense can create positive or negative associations for the members of the congregation. Whether incense is used or not, scent continues to be central to all human interactions. And incensation is the action transmitted by our tradition. It expresses adoration and prayer to God, as well as honor and reverence to the holy people and holy elements of our congregation. It is our community's nonverbal way of expressing esteem for the remains placed in the coffin, for the table of the Lord, for the congregation gathered in song at Evening Prayer. The more we recognize the need to engage the whole body and all the senses in common action, the more local communities probably will use incense and other kinds of fragrance.

Charcoal

Lit charcoal has long been the Church's preferred method of burning incense. It is generally available in "self-lighting" briquettes, pieces treated so that only a brief touch of flame is necessary to start the charcoal burning. Since this treatment usually is on the top of the briquette or the edges, it is better to light the tops. Ignition will take longer if the charcoal is chipped or damp. Some charcoal may give off sparks when lit, so long sleeves should be rolled back. Metal tongs can hold the briquette firmly without cracking it. A candle on a tabletop provides a steady source of flame. Depending upon the size and the burning time of the charcoal, and the size of the censer, more than one piece may be lit.

The best kinds of briquettes are shaped with a well or depression on one side to cradle incense grains. Obviously, when such a briquette is placed in the brazier, the depression should face up. Foil wrapping or packaging that retards moisture, boxes that prevent crumbling, and as large a size as will fit in the censer are all good qualities.

Incense

This mixture of solidified resin and other sweet-smelling particles is used three ways in the liturgy. Incensation, the principal usage, normally means the swinging of smoke toward someone or something. A secondary use is related but stationary (the insertion of incense grains in a brazier containing many lit coals; this form is called for in the *Dedication of a Church and an Altar*). The third use is discussed on page 62—large grains inserted in the paschal candle.

No exact mixture or scent is specified for the incense itself, though frankincense and myrrh, the gifts of the Magi to the infant Christ, certainly have pride of place. Even if local churches are quite satisfied with their current scent, sacristans can periodically experiment with other possibilities. The unity of a liturgical time (Christmas Time, for example) may be celebrated by using the same scent through-out the weeks. Having several scents on hand makes it possible to use a different scent for each liturgical time, giving each liturgical time its own, distinct aroma. One scent can be used for Advent, another for Christmas Time, still others for Lent, Easter Time, and Ordinary Time. Once again, there are no specifications mandated, but certain traditions and the ambience of each liturgical time might suggest specific scents. For example, many Orthodox churches could use gardenia (available from Orthodox church supply stores) for the Easter Vigil and Sundays throughout the liturgical time. Rose is traditional for the later part of Easter Time and on the Solemnity of Pentecost. Once selected, the "seasonal" choice can be used in all the incensations of a parish on those days.

Another factor in incense selection is the actual use of the perfumed smoke at a given rite. For Entrance Processions and for the incensation of all persons at Mass or Evening Prayer, a long period of smoke is desirable. At the Gospel Procession, or for the incensation just at the one moment of Eucharistic benediction, a shorter burst of smoke is better. Powder-like incense often produces aroma immediately and burns only for a brief time; grains usually burn longer after a slower start; very large grains or pellets often take a long time to produce smoke, but they burn for a very long time and with a very rich fragrance.

A word about potential health hazards in smoke: The incense normally used in churches contains nothing harmful, although certain ingredients can affect persons with allergies. All incense—even the incense professing to be "hypoallergenic"—releases particulate matter into the air, and can cause a reaction for people with severe asthma or other respiratory problems. Ways of accommodating these persons might include identifying places for them in the congregation area where they will be less affected by the smoke, or by designating at least one of the parish's regular Masses as an "incense-free" Mass.

Some studies of cheaper kinds of incense, rarely used in churches, show that sandalwood sawdust and aromatic oils might give off hazardous substances. Reputable producers should be able to provide documentation on the safety of their ingredients.

Thuribles and Other Burners of Incense

HISTORY   Several forms of charcoal pans and perfume burners have been used in churches over the centuries.

Stationary vessels or pans purified the air, added scent, and honored a particular place or shrine. These were sometimes vases or urns with perforated covers, but without handles. In the old rite at Lyons (France), one urn stood at either side of the altar and grains were added at different points of a service. In other places, vessels were suspended from the ceiling or from wall brackets. Still others resembled braziers on stands.

Portable vessels have been either vessels on chains (our thuribles) or bowls, often shallow and fitted with a long, insulated handle. The bowls allowed the use of many coals, but were more stationary than mobile. As thuribles became more prevalent, the varied movements and numbers of swings were regularized.

CURRENT USE   We should have thuribles that fit the scale of our facilities, as well as the uses made of them in local rites. More smoke and larger gestures call for more coals and incense to be spread over the pan. Certain processions call for more than one thurible; for example, two thuribles are suggested for the processions with the Blessed Sacrament on Thursday of Holy Week and on the Solemnity of the Most Holy Body and Blood of Christ (*Corpus Christi*).

If braziers or other stationary vessels are desired for a particular environment or feast, they are available from church suppliers in insulated ceramics and other materials. In most cases, however, sand added to existing vessels, wide-mouthed vases or pots can provide a fine burner for charcoal.

Boats and Other Vessels for Incense

The old containers for incense dust or grains were usually metal and equipped with a spoon that was narrow, but long enough not to slide down into the vessel. One of the prevalent shapes led to the odd name "boat" for the vessel used to contain the incense. Any metal box or container that can be properly handled is acceptable. Some boats match the thurible, but this is not necessary.

Other Fragrances

Fragrances other than incense can be considered as local churches examine ways to mark each liturgical time, to heighten festivity on solemnities, and to foster the involvement of all the senses. There are no specific rules governing these alternatives except common sense.

Outdoor processions of sanctoral images or the Eucharist can move on pathways strewn with flowers or plants that release their perfume when trod upon. In pre-Reformation England, such plants as lavender, hyssop, sage, and rue provided materials for this "odorizing." In our country, strewing is considered odd, but it may provide fertile ideas for adaptation. In general, however, these ideas will not work indoors, especially in churches that are carpeted.

The Care and Storage of Materials Related to Incensation

The same metal cabinet used for candles might also house the materials related to incensation. Inside these cabinets, parishes generally need the following:

- ❏ one or more thuribles, best hanging from hooks after cooling down outside the cabinet
- ❏ incense in various powders and grains
- ❏ charcoal briquettes, packaged to avoid moisture
- ❏ one or more boats and spoons
- ❏ tongs
- ❏ matches
- ❏ candles and a candle stand for igniting charcoal
- ❏ fire extinguisher nearby (page 156)
- ❏ a high-quality and worthy stand to be used in the congregation space for the thurible and boat
- ❏ canisters or receptacles for used (and still hot) charcoal

A further piece of furniture is most useful in every sacristy—a strong table, with a surface of metal or stone, for preparing thuribles and cleaning them soon after each liturgy.

In cleaning thuribles, manufacturers' instructions must be followed. If old thuribles need attention, the traditional method for cleaning them is to dip the vessels in boiling water and then dry them immediately.

Chapter Twenty-six

Flowers

The sacristy should have space for the preparation and care of flowers. (Review pages 30–32 on flowers as liturgical art.)

Acquiring Flowers

A parish needs a clear plan for funding and acquiring these festive additions to the church complex. The best plan will draw on community members with expertise in arranging flowers, freeing the sacristans to perform the many other tasks in liturgical preparation, although some sacristans may enjoy the additional responsibility of handling flowers. Most parishes use one or more of the following approaches:

- Special agreements can be drawn up for a given year with a florist who is sensitive to the scale of the church building and the inherent timing of the times of the liturgical year. Such an arrangement often gives the church a priority of attention, fosters accountability, allows for the delivery of material just before it is needed (Christmas Time just before Christmas Eve, Easter Time on Holy Saturday) and is easier on bookkeepers. The florist could even take responsibility for the removal of old flowers and plants. This contract or understanding can be reviewed each year, perhaps even with specifications set down and bids solicited from several vendors.

- Volunteers can be solicited to provide funding or particular arrangements on given days. It might be helpful to include a regular announcement in the parish bulletin or to post a sign-up sheet in a prominent place. Groups or households could also sign up to assume responsibility for an entire liturgical time, and even participate in the liturgical time preparation session. This registration might include the possibility of funds for a day or liturgical time being donated in memory of a deceased loved one or in honor of a special anniversary. The names of donors or the persons honored could be noted later in the Sunday bulletin. Whatever arrangement is chosen, it is important to practice clear communication throughout.

- For certain festivals, and for special zones in the parish buildings, every member of the parish may be invited to bring flowers of his or her own—sometimes specified by type and sometimes leaving conditions open for a wide variety. These could form a panoply of blossoms and greens before the shrine of the titular saint on his or her feast. The flowers could be strewn on the path of an outdoor Marian or Eucharistic procession. Or they might be placed in a grand circle of roses put in vases all around the congregation on Pentecost.

- Flowers brought to church by families for funerals and weddings can be regulated by local guidelines, so long as these are distributed widely and early.

- After Christmas Time and Easter Time, as well as after other major solemnities and feasts, potted plants can be put in the entrance hall for any gardeners to take. If any are nurtured back to life for the following year, they might be brought back to the congregation.

- Suburban or rural parishes sometimes have their own flower (and vegetable) gardens, tended by volunteers and planted with items appropriate for the liturgy and for the soup kitchen.

- While some silk or metal "flowers" are of exquisite quality and fine materials, they are not flowers. The liturgy needs materials that are honest and natural; floral arrangements should use only real flowers and greens.

The Preparation of Floral Arrangements

The best and most up-to-date advice on floral arranging can be found in local programs of continuing education and in local libraries. There we can learn whatever we need to know about stem preparation, supports, water, forcing or retarding growth, texture and color in arrangements, and the materials best suited for large-scale architecture. These all need to be interpreted in terms of specific sites. In our sacristies, this means that liturgical as well as aesthetic criteria must be met. Those who are qualified to pass on knowledge of large floral displays do not teach abstract principles; they show how the given context of public action must determine the look.

As floral decorations are prepared for one day or an entire liturgical time, preparations must include a specific understanding of who will get the materials, arrange them and place them, water or care for them, and remove them at an agreed-upon time. For this work, sacristies usually should have the following equipment on hand: clippers and scissors, tape, florist foam, spikes, watering cans, and water dishes to place under all pots. A table or countertop is also important to have, and there should be receptacles for trash, recyclable materials, and compost nearby. In many settings, a table with a metal or stone top is needed. The table used for candles and incense may be large enough for the preparation of the flowers as well. Otherwise the sideboard of a sink is often the right size and material.

Most parishes have vases and vessels of their own for flowers, and this is wise if they are congruent with the local architectural style and with the exact placement of the flowers. Some communities also have a good-sized collection of pedestals and bases. These pieces of furniture should never be so large as to seem like tables, nor should they compete with the central furnishings of the church building. For this same reason, they are best used in open places like the entrance hall, rather than in the sanctuary. If the parish has many vessels and pieces of furniture, they should be neatly stored in an accessible cabinet.

Chapter Twenty-seven

Maintenance and Housekeeping

Maintenance Program

In the daily work of the sacristan, many priorities vie for his or her attention. Three values related to maintenance should be remembered by all sacristans. As the *Ceremonial of Bishops* (#38) states, "The first of all the elements belonging to the beauty of the place where liturgy is celebrated is the spotless cleanliness of the floor and walls and of all the images and articles that will be used or seen during a service." Second, the parish pastoral council, finance council, facilities committee, and pastor must know that deferred maintenance is both dangerous and more expensive, and this applies to *all* worship places, not just to older ones. Third, the time and money spent to preserve the liturgical facility should never be considered as competing with funding for the poor. Our facilities should be preserved precisely as part of our gift to the poor.

When we apply such serious concerns to the sacristy, we have at least seven levels of activity that should be ongoing:

1. *Immediate, Emergency Repairs.* These are understood by all and, due to their unpredictability, mean that everything else must wait for them to be completed. Such "band-aids" are a direct service to the congregation and to ministers who may need the repair completed for the liturgy to proceed.

2. *"Once-over" Tours.* Before the weekend or before a major service, a tour of the facility should take place. This work is also very important to the liturgical action and includes such things as cleaning any debris from the entryway and congregation seating, making sure that the furnishings are positioned properly, pulling wilted pieces from plants, and tending to other next-to-the-last-minute details.

3. *Preparing for Future Events.* A careful listing (and checking) of all the facilities, furnishings, and artifacts needed for a given event allows the sacristan to identify items that need to be fixed in advance.

4. *Regular Housekeeping and Cleaning.* This often is done by custodians or volunteers other than the sacristan, but the sacristan should nurture a productive collaboration with those who carry out this work. Every community should have a regular system for routine cleaning, and this must be understood by all involved, so it can be done even when the supervisor is away on vacation.

5. *Special Campaigns or Sessions to Tackle One Job or Prepare for One Feast.* Before Christmas Time and Easter Time, and perhaps before some other great days or liturgical times of the liturgical year, parishioners are generally quite willing to volunteer their time for a day or evening of communal cleaning and preparation. Apart from those few holy times, special sessions can be scheduled for volunteers to join the regular sacristy crew in polishing all the vessels, mending textiles (linens, vestments, and decorative hangings), cleaning the sacristy, washing or otherwise cleaning pews. These are not just opportunities to have many hands make light work; they are invaluable times to build community. New members of the parish should be made especially welcome.

6. *Periodic Inventory of Materials in the Church Complex.* A database can be developed to list each item and its location, which can be supplemented with photographs of valuable items and regularly updated. Photos and descriptions should be stored away from the facility. (This is also the time to involve insurance representatives or diocesan agents in updating policies.)

7. *Preventive or Routine Maintenance of Facilities.* This program will differ from place to place, being determined by the local materials and properties, climate, and other conditions. This suggests the keeping of a central file with all maintenance manuals for products purchased, with records of the building's construction, and with reports from building experts. While this last level is seldom the province of sacristans, we should be a part of the preparation, or at least know the schedule of the work to be done.

Maintenance and Miscellaneous Items for the Sacristy

These are additional tools that might facilitate work in the sacristy and vesting room. They do not generally repeat items described in earlier chapters. Local circumstances might expand or abbreviate these lists; they are just starters.

POWER   long electrical extension cords of the proper strength, back-up batteries in all the sizes needed, battery tester, flashlights

FASTENING   string (various weights), tapes and dispensers (duct, electrical, florist, masking, removable, scotch), tacks, screws and screwdrivers of various types, nails and hammer, glue (regular and wood), paper clips

SECRETARIAL   paper, index cards, self-stick notes of various sizes, pencils and sharpener, pens, magic markers, correction tape, scissors, schedules posted for various tasks and ministers

CLEANING   vacuum cleaner with bags, dust buster with bags, carpet sweeper (if any rugs), dry mop, wet mop and bucket, hand broom, dust pan and brush, rags, dust cloths, brushes of various kinds, wastebaskets and large barrels, garbage bags, basins for washing water, rubber gloves, sponges, knives (butter, paring, X-ACTO razor), strainer on pole for font, cleaning fluids (for brass, for floor, furniture polish, tile cleaner, window cleaner)

VESTMENTS AND LINENS   steam iron and ironing board, steamer, sewing kit, scissors, lint rollers or brushes, spot remover, pins (hat, safety, straight).

Chapter Twenty-eight

Security and Health

We need a range of materials to assist in health, hygiene, and security for the parish, as well as security for the liturgical objects that serve the community. Not every sacristy or vesting room will have all of these materials. Many will need fewer; some will need more. Here are some ideas to stimulate list makers.

Inclement Weather

The clearing of ice, snow, or other hazards from public ways, including sidewalks, is, like other matters of public safety, an important concern of the local church. This concern must be translated into systems that coordinate volunteers or contractors to clear public and parish-owned surfaces for walking as soon as possible after any storm. If certain areas of a parking lot are prone to quick flooding during showers, then the drainage should be improved, and visitors would need to be alerted to not park there until such improvements are made. Sacristans should collaborate on these matters with members of the pastoral staff or facilities committee. Hospitality begins before people get to the church doors.

Health and Hygiene

We should know if any members of the congregation, especially ministers and members who are regular participants, are trained in current methods of CPR and emergency response. Then these materials, or some equivalent, should be in every vesting room or entrance hall:

- a large, complete first aid kit, freshly stocked, especially with bandages of every size

- a defibrillator (this has become part of the emergency resources in most public places)

- paper cups and a bottle of water for taking medications, if sinks and water coolers are far removed

- material to cover and absorb vomit and other liquid spills (sawdust is traditional, but suppliers have newer mixtures available)

- latex gloves of various types and sizes (to be worn when using certain cleaning liquids, or picking up refuse)

Security

The key to the tabernacle must be kept safely, entrusted only to sacristans and those who need access to the tabernacle to take Communion for the sick. Other keys to the church building should be kept in a secure place as well, preferably on a key panel where the numerous keys are hung and labeled in logical order.

If there are many valuable vessels, the sacristy might be equipped with a metal safe. This may be too expensive an item for new sacristies, but many older churches already have one. The safe should be utilized for all valuables, including the collection funds if this is the most secure spot on the property.

Fire extinguishers need to be positioned for easy visibility and access, especially near sources of open fire or candlelight (baptistry, congregational area, sacristy). If new extinguishers are being purchased, the best models often are the ones that are simplest to operate. With ushers or greeters, and with members of the pastoral staff, we may need to review (at least annually) local procedures for the evacuation of the congregation. All concerned need to know the locations of fire extinguishers, fire alarms, and telephones for summoning emergency assistance. Exit signs, extinguishers, and emergency lights need to be maintained on a regular schedule. (See page 160 for alarm and sprinkler systems.)

In the coat room, vesting room, or some other logical place, there needs to be a "lost and found," where found objects can be kept for later retrieval by their owners. If unidentified items are not claimed after a long time, they can be given to local shelters or charities. Larger objects might be turned in to the police, or at least reported to them by phone.

In places subject to civil disorder or disruptive protests, everything possible should be done to be hospitable despite security restrictions, to ensure a liturgy as unimpeded by barriers as possible. The right of the community to assemble for liturgy must be upheld, even though demonstrators might disagree. Such concerns must be translated into very clear policies when parish leaders, ushers, and sacristans meet with police about access, disruptions of the congregation, suspicious parcels, security for the collection, or the presence of disruptive or mentally ill persons.

Contact Information

Current directories for area telephone numbers, email addresses, and Web sites for the diocese should be available. A bulletin board in the vesting room or sacristy should have a list of these numbers:

- emergency services (one number if used in area; otherwise, separate numbers for ambulance, fire, poison center, police)
- civic officials (fire marshal, department for parade permits, police offices, transportation and parking departments, trash collection agency/department)
- contractors regularly used by the parish (audio system, electrical, heating, ventilation, air conditioning, plumber, trash collection if not handled by municipality)
- diocesan offices (Bishop, building commission, liturgy office)
- parish leaders, liturgical ministers, and regular volunteers (be sure to obtain their permission to post information)
- shelters and dining facilities for the homeless
- suppliers of liturgical elements like bread, wine, and candles
- transportation (bus or transit schedules, taxi)
- utilities, especially the numbers to use in case of outages (electricity, gas, oil, telephone, water)

Chapter Twenty-nine

Mechanical Systems

The mechanical systems that serve the liturgy differ widely from place to place. The basic liturgical criteria are quality and appropriateness. In appearance and function, all systems must be appropriate to the liturgy. They must be the best systems obtainable in terms of the economy of natural resources and parish funds. The parts that are seen by the congregation should contribute to the overall decor, not neutralize it or detract from it.

Light

Under no conditions can the altar candles, paschal candle, lamp before the tabernacle, or other liturgical elements be replaced by electricity. But artificial lights can serve other important functions. They can highlight certain architectural forms or features and bring attention to the images of saints. More importantly, they can provide light for the congregation in places and directions that unify and facilitate its action. For example, lighting around the seats should not be dark while the sanctuary is bright, as in a theater. Good light for the congregation can remind us that we are part of the liturgy, called to full, conscious, and active participation. Spotlights should not blind preachers from seeing listeners.

In addition to these general principles of liturgical appropriateness, other requirements will need to be set in each local Church. Exterior lights should provide sufficient security for all services and meetings held after dark, yet there should be a way to have the Easter fire in darkness. Indoors, the configuration of rooms and rites should indicate the many places that electrical receptacles might be useful. All switches on the light panel should be clearly labeled.

Sound

Audibility in an active congregation involves much more than installing a sound system. First, the inherent acoustics of the building needs to be maximized. That means studying the acoustics with others who prepare the liturgy, helping lectors, readers, Priest Celebrants, and have other presiders learn the art of proclamation, encouraging the congregation to gather more closely to one another, and avoiding the use of carpeting. In many small church buildings or in liturgies that take place in smaller spaces such as the baptistry or chapel of reservation, microphones may not be needed at all. The absence of amplification can be a blessing; too often they force people to focus on just one speaker, to hear the rite as a transmitted message. And they rarely allow communities to hear themselves sing.

Where communities elect to use amplification systems, the amplified sound should be as clear and natural as possible. Microphones should not impede the movement that is necessary during the liturgy (wireless microphones are widely available and can allow the Priest Celebrant to move from chair to altar to font unimpeded by cords and microphone stands). Ideally, the source of the sound will be related to the direction from which people are hearing it. For example, when the congregation faces the door, as at a funeral when the body is received, it is disorienting to hear the voice of the Priest Celebrant coming from behind them.

Air

The air in any place of congregation needs to be fresh and uncontaminated. When air is heated, it should be comfortable for gathering without coats and gloves, with humidity regulated for the preservation of the building's fabric and contents. When air is circulated by fans, these devices should be neither visually nor aurally obtrusive. When air is cooled, the controls should be accessible. An extra-large crowd may require a lower setting; an extra-long liturgy may require the manual override of the automatic shut-off.

Security

The mechanical systems for security should be similarly unobtrusive and conducive to liturgical gatherings. (For notes on other security arrangements, see page 156.) Systems related to fire (smoke detectors, heat detectors, alarms, sprinklers) should be set to allow for the use of full incense and congregational candles. Security alarms should be set up to minimize accidental soundings, and then monitored so that those inside and neighbors outside are not subjected to unnecessary noise. Emergency lights and signs should be placed according to code, but as unobtrusively as possible.

Visual Displays

In some Christian denominations today, worship looks and sounds more like a concert or lecture than a shared prayer. Screens and theater seating dominate the space; videos and texts are projected on large screens; and racks of theatrical lighting lend color and drama as the service unfolds. The Catholic Church has certainly used the Internet and even social networking Web sites to help spread the Gospel, but she has been very wary of bringing technology into worship. While some parishes save money and paper by projecting hymn numbers or even hymn texts on screens, there are more questions than answers when it comes to the use of such technologies. Our culture is dominated by media, which inundates us with imagery and information, but which leaves us as passive observers, not engaged participants. The liturgy is so different from this passivity: the congregation is not an audience, but the Body of Christ, gathered together by God for worship, sacrament, and mission. The use of TV screens can set up barriers and discourage the full, conscious, and active participation of the congregation.

Virtually everything we use for the liturgy is set apart for worship. We set apart our church buildings and consecrate them to one use—the worship of God. The chalices, patens, linens, candles, and books we use in the liturgy are all set apart for this noble purpose. They are not the same cups and plates, linens, and candles we might use in other settings, even for the most festive meal. The use of electronic media—fleeting and disposable by its very nature—lacks this dignity and permanence.

Parishes using such technologies, especially for hymn texts, should be sure that they are in full compliance with copyright laws, which apply as much to electronic media as it does to print media.

Chapter Thirty

Liturgical Items No Longer in General Use

This chapter contains a list of items not used in the Ordinary Form of the Roman Rite, though some of them may still be used in celebrations of the Extraordinary Form. It is important for the sacristan to understand what each item in the sacristy is, and the history of its use. This will enable the sacristy team to make informed decisions about whether unused items should be kept, given to another parish or to an archive or diocesan museum, or reverently discarded.

Decorations and Furniture

1. ALTAR CANOPY Some older churches still have some form of architectural canopy over the altar area; the most famous is at the main altar at St. Peter's in the Vatican. Canopies usually took one of two forms:

- **A civory, or ciborium** (the original meaning of that word), a roof held up over the altar area by four or more columns. The one designed by Bernini at the

Vatican still accomplishes its task of calling the attention of the congregation to this place and giving it shape and force.

- **A baldaquin, or tester**   a smaller roof of metal or wood that is hung over the altar. It is either suspended by cables from the ceiling or fixed to a rear wall.

With free-standing altars now the rule, only the civory form is still possible in new constructions. These work best in large, open spaces. In existing churches, an old canopy over a still extant but unused "high altar" serves no liturgical purpose. A decision to move or to remove this whole construct rests more on emotional and artistic preservation questions. If neither removal nor reutilization is possible, then such existing monuments should be diminished in importance by being stripped of anything that would call attention to them: cloths, lights, flowers, and any other adornments.

2. Communion Railing   Sometimes called a sanctuary rail or altar rail, these low fence-like structures are still seen in some older churches. Reasons for their introduction included the protection of the altar from profanity and the reservation of the sanctuary for certain persons and rites. Later rails were of a height and width to serve as leaning places for those kneeling to receive Holy Communion. Many Communion rails were removed in the wake of the liturgical reforms of the Second Vatican Council in an effort to emphasize the unity, as opposed to the separateness, of all those at liturgy. The removal also accompanied the transition to standing for Holy Communion—the ancient posture of praise.

See page 35 for more on the unity of the space for the congregation—nave and sanctuary—and the usefulness of keeping some artistic demarcation or distinction for the sanctuary.

3. Rood Screen   These architectural barriers or veils often closed off the entire sanctuary and choir area from the rest of the congregation place. The name for them is related to the cross erected at the summit of the partition. Most of these screens were rightly dismantled decades ago. Where rood screens remain, planners need to treat each side as a separate room in the church complex, perhaps using the choir area for weekday Masses, and the nave for larger assemblies.

4. Catafalque   In liturgical lexicons, this was a piece of wood shaped like a coffin, set on a stand and covered with a pall as if it were a coffin. They were used for memorial services or funerals without a body present. Due to their (literally) empty symbolism, they were discontinued. The dead body is what should be honored with signs of farewell—the actual remains, not a picture or representation of the deceased. In some dictionaries, the word *catafalque* is defined as a platform, not for an empty coffin, but for the actual coffin or corpse.

5. Statues and Images   No less a document than the *Constitution on the Sacred Liturgy* (#124) called for the removal of artistic works that are "repugnant to faith and morals and to Christian devotion," works "that offend true religious sense either by their grotesqueness or by the deficiency, mediocrity, or sham in their artistic quality." (See pages 20–32 for descriptions of the legitimate role of images in the reformed rites.) Works of quality can be used within these standards, perhaps during specified liturgical times or on related feasts.

Sound-makers

6. SANCTUS BELLS   One of the functions assigned to exterior bells in the medieval period was to signal that certain important actions were taking place in the church building. Through the centuries, this came to be imitated by the ringing of a hand-held bell in the sanctuary. The Sanctus, or "sacring," bells passed on to us in many older churches are triple bells with many tongues, chimes, or gongs. The bells are optional for use in the Ordinary Form of the Roman Rite, and may be rung just before the consecration (at the epiclesis of the Eucharistic Prayer) and at the elevations of the host and the chalice (see the *General Instruction of the Roman Missal*, 150).

7. CLAPPERS   In the centuries when small bells were rung in sanctuaries during Mass, hinged pieces of wood were substituted on the Thursday and Friday of Holy Week.

8. SACRISTY BELL   Many sacristies had a bell hung by the door to the sanctuary, rung to signal the start of a service. We have other cues now. One is the ancient and beautiful tradition of ringing the tower bells.

Texts

9. ALTAR CARDS   In the Tridentine order of Mass, a large card was used at the center of the altar, in front of the tabernacle, with some standard texts to assist the priest's memory. In the seventeenth century, two smaller cards were added, one on each side of the altar. These were sometimes very elaborately decorated. Depending on their quality, they may be museum or archival material.

Vessels

10. COMMUNION PLATES   In the Tridentine Rite, a white linen cloth was spread on the Communion rail for the distribution of the Eucharist. Its purpose was to catch any falling particles, as well as to carry over the appearance of the covered altar. In the late nineteenth century, the Vatican "tolerated" the substitution of a metal plate, a paten with side handles, passed from communicant to communicant and held under his or her own chin. In 1929 this was formally adopted for all churches, but not as a substitute for the cloth. Both were used as precautions for particles. Except at solemn Masses when the actual chalice paten was held under chins by the deacon, communicants themselves passed along this Communion paten. It was to be kept dust-free in a cloth bag (burse) when not in use. This came to be a significant bit of bodily action on the part of communicants, who now had to do more than just open their mouths. Later, a long handle was added and this role was taken over by a server, who moved from chin to chin in tandem with the Communion minister. These are given brief mention in the current rite but have been largely discontinued in present practice.

11. REPOSITORY TABERNACLE   During the Paschal Triduum, ancient customs require the Eucharist to be reserved away from the altar of celebration. If the only tabernacle was on the main altar, then this large vessel was used at a side altar or shrine decorated with many candles and flowers. The purpose was not to create a shrine distinct to the Triduum; it was to have a place of reservation away from the altar. Today, in churches with a separate Blessed Sacrament chapel, the regular tabernacle is used on Thursday of Holy Week evening as well.

12. THRONE OF EUCHARISTIC EXPOSITION This is a small stand or elevated platform equipped with a back that supports a canopy over the monstrance. Communities with perpetual exposition had permanent thrones over the altar. All others were to use moveable ones so that an empty throne would not distract from the celebration of the Mass (the same logic that later motivated the transfer of the tabernacle from the altar). The preferred form suggested in the current rite of exposition is for the monstrance to rest directly on the altar. Old thrones are really portable niches and might, depending on their design, hold statues, relics, or holy oils in a different part of the church complex.

13. EUCHARISTIC TUBE OR STRAW The *General Instruction of the Roman Missal* (#243–249) and ancient traditions suggest four possible methods of Eucharistic cup-sharing: directly from the chalice, through a tube or straw, in a spoon, or by intinction—dipping the bread in the wine. Today, Holy Communion directly from the chalice and by intinction are both permitted, though the latter is quite rare (see GIRM, 284–287). Some sacristy collections may have a tube or straw formerly used for Holy Communion from the cup.

14. EUCHARISTIC SPOON This, too, is an artifact used in one of the alternative means of sharing the cup. The minister would pour wine from the spoon directly into the communicant's mouth, taking care not to let the spoon touch the communicant's lips or tongue.

15. INTINCTORIUM This was the name coined for the odd vessels invented to give Holy Communion by dipping the host into a small cup fixed in the middle of a paten (like a platter with a dipping bowl). These are generally not used, and such patens can have the cups removed to resume service as regular patens.

16. WATER SPOON These tiny spoons, with long handles, were used by a few priests, who wanted to be sure that only a drop or two went into the chalice. The spoon-bowl is often attached at a right angle to the spoon-handle for dipping into narrow-necked cruets.

17. HOLY WATER SPRINKLERS Today, most parishes use a bucket with separate sprinkler for the blessing with holy water. But the sacristy may also include a one-piece sprinkler with a reservoir, looking something like a microphone. These sprinklers can still be used, especially when the priest or deacon goes outside of the parish; for example, when he blesses a home or car, or for the blessing of a grave at the cemetery.

18. SMALL VIAL OR VESSEL WITH SAND The current *Order of Christian Funerals* states that the Rite of Committal (lowering the body into the vault or earth and burying it) should take place either in the middle of the rite of committal or at the conclusion of the rite (#209). Though it is a deeply religious and communal act, it is too often left for cemetery workers and bulldozers. If a committal is not possible with the gathered community, the "gesture of final leave-taking" envisioned in the rite could be "placing flowers or soil on the coffin" (#210). The earth need not come from a vial or flask carried by the mortician or Priest Celebrant. It can be taken from the site and tossed into the grave by hand or with a shovel or something similar. If the coffin is in a cemetery chapel, the gesture of leave-taking could consist of placing flowers on the coffin.

Vestments and Other Textiles

19. BIRETTA AND VARIOUS HATS (See page 129 regarding the miter and skull cap for Bishops at liturgy.) In the Tridentine Rite, there were many rules for the wearing and handling of hats for the ordained, generally the biretta. The red cardinalatial hat (galero) was abolished in 1969.

20. TUNIC OR TUNICLE This was the tunica alba of ancient days, modified and worn by subdeacons until that order was suppressed in 1972. See page 122 regarding the evolution of the same tunica alba into both the alb and the dalmatic. Sometimes these tunics have lines and decor appropriate to modern vesture and can be used as dalmatics by the deacon.

21. MANIPLE This is a small vestment, about three inches wide and about two feet long, looped over the left wrist and fastened there by a loop or button. They began their existence in antiquity as linen rectangles, handkerchiefs carried or worn simply for the convenience of the Priest Celebrant. By the Middle Ages, clerics used other cloths to wipe vessels, noses, and hands; the maniple became an ornament of rank.

22. LITURGICAL GLOVES, HOSIERY, FOOTWEAR OF BISHOPS The decorated gloves with large cuffs, the caligae (also called buskins or stockings) of the day's liturgical color, and various forms of decorated sandals (also called soleae, campagi, calcei or sandalia) were used for a thousand years as signs of office, dignity, and tradition. These items have no function in the Ordinary Form of the Roman Rite.

23. COMMUNION CLOTH In the Tridentine Rite, a white linen cloth had to be draped over the Communion rail during the distribution of Communion. It often made a visual link between the covered altar and the reception of Communion.

24. ALTAR CLOTHS ON SIDE ALTARS OR FORMER MAIN ALTARS There is only one altar in a church building, and only it should be covered with an altar cloth. Decorative or side altars should no longer be constructed; existing ones should not be given the mark of respect reserved for an altar: a cloth, candles, or a cross. Cloths on these other surfaces, especially when they hang down the front (antependia) or sides, draw undue attention and confuse the notion of one altar per church.

25. PILLOW(S) FOR GOOD FRIDAY These are no longer required for the act of prostration that should begin the celebration of the Lord's Passion. Depending on their design, they can be used as part of other decorations. Otherwise, they should be retired.

Candles

26. BUGIA   This was a candle, normally with a small base and long handle, that was held near the Bishop by an assisting minister for the reading of certain texts. It obviously had a practical purpose before electricity, but it was abolished in 1968 ("unless needed"). Something similar is often needed near the text of the *Exsultet* while it is being sung. Assisting ministers should not hesitate to give such help when needed.

27. CANDELABRA   This object, with five or seven candles, is often used for eucharistic exposition, though the rite today only calls for four or six candles. Candelabra do not need to be reserved for exposition. They can also be used for festal decor at saints' shrines, "seasonal" illumination in the entrance hall, or other appropriate uses. The special stand of candles for *Tenebrae* can still be used at that combined liturgy of the Office of Readings and Morning Prayer on Friday of Holy Week and Holy Saturday.

28. CANDLE FOR THE EUCHARISTIC PRAYER   This "Sanctus" candle used to be mounted on a wall bracket of the sanctuary or on the credence table. It remains lit from Sanctus to the end of the Communion Rite. Its lighting is no longer a part of the rite. Any wall-mounted candle can be lit throughout the services on feasts as part of the overall decorative program.

Part Four
Checklists

Chapter Thirty-one

The Liturgical Year and the Sacristy

Calendars

Our lives are deeply influenced by many calendars. They organize and comfort us. Sometimes they compete with one another for our attention, as when the Christmas lights twinkle in the malls before the violet of Advent appears. Calendars beckon us toward special treats. How we longed as children for Halloween on October 31! Calendars can also make us dread the turn of a month's or week's page; say, to April 15, tax day in the United States of America. They always provide ways to understand the flow of time, frames for interpreting events. They shape us as communities and as individuals.

The seven-day week is the basic structure for dividing time in our world. For Christians, Sunday is the source and summit of the week, the first day on which God began the creation, the day on which Christ rose from the dead, the day on which the Spirit rushed upon the Church, and the symbol of the eighth day—that day of eternity in which we will enjoy life in the new Jerusalem.

For us Christians, the year of Sundays is arranged in another calendar besides the January-to-December one—the liturgical calendar.

The liturgical year calls communities to remember the life of Jesus and invites us into our own identity as holy ones of God. It is a way to organize time that can inspire and enliven all the other schedules that shape our lives; it helps form us as a Christian people. In each period of liturgical time, we are put in touch with another aspect of life in faith. We hope for the coming of Christ always, but Advent lets us sense that hope more tangibly. In Lent and Easter Time we experience and express more intensely the penitence and joy that our Baptism brings us year-round. These intense experiences are facilitated by the communal symbols and actions proper to each liturgical time.

The liturgical year, in its delineation of liturgical times and days, structures our work as sacristans. We do not prepare artifacts for an ethical society gathered to hear about abstract concepts like hope, commitment, and new life. Instead, we prepare the place for a Church gathered to embrace Advent's hope, to become flesh for the world at Christmas Time, to change hearts in Lent, to experience new life over the Triduum, and to be enflamed by the Holy Spirit through Easter Time. Each liturgical time has a distinct ambience of texts and colors, artifacts and songs. We need to know the liturgical year because our work and all of the elements we prepare can truly enhance our community's experience of the liturgical time.

Our appreciation for the liturgical year must quickly take on very practical forms. As we do more and more sacristy work, living through each year's progression of days, we must learn to think about the liturgical times long before its opening day. This is a discipline central to all ministers serving the community through preparatory work. We must read the scriptures, review the texts of *The Roman Missal*, and most importantly, list the necessary artifacts in advance. As local traditions form and careful files are kept, this will be easier. There is no need for liturgical times or individual feasts to be reinvented over and over. Instead, we pass on notes from year to year to let our discipline of preparation be more and more expressive of local traditions and cherished patterns of action.

System for the Liturgical Year

Though Sunday is the building block of all Christian calendars, various denominations and liturgical traditions structure their respective liturgical years in slightly different ways, with various demarcations of liturgical times and particular lists of saints. The Roman Rite follows the calendric system described in the *Universal Norms on the Liturgical Year and the General Roman Calendar* (a document found at the front of *The Roman Missal*).

Our system includes six periods of liturgical time —Advent, Christmas Time, Lent, Triduum, Easter Time and Ordinary Time. Various days within the 365 have more or less importance in our tradition. For example, Christmas is more important than Wednesday of the Fourteenth Week in Ordinary Time. Texts for all of these days appear in the "Proper of Time" (formerly known as the "Proper of Seasons") section of *The Roman Missal*, *Lectionary for Mass*, and Liturgy of the Hours. Other requisites appropriate to days of a liturgical time are listed in the various rites. The decorative program for a period of liturgical time is rarely set by universal norms, but traditions are shared by many local churches. Some lists of texts, requisites, and decorations follow in this manual as examples or guidelines.

Since the earliest days of Christianity, communities have marked liturgical time with local color. Energy and variety were brought by schedules paralleling the liturgical times—days remembering church dedications and the anniversaries of the death of holy ancestors. These local lists were shared among urban areas, with reverence shown to another city in the adoption of feasts for their honored saints. Through the centuries, some aspects of Jesus' life (for example, the Presentation) were added to these calendars. These lists came to be called in *The Roman Missal* the "Proper of Saints."

The general calendar issued by Rome has a few hundred saints on it; it is printed at the front of every edition of *The Roman Missal*. In our tradition, this basic list is meant to be supplemented with local lists drawn from the thousands of other saints and blessed. The Bishops' conference of the United States has added about 20 other days, generally of saints and blessed with particular connections to the United States. They also are listed at the front of every edition of *The Roman Missal*. Some dioceses have added a few more. In each parish, the anniversary of dedication and the day celebrating the parish name also are to be added. The general list plus the local supplements form the Proper of Saints.

The interaction of the two lists, the Proper of Time and Proper of Saints, gives a distinctive quality to each year. Liturgical times and days all have various levels of importance, with set orders of precedence. For example, Sundays of Advent, Christmas Time, Lent, and Easter Time always take precedence over saints' days; weeks like Holy Week and the octave of Easter are similarly important. Because Sundays and Easter Sunday are on different dates each year, each year some saints' feasts are eclipsed. There are also special relationships and connections to be discovered each year—a certain saint's day falling on Thanksgiving, or Memorial Day falling on the day after Pentecost, for example.

To ensure the observance of the most important feasts and to show the lesser status of other days, all observances are ranked:

- solemnities (They are always celebrated—for example, if March 25 is Friday of Holy Week, the Annunciation is moved to the first available day, right after Easter week.)

- feasts (Feasts of the Lord take precedence over Sundays in Ordinary Time; all other feasts are eclipsed only by Sunday or the weeks surrounding Easter.)

- obligatory memorials (These are kept on weekdays by all parishes, except in the two weeks surrounding Easter.)

- optional memorials (Communities decide which to keep.)

Using an Ordo

A liturgical almanac (called an *Ordo*, Latin for *order*) is issued annually by several dioceses and publishers. (The "order" referred to is the order of rites and actions to be used throughout the year.) Even when an *Ordo* is published by a national company, it often comes in regional or diocesan editions, with the particular observances of the diocese (for example, diocesan patron) listed at the appropriate date. These are very informative and convenient, but they are by no means magical. Anyone with a clear understanding of the liturgical times, the table of precedence, and calendar lists could interpolate the liturgical observances onto a civil calendar. *Ordos* are not meant to mystify, but to save a lot of work and list making.

The lineup of feasts in a week and weeks in a period of liturgical time should always be considered in liturgical preparation and in the scheduling of non-liturgical parish events. *Ordos* regularly give even more than the basic name or observance for each day. The following information is found in any good *Ordo*. If one is unavailable, the information must be secured from another source. All of these elements provide direction for work in the sacristy.

LITURGICAL TIME   The boundaries for a period of liturgical time are clearly listed. This helps us prepare ahead for decorations: when they go up, when they come down, and how long they must last. Advent can be anywhere from 22 to 28 days. Christmas Time is 15 to 20 days. Other liturgical times run for fixed numbers of days: Lent (43), the Triduum (3), and Easter Time (50). It is important to respect these parameters, for the decorations should not transmit a message or create an attitude that is at odds with the texts and music of the liturgy. For example, any decision to let the Christmas Time decor go up early, in mid-Advent, betrays a seriously wrong attitude: Either we think that Advent is not important, or we think that decorations are just trivial dressings without power. Changing the decorations between Easter Time and Pentecost can divide the liturgical time and turn Pentecost into a separate feast instead of the conclusion of Easter Time.

THE DAY   Before the reforms of Second Vatican Council, observances falling on the same day might have been merged into one liturgy, with prayer texts for both. Now there is one observance each day. This happens in one of three ways:

- In many cases, one day is set for everyone to observe—a day from the Proper of Time or a day ranked as a mandatory memorial or higher from the Proper of Saints.

- At the start of each year, those who prepare the liturgy need to chart those days that are particular to the diocese and to the parish. The diocesan dates are in regional editions of the ordo or on diocesan mailings. The particular parish feasts are not in the ordo but are significant days. The most important are as follows:

- the anniversary of dedication—a solemnity (generally on the Sunday nearest the dedication date if in Ordinary Time, or on the Sunday before All Saints)

- the anniversary of dedication of the cathedral church—a solemnity in the cathedral itself, generally observed as a feast everywhere else in the diocese

- the day celebrating the local titular—a solemnity (often this is a patron saint, but it might also be a title of Jesus or of Mary; generally celebrated on the preceding Sunday in Ordinary Time or on the actual date)

- solemnities or feasts related to religious orders assisting in the parish.

On other days, several choices are offered, and the local community must choose which one will be observed on that date. This happens only on some weekdays, when one or another optional memorial might be chosen instead of the ordinary weekday. If an optional memorial is chosen, it is then the memorial for that place and time. If all of the optional memorials are bypassed in favor of the ordinary weekday, then they are no longer factors in preparing for that day. This choice should be made intentionally, perhaps as part of a review of the year as a whole, not just by the Priest Celebrant a few minutes before Mass. Those in the community who use the Liturgy of the Hours for daily prayer and those who prepare ahead for weekday liturgies would benefit from knowing in advance what options are being followed locally.

THE SCRIPTURE TEXTS FOR MASS   Ordos and most liturgical desk calendars cite references for these. The semicontinuous Lectionary of the Proper of Seasons (Sunday or weekday; note that the Lectionary currently retains the title "Proper of Seasons" whereas *The Roman Missal* uses "Proper of Time") is followed on most days, even on a majority of the memorials of saints. On a few days (solemnities and feasts and a rare few memorials), readings come from those days in the Proper of

Saints. When the continuous pattern is interrupted by such a day, Priest Celebrants, other presiders, and those who prepare the liturgy can interpolate the lost passages into an adjoining day. This is particularly important when the surrounding days have First Readings with dramatic narratives and the skipped passage contains an important element. We should always be in communication with those who decide such matters to see how the Lectionary should be set.

For some days and rites, a choice of readings is given for the observance. When selected, they might be marked in the Lectionary with a self-sticking note or flag, especially if several readings appear on a page.

THE PRAYER TEXTS FOR MASS Once the day is ascertained (see above), many texts can be selected for their "seasonal" or topical connections, sometimes in prior preparation, at other times in the sacristy before Mass (the Preface of the Eucharistic Prayer, the Eucharistic Prayer itself, the form of blessing). Other texts are prepared locally; for example, the Universal Prayer (Prayer of the Faithful). (See page 102 for information on setting ribbons and notes in *The Roman Missal*.) The Presidential Prayers (Collect, Prayer over the Offerings, Prayer after Communion) for the given day are determined according to this pattern:

a. Most days have a set of prayers assigned to them and positioned with that title in the Proper of Time or Proper of Saints.

b. Some days in the Proper of Time have only a Collect that is assigned (that is, "proper"); a few have no assigned prayers. A reference always is made under their title in *The Roman Missal* (and in *Ordos*) to the sections of general texts (Commons) from which prayers can be drawn. When a couple of possible Commons (for example, pastor or doctor) or several texts in a Commons are available, selections should be made according to both the life of the saint or blessed and the needs of the community.

c. Weekdays in Ordinary Time with no saint's observance (or with an optional memorial passed by) offer a variety of choices for the Presidential Prayers:

- Use prayers from the prior Sunday in Ordinary Time (but not from a feast falling on Sunday).

- Use one of the Votive Masses (found after the Commons in *The Roman Missal*).

- Use Masses and Prayers for Various Needs and Occasions (printed after the Commons).

- Choices for the Liturgy of the Hours. Many *Ordos* contain notes on special choices for the various hours. As with Mass texts, texts for the hours should flow from the day being observed. This is usually obvious, but when optional memorials are offered in the calendar, those praying should know the option selected.

COLOR OF VESTMENTS These are usually listed in *Ordos*. The logic informing the assignments is outlined on pages 118–119. If the day's color differs from the color for the liturgical time, it is neither necessary nor advisable to change the whole decor for one day. Instead, the contrast can indicate, for example, that Saint Joseph is being celebrated in Lent.

The Lists in This Manual

The pages that follow describe the physical requisites for some of the most important or unusual days in our liturgical year. The first list is a basic list for celebrating Mass at any time. Then follow lists for the specific liturgical times and feasts. These are all meant as general examples; local plans and customs will always call for adaptations. All lists should be prepared and reviewed with the Priest Celebrant and those who prepare the liturgy long before the day of celebration.

Chapter Thirty-two

Basic Checklist for Celebration of the Eucharist and Other Rites

PLACE FOR EUCHARISTIC ACTION

Seating:

- ❏ hymnals

Altar:

- ❏ covered with one white cloth, if a festive colored cloth is used, the upper-most cloth must be white
- ❏ *Book of the Gospels* with text marked, if used and not carried in procession
- ❏ nearby: any candles, candlestands not carried in procession
- ❏ nearby: stand for processional cross

Credence Table:

- ❏ vessel of water and sprinkler, if rite of sprinkling will be performed
- ❏ large chalice (can be covered by pall and/or white veil)
- ❏ purificator
- ❏ corporal
- ❏ book stand, if needed
- ❏ water in small cruet
- ❏ basin, pitcher of water, towel
- ❏ additional cups and purificators for the congregation (on tray)
- ❏ additional patens for the congregation

Priest Celebrant's Chair:

- ❏ *The Roman Missal* (after review in vesting room)
- ❏ hymnal and/or printed worship aid, if not carried in procession

Ministers' Seats:

- ❏ texts for concelebrants, if any
- ❏ hymnals and/or worship aids, if not carried in procession

Ambo:

- ❏ Lectionary with texts marked
- ❏ Psalm setting for cantor (unless carried there for this action)
- ❏ Universal Prayer (Prayer of the Faithful) if announced here

Music Stand (or Secondary Podium):

- ❏ Universal Prayer (Prayer of the Faithful) if announced here

SACRISTY

- ❏ if incense is used: charcoal lit in thurible, then put in vesting room
- ❏ if incense is used: extra charcoal (and tongs, matches) for adding during Mass
- ❏ controls set for air, sound, lights
- ❏ microphones put in place, turned on, and tested

VESTING ROOM

- ❏ vesture (see page 130); chasuble, dalmatic of day's color
- ❏ lavaliere microphones, if any
- ❏ Lectionary with texts marked
- ❏ *Book of the Gospels* with texts marked, if carried in procession
- ❏ local texts (dismissal of catechumens, intercessions) prepared in binder
- ❏ Other texts marked in *The Roman Missal* for review before placement by chair
- ❏ if incense is used: thurible, with lit charcoal
- ❏ if incense is used: vessel of incense, "seasonal" scent
- ❏ processional cross
- ❏ two or more processional candlesticks with lit candles

Table with Gifts:

- ❏ patens, bowls, or ciboria with large host, additional hosts for the faithful
- ❏ vessels containing wine for the Priest Celebrant and the faithful, to be poured into chalices at the Preparation of the Gifts

Other:

- ❏ collection baskets ready
- ❏ worship aids, bulletins, or other handouts

CATECHUMENEON

- ❏ opened and prepared, if catechumens present

Chapter Thirty-three
Checklists for Liturgical Times and Other Days

Advent

THE LITURGICAL TIME: Advent is described in our official books:

> Advent has a twofold character, for it is a time of preparation for the Solemnities of Christmas, in which the First Coming of the Son of God to humanity is remembered, and likewise a time when, by remembrance of this, minds and hearts are led to look forward to Christ's Second Coming at the end of time. For these two reasons, Advent is a period of devout and expectant delight. . . .

> The weekdays from December 17 up to and including December 24 are ordered in a more direct way to preparing for the Nativity of the Lord. (*Universal Norms on the Liturgical Year and the General Roman Calendar,* 39, 42)

> During Advent, the playing of the organ and other musical instruments as well as the floral decoration of the altar should be marked by a moderation that reflects the character of this liturgical time, but does not anticipate the full joy of Christmas itself (*Ceremonial of Bishops,* 236).

VESTURE In former centuries, Advent was penitential. Though violet has been maintained as the color to use during this time, Advent should not be the same as Lent, and decorations or vestments that use images of Christ's Passion should be reserved for Lent. The retention of rose as an optional color for the Third Sunday of Advent allows a welcome infusion of joy midway through this liturgical time.

DECORATIONS Decorations should reflect our anticipation, not the fullness of Christmas splendor. Despite the full-throated carols of praise sounding through malls, the Churches holding to Advent require of their sacristans (and musicians) a certain discipline. We must hold back from Christmas decorations until after the Fourth Sunday of Advent, and let our communities savor Advent longing for weeks before we leap into the full-throated praise of the Incarnation at Christmas Time.

The Advent wreath is a well loved and highly recommended part of the Advent decor. The wreath and candles hint at the greens and lights of Christmas, the light of Christ, the brilliance of the end time, and the progress of this period of preparation. The wreath should be fashioned from real greens, which may be replaced halfway through the time, if necessary. True smell and honesty of form are important. The *Book of Blessings* (#1510, 1512) describes the Advent wreath:

> Customarily the Advent Wreath is constructed of a circle of evergreen branches into which are inserted four candles. According to tradition, three of the candles are violet and the fourth is rose. However, four violet or white candles may also be used.

If the Advent Wreath is to be used in church, it should be of sufficient size to be visible to the congregation. It may be suspended from the ceiling or placed on a stand. If it is placed in the presbyterium [sanctuary], it should not interfere with the celebration of the liturgy, nor should it obscure the altar, lectern, or chair.

If the local wreath is the proper scale, then few other decorations, if any at all, are needed. Other customs may include the following:

- a Jesse tree (in the entrance hall, decorated with representations of the ancestors and prophets, not arcane symbols of virtues)

- highlighted statues or windows of John the Baptist, images of Isaiah or of the other prophets

- candles by the Marian shrine, especially if the image there follows one of the eschatological images so central to Advent (Immaculate Conception, Our Lady of Guadalupe)

- a wall in the narthex dedicated to signing up volunteers for the various tasks of Christmas

- outdoor decor that announces Advent (violet strips of cloth, an outdoor tree with "Jesse" figures).

Christmas Time

THE LITURGICAL TIME   Christmas Time provides us each year with two or three weeks for high festivity. All our preparations and decorations should help encourage and sustain the expressions of joy called for in the liturgy. At Christmas, we rejoice in the birth of Jesus, his manifestation as Messiah and Lord, and from our sharing in divinity through our participation in his Paschal Mystery. God took human flesh to raise this very flesh to divine dignity.

A devout and fully Christian observance of these days thus calls for more than pious emotions before the manger scene. We must also thrill to the retelling of Christ's other manifestations, and sing in wonder of our new dignity. These aspects will be seen more fully if Christmas is more than a day, if the decorations and other artifacts give external cohesion to the inner unity of the days from Christmas Eve to the Feast of the Baptism of the Lord. Festal decorations must be held back until just before Christmas Eve. Their ability to last until the end of the liturgical time must be a factor in their selection. The Feast of the Baptism of the Lord, the final day of the liturgical time, is somewhat over two weeks after Christmas Day—on the Sunday after the Solemnity of the Epiphany of the Lord (unless the Solemnity of the Epiphany of the Lord is as late as January 7 or 8, with the Feast of the Baptism of the Lord on the very next day, Monday, January 8 or 9).

VESTURE   White is assigned for this liturgical time. As always, gold or "more precious vestments" can be worn on solemn occasions such as Christmas and Epiphany. Red is often associated with Christmas in today's culture, and can be used as part of the decor, but in vesture for this liturgical time it is used only for the martyrs' days.

DECORATIONS   The decor should show the unity of these 15 to 20 days, facilitate the joyful experience of the sacred mysteries, and draw the congregation into a sense that Christ is still coming among us. From the shepherds and the Magi to our day, we see the Lord. Traditional decorations often are best:

Manger. The manger scene can be a reminder of Bethlehem, but also, with a touch of glorious decoration, a signal of the paradise promised and brought on that holy night. The *Book of Blessings* (#1544) sensibly notes that the manger must not be placed in the sanctuary. It can be outdoors or in an easily accessible part of the interior that is conducive to visits and prayer.

Christmas tree. Whether an evergreen tree is outside the church complex or one is brought indoors, the lit tree is a marvelous sign of the tree of paradise, the tree of life and light. It is perhaps the best non-verbal invitation to hope and brilliant rejoicing. It certainly does more than turn us back in nostalgia; it draws us forward to the kingdom of fullness and light. It is also a strong signal of the time's dates when lit from Christmas Eve to Epiphany or the Baptism of the Lord. Of course, an indoor tree should neither interfere with liturgical actions nor violate fire and egress codes.

Flowers. Where poinsettias are traditional, they certainly should be used. Traditions are hard to invent and should be respected and enjoyed when found. Creativity would be well spent in arranging them for color throughout the congregation space, not crowded up against the altar.

Exterior decorations. When preparing the decor for any liturgical time, the exterior should always be included. Possibilities for Christmas include the following: a weatherproof banner, lights on a large evergreen tree, an outdoor manger, garlands or fabric over the entries, luminarias along the parish walkways (lit at night on Christmas and Epiphany), or a huge wreath on the facade or tower.

Christmas Eve: Vigil and Mass during the Night

Mass during the Night is often preceded by a vigil service—the Office of Readings ("vigils") or some form of a service lessons and carols before Mass. Here is a checklist for items other than decorations, which were discussed above:

PLACE FOR EUCHARISTIC ACTION

Seating:

❏ hymnals or special service booklets

Open Space:

❏ dedication candles lit (optional), pew candles lit (if any), Advent wreath lit (if kept)

❏ créche prepared outside the sanctuary

Altar:

❏ covered with one white cloth, unless this comes at Preparation of the Gifts

❏ *Book of the Gospels* with text marked, if used and not carried in procession

❏ nearby: any candles, candlestands not carried in procession

❏ nearby: stand for processional cross

Credence Table:

❏ large chalice (can be covered by pall and/or white veil)

❏ purificator

❏ corporal

❏ book stand, if needed

❏ water in small cruet

❏ basin, pitcher of water, towel

❏ any bread, wine, not in procession of gifts

❏ additional chalices and purificators for the congregation (on tray)

❏ additional patens or ciboria for the congregation

Priest Celebrant's Chair:

❏ *The Roman Missal* (after review in vesting room)

❏ hymnal or booklet, if not carried in procession

❏ candle, bobeche (if light service is done)

Ministers' Seats:

❏ texts for concelebrants, if any

❏ hymnals or booklets, if not carried in procession

❏ candles, bobeches for all (if light service is done before Mass)

Ambo:

❏ Lectionary with texts marked

❏ Psalm setting for cantor (unless carried there for that action)

❏ Texts for Universal Prayer (Prayer of the Faithful), if done here

❏ *The Nativity of Our Lord Jesus Christ* (Christmas Proclamation), if sung

Music Stand (or secondary podium):

❏ Texts for Universal Prayer (Prayer of the Faithful), if done here

SACRISTY

❏ charcoal lit in thurible, then put in vesting room

❏ extra charcoal (and tongs, matches) for adding during Mass

❏ controls set for air, sound, lights

❏ microphones put in places, turned on, and tested

VESTING ROOM

- ❏ vesture (see page 130); chasuble, dalmatic of white or gold
- ❏ lavaliere microphones, if any
- ❏ *Book of the Gospels* with texts marked, if carried in procession
- ❏ local texts prepared (dismissal of catechumens, Universal Prayer) and other texts marked in *The Roman Missal*, for review prior to placement by chair
- ❏ thurible, with lit charcoal
- ❏ vessel of incense, Christmas scent
- ❏ processional cross
- ❏ two or more candlesticks with lit candles

Table with Gifts:

- ❏ bread for all in patens, bowls, or ciboria, if in procession
- ❏ wine for all, if in procession

Other:

- ❏ collection baskets ready
- ❏ booklets, bulletins or other handouts
- ❏ candles, bobeches for all, if service of light will be celebrated before Mass

CATECHUMENEON

- ❏ opened and prepared, if catechumens present

Solemnity of the Epiphany of the Lord: Mass

The liturgical books suggest these additional elements: extra candles in the room, a proclamation of the year's movable feasts, and a special presentation of gifts.

PLACE FOR EUCHARISTIC ACTION

Seating:

- ❏ hymnals and worship aids

Open Space:

- ❏ as many candles lit as possible (dedication candles, pew candles also)
- ❏ créche outside the sanctuary; Magi added now

Altar:

- ❏ covered with one white cloth, unless this comes at preparation rite
- ❏ *Book of the Gospels* with text marked, if used and not carried in procession

❏ nearby: any candles, candlestands not carried in procession

❏ nearby: stand for processional cross

Credence Table:

❏ vessel of water, if rite of sprinkling occurs

❏ large chalice (can be covered by pall and/or white veil)

❏ purificator

❏ corporal

❏ book stand, if needed

❏ water in small cruet

❏ basin, pitcher of water, towel

❏ any bread, wine, not in procession of gifts

❏ additional chalices and purificators for the congregation (on tray)

❏ additional patens, bowls, or ciboria for the congregation

Priest Celebrant's Chair:

❏ *The Roman Missal* (after review in vesting room)

❏ hymnal, if not carried in procession

Ministers' Seats:

❏ texts for concelebrants, if any

❏ hymnals, if not carried in procession

Ambo:

❏ Lectionary with texts marked

❏ Psalm setting for cantor (unless carried there for that action)

❏ Universal Prayer (Prayer of the Faithful), if done here

❏ additional texts (*The Announcement of Easter and the Moveable Feasts* [Epiphany Proclamation], if sung)

Music Stand (or Secondary Podium):

❏ Universal Prayer (Prayer of the Faithful), if done here

SACRISTY

❏ charcoal lit in thurible, then put in vesting room

❏ extra charcoal (and tongs, matches) for adding during Mass

❏ controls set for air, sound, lights

❏ microphones put in places, turned on, and tested

Vesting Room

- ❑ vesture (see page 130); chasuble, dalmatic of white or gold
- ❑ lavaliere microphones, if any
- ❑ *Book of the Gospels* with text marked, if carried in procession
- ❑ local texts prepared (dismissal of catechumens, intercessions) and other texts marked in *The Roman Missal,* for review prior to placement by chair
- ❑ thurible, with lit charcoal
- ❑ vessel of incense, Christmas scent
- ❑ processional cross
- ❑ two or more lit candles; more suggested for this day

Entrance

Table with Gifts:

- ❑ bread for all in patens, bowls, or ciboria, if in procession
- ❑ wine for all, if in procession
- ❑ water in small cruet, if in procession

Other:

- ❑ collection baskets ready
- ❑ booklets, bulletins, parish calendars for the new year

Catechumeneon

- ❑ opened and prepared, if catechumens present

Lent

The Liturgical Time   Lent is the time to prepare for Easter Time, stretching from Ash Wednesday to the start of the Sacred Paschal Triduum on Thursday of Holy Week. During Lent, the community prays over the catechumens with heightened intensity and frequency. All who truly keep Lent prepare themselves, through a spirit of repentance, to renew their Baptism at Easter. The baptismal and penitential aspects of Lent have given rise to many customs and practices related to our work in the sacristy.

Just as Advent—the other preparatory liturgical time—shifts to a more intense mode on December 17, Lent has an internal structure to help us build our devotion and fervor as Easter Time draws near. Ash Wednesday and the next three days form a solemn prelude. Later, there is a shift as we move from first four weeks of Lent to the final two weeks, when attention to the Passion of Christ inspires our renewal. The culmination of the entire liturgical year comes with the Sacred Paschal Triduum. Its intense remembering does more than point us back to a Cross two millennia ago. It brings us to a living reality, a Cross and Resurrection that shapes us and all who will ever live. The internal movement of these liturgical times does not necessarily need to be reflected in decorations. But we should all appreciate the fundamental unity and purpose of this entire 43-day period.

EQUIPMENT FOR ASHES AND PALMS   For Palm Sunday, we need suitable receptacles to hold palms. Consider buying whole fronds and inviting volunteers to cut them into sizable pieces—the emotional attachment of Catholics to this sacramental is marvelous, and we should do all that we can to involve volunteers and to encourage physical contact with the symbols of our prayer. After Palm Sunday, we need containers or bags in which to save remaining palms for the following Ash Wednesday.

Early in the new year invite parishioners to bring their used palms to church by the Sunday before Ash Wednesday. Baskets will be needed to receive these palms. The palms can be burned in a large brazier or clean outdoor grill, with parish members gathered around and singing, or more quietly over the next two days. The ashes should be kept in a covered jar to store them safely until Wednesday. For the services on Ash Wednesday, we need a large bowl for the ashes, smaller vessels for ministers, and a large spoon. In such practical ways, we allow this eloquent dirt to tell of death, penitence, and the start of a new liturgical time in our lives.

VESTURE   If possible, the violet vesture used in Lent might well be different from that used in Advent. Austerity is important everywhere in this liturgical time, and appliquéd symbols of the Passion on vestments or banners do not necessarily enhance the liturgical time. The white vesture used on the few solemnities should be as plain as possible. The red for Palm Sunday of the Lord's Passion should not have Pentecost symbols.

DECORATIONS   Emptiness speaks as forcefully as any of the floral arrangements used over the rest of the year. By customs firmly restated in the liturgical books, this is the liturgical time for bare buildings and for avoiding all manner of flowers. In the midst of this austerity, three elements at the core of Lent can be highlighted: the collection place for alms, a place of prayer for the elect preparing for Baptism at Easter, and exterior signs with clearly worded invitations to the coming celebrations of Holy Week.

Ash Wednesday: Celebration of the Eucharist

If ashes are distributed apart from Mass, at a Liturgy of the Word following the order found in Chapter 52 of the *Book of Blessings,* use this checklist, except for those items particular for Mass.

PLACE FOR EUCHARISTIC ACTION

Seating:

❑ hymnals

Open Space:

- ❏ spaces designated for ministers to distribute ashes

Altar:

- ❏ covered with one white cloth, unless this comes at Preparation of the Gifts
- ❏ *Book of the Gospels* with text marked, if used and not carried in procession
- ❏ nearby: any candles, candlestands not carried in procession
- ❏ nearby: stand for processional cross

Credence Table:

- ❏ vessel of water with sprinkler (for ashes)
- ❏ bowls containing ashes, perhaps arranged on trays for the blessing
- ❏ basins with small bars of soap, pitchers of water, towels (as many as needed—all ministers distributing ashes wash hands)
- ❏ large chalice (can be covered by pall and/or white veil)
- ❏ purificator
- ❏ corporal
- ❏ book stand, if needed
- ❏ water in small cruet
- ❏ any bread, wine, not in procession of gifts
- ❏ additional chalices and purificators for the congregation (on tray)
- ❏ additional patens, ciboria, or bowls for the congregation

Priest Celebrant's Chair:

- ❏ *The Roman Missal* (after review in vesting room)
- ❏ hymnal, if not carried in procession

Ministers' Seats:

- ❏ texts for concelebrants, if any
- ❏ hymnals, if not carried in procession

Ambo:

- ❏ Lectionary with texts marked
- ❏ Psalm setting for cantor (unless carried there for this action)
- ❏ Universal Prayer (Prayer of the Faithful), if done here

Music Stand (or secondary podium):

- ❏ Universal Prayer (Prayer of the Faithful), if done here

SACRISTY

❏ charcoal lit in thurible, then put in vesting room

❏ extra charcoal (and tongs, matches) for adding during Mass

❏ controls set for air, sound, lights

❏ microphones put in place, turned on, and tested

VESTING ROOM

❏ vesture (see page 130); chasuble, dalmatic of violet

❏ lavaliere microphones, if any

❏ *Book of the Gospels* with texts marked, if carried in procession

❏ local texts prepared (dismissal of catechumens, intercessions) and other texts marked in *The Roman Missal,* for review prior to placement by chair (the *Book of Blessings* instead of *The Roman Missal,* when the celebration is not Mass)

❏ thurible, with lit charcoal

❏ vessel of incense, Lenten scent

❏ processional cross

❏ two or more candlesticks with lit candles

ENTRANCE

Table with Gifts:

❏ bread for all in patens, bowls, or ciboria, if in procession

❏ wine for all, if in procession

Other:

❏ booklets, bulletins or other handouts

CATECHUMENEON

❏ opened and prepared, if catechumens present

First Sunday of Lent with Penitential Procession

This outline provides for a procession of the entire congregation to begin Mass and signal the start of Lent. As called for in official documents (*Paschale Solemnitatis,* 23; *Ceremonial of Bishops,* 261), all gather in a separate place for a hymn, an introduction to Lent, and prayer. Then a solemn procession of all is accompanied by the litany of the saints. At Masses with catechumens present, a Rite of Sending for Election is provided for this day in the *Rite of Christian Initiation of Adults.*

PLACE FOR EUCHARISTIC ACTION

Seating:

- ❏ special seats for catechumens after the procession, if reserved hymnals or booklets, unless these are in other gathering place

Open Space:

- ❏ area set for catechumens and sponsors, when called forward

Altar:

- ❏ covered with one white cloth, unless this comes at the Preparation of the Gifts
- ❏ *Book of the Gospels* with text marked, if used and not carried in procession
- ❏ nearby: any candles, candlestands not carried in procession
- ❏ nearby: stand for processional cross

Credence Table:

- ❏ large chalice (can be covered by pall and/or white veil)
- ❏ purificator
- ❏ corporal
- ❏ book stand, if needed
- ❏ water in small cruet
- ❏ basin, pitcher of water, towel
- ❏ any bread, wine, not in procession of gifts
- ❏ additional chalices and purificators for the congregation (on tray)
- ❏ additional patens, bowls, or ciboria for the congregation

Priest Celebrant's Chair:

- ❏ nearby: violet chasuble, if cope worn in procession
- ❏ hymnal, if not carried in procession

Ministers' Seats:

- ❏ texts for concelebrants, if any
- ❏ hymnals, if not carried in procession

Ambo:

- ❏ Lectionary with texts marked
- ❏ Psalm setting for cantor (unless carried there for this action)

- ❏ intercessions for the catechumens and candidates, if rite of sending is celebrated, and if done here
- ❏ Universal Prayer (Prayer of the Faithful), if done here

Music Stand (or Secondary Podium):

- ❏ intercessions for the catechumens and candidates, if Rite of Sending is celebrated, and if done here
- ❏ Universal Prayer (Prayer of the Faithful), if done here

SACRISTY

- ❏ charcoal lit in thurible, then put in vesting room
- ❏ extra charcoal (and tongs, matches) for adding during Mass
- ❏ controls set for air, sound, lights
- ❏ microphones put in places, turned on, and tested

VESTING ROOM

- ❏ vesture (see page 130); cope or chasuble, dalmatic of violet
- ❏ lavaliere microphones, if any
- ❏ *Book of the Gospels* with text marked, if carried in procession
- ❏ local texts (introduction to Lent, Rite of Sending for Election, intercessions) prepared, *The Roman Missal* placed here for review prior to placement in gathering area
- ❏ thurible, with lit charcoal
- ❏ vessel of incense, Lent scent
- ❏ processional cross
- ❏ two or more candlesticks with lit candles

ENTRANCE

Exterior:

- ❏ signs directing congregation to special gathering place

Table with Gifts:

- ❏ bread for all in patens, bowls, or ciboria, if in procession
- ❏ wine for all, if in procession

Other:

- ❏ collection baskets ready
- ❏ booklets, bulletins, Triduum schedule or other handouts

Catechumeneon

❑ opened and prepared, if catechumens present

Other Gathering Place

❑ place arranged for entire congregation

❑ place reserved for instrumentalists and other leaders of music

❑ place reserved for the Priest Celebrant and other ministers

❑ *The Roman Missal* (carried there by assistant)

❑ hymnals or booklets for all

First Sunday of Lent: The Rite of Election

This rite normally takes place in the cathedral on the First Sunday of Lent. It can be combined with the Rite of Calling the Candidates to Continuing Conversion (for Confirmation, Eucharist, reception into full communion) previously baptized. The list here presumes a diocesan-wide gathering, where the Liturgy of the Eucharist normally does not follow (*Rite of Christian Initiation of Adults,* 560).

Place for Congregation

Seating:

❑ hymnals or booklets

❑ signs indicating positions, if parish-by-parish seating plan

❑ reserved seats for chief catechists or others as needed

Open Space:

❑ area arranged for those to be called forward

❑ requisites to meet local procedures related to book of elect, for example, fairly high table or stand with *Book of Elect* and pens

❑ place determined for the person or persons presenting the catechumens (and other candidates) by name

Altar:

❑ *Book of the Gospels* with text marked, if used and not carried in procession

❑ nearby: any candles, candlestands not carried in procession

❑ nearby: stand for processional cross

Cathedra:

❑ hymnal or booklet

❑ places nearby for ministers assisting with miter, pastoral staff, and ritual book

Other Ministers' Seats:

❏ hymnals or booklets (if not carried in procession)

Ambo:

❏ Lectionary with texts marked

❏ Psalm setting for cantor (unless carried there for this action)

❏ text of intercessions, if done here

Music Stand (or Secondary Podium):

❏ text of intercessions, if done here

SACRISTY

❏ charcoal lit in thurible, then placed in vesting room

❏ controls set for air, sound, lights

❏ microphones put in place and turned on

VESTING ROOM

❏ cope, dalmatics of violet

❏ lavaliere microphones, if any

❏ *Book of the Gospels* with texts marked, if carried in procession

❏ texts marked in ritual book, for review prior to assistant carrying it

❏ texts, lists of names for person(s) presenting catechumens

❏ thurible, with lit charcoal

❏ vessel of incense, Lenten scent

❏ processional cross

❏ two or more candlesticks with lit candles

❏ Entrance booklets, bulletins or other handouts

❏ table(s) for registration or for diocesan information

❏ clear charts posted, if parish-by-parish seating plan followed

Scrutinies and Mass on the Third, Fourth, and Fifth Sundays of Lent

The word *exorcism* may bring to mind fantastic ideas of demons from Hollywood films. But exorcisms remain a significant part of our liturgical tradition, most prominently in the Rite of Baptism and in the Scrutinies, public rites of the congregation and those elected for initiation at Easter. Neither fantastic nor bizarre, they are public statements of the reality of evil in our lives and of Christ's power. Through self-searching and repentance, but chiefly through a shared reliance on God, our communities prepare for Easter.

PLACE FOR EUCHARISTIC ACTION

Seating:

- ❏ hymnals
- ❏ designated seats for catechumens and elect, if reserved

Open Space:

- ❏ space designated for the elect and their sponsors to stand (and kneel) after coming forward; this does not need to be near the altar but might be closer to congregation in center aisle

Altar:

- ❏ covered with one white cloth, unless this comes at preparation rite
- ❏ *Book of the Gospels* with text marked, if used and not carried in procession
- ❏ nearby: any candles, candlestands not carried in procession
- ❏ nearby: stand for processional cross

Credence Table:

- ❏ large chalice (can be covered by pall and/or white veil)
- ❏ purificator
- ❏ corporal
- ❏ book stand, if needed
- ❏ water in small cruet
- ❏ basin, pitcher of water, towel
- ❏ any bread, wine, not in procession of gifts
- ❏ additional chalices and purificators for the congregation (on tray)
- ❏ additional patens, bowls, or ciboria for the congregation

Priest Celebrant's Chair:

- ❏ *The Roman Missal* (after review in vesting room)
- ❏ hymnal, if not carried in procession

Ministers' Seats:

- ❏ texts for concelebrants, if any
- ❏ hymnals, if not carried in procession

Ambo:

- ❏ Lectionary with texts marked
- ❏ Psalm setting for cantor (unless carried there for this action)
- ❏ intercessions for the elect, if done here
- ❏ Universal Prayer (Prayer of the Faithful), if done here

Music Stand (or Secondary Podium):

- ❏ intercessions for the elect, if done here
- ❏ Universal Prayer (Prayer of the Faithful), if done here

SACRISTY

- ❏ charcoal lit in thurible, then put in vesting room
- ❏ extra charcoal (and tongs, matches) for adding during Mass
- ❏ controls set for air, sound, lights
- ❏ microphones put in place, turned on, and tested

VESTING ROOM

- ❏ vesture (see page 130); chasuble, dalmatic of violet (rose optional on Fourth Sunday of Lent)
- ❏ lavaliere microphones, if any
- ❏ *Book of the Gospels* with text marked, if carried in procession
- ❏ local texts (Scrutinies, Universal Prayer [Prayer of the Faithful] prepared, and other texts marked (ritual Mass, "For the Celebration of the Scrutinies") in *The Roman Missal*, for review prior to placement by chair
- ❏ thurible, with lit charcoal
- ❏ vessel of incense, Lenten scent
- ❏ processional cross
- ❏ two or more candlesticks with lit candles

ENTRANCE

Table with Gifts:

- ❏ bread for all in patens, bowls, or ciboria, if in procession
- ❏ wine for all, if in procession

Other:

- ❏ collection baskets ready
- ❏ booklets, bulletins, Triduum schedules, or other handouts

❏ opened and prepared for sharing after dismissal of catechumens

Palm Sunday of the Passion of the Lord (with Procession)

The first form of the Commemoration of the Lord's Entrance into Jerusalem is the traditional procession of palms, which may take place only once in each church, though the second form, the solemn entrance, can (and should) take place at all other Palm Sunday Masses in the church. According to *The Roman Missal*, it should begin "at a smaller church or other suitable place other than inside the church to which the procession will go."

PLACE FOR EUCHARISTIC ACTION

Altar:

❏ covered with one white cloth, unless this comes at Preparation of the Gifts

❏ nearby: any candles, candlestands not carried in procession

❏ nearby: stand for processional cross

Credence Table:

❏ large chalice (can be covered by pall and/or white veil)

❏ purificator

❏ corporal

❏ book stand, if needed

❏ water in small cruet

❏ basin, pitcher of water, towel

❏ any bread, wine, not in procession of gifts

❏ additional chalices and purificators for the congregation (on tray)

❏ additional patens, bowls, or ciboria for the congregation

Priest Celebrant's Chair:

❏ nearby: red chasuble, if cope worn for procession

❏ hymnal or booklet, if not carried in procession

Ministers' Seats:

❏ texts for concelebrants, if any

❏ hymnals or booklets, if not carried in procession

Ambo:

❏ Lectionary with texts marked

❏ Psalm setting for cantor (unless carried there for this action)

❏ books for singing the Passion (or reading in parts), if used (secondary lecterns for those taking parts, or reading desks added to large ambo area)

❏ Universal Prayer (Prayer of the Faithful), if done here

Music Stand (or Secondary Podium):

❏ Universal Prayer (Prayer of the Faithful), if done here

SACRISTY

❏ charcoal lit in thurible, then put in vesting room

❏ extra charcoal (and tongs, matches) for adding during Mass

❏ controls set for air, sound, lights

❏ microphones put in place, turned on, and tested, including additional microphones for Passion readers

VESTING ROOM

❏ vesture (see page 130); cope or chasuble, dalmatic of red

❏ lavaliere microphones, if any

❏ local texts (dismissal of catechumens and elect, intercessions) prepared texts marked in *The Roman Missal* (including texts for the Lord's entry into Jerusalem); reviewed prior to placement in (or procession to) special gathering area

❏ thurible, with lit charcoal

❏ vessel of incense, Lenten scent

❏ processional cross, decorated with palm branches

❏ two or more candlesticks with lit candles

ENTRANCE

Exterior:

❏ signs directing congregation to special gathering place

❏ arrangements made for procession: permit secured for use of public streets or sidewalks, traffic guards, special regulations for parking

Table with Gifts:

❏ bread for all in patens, bowls, or ciboria, if in procession

❏ wine for all, if in procession

Other:

❏ collection baskets ready

❏ booklets, bulletins, Triduum schedules, or other handouts

CATECHUMENEON

❏ opened and prepared, if catechumens and/or elect present

OTHER GATHERING PLACE

❏ space prepared for entire congregation

❏ space set for instrumentalists, other leaders of music, Priest Celebrant, other ministers (near table/podium)

❏ palm branches for all, in baskets or other receptacles

❏ hymnals or booklets for all

Table or Stand:

❏ vessel of water and sprinkler

❏ palms for Priest Celebrant and ministers who proceed from vesting room

❏ *The Roman Missal*

Podium:

❏ Lectionary or *Book of the Gospels* (unless carried in procession from vesting room)

Chrism Mass

PLACE FOR EUCHARISTIC ACTION

Seating:

❏ hymnals or booklets

Open Space:

❏ table for the vessels of oil

Altar:

❏ covered with one white cloth, unless this comes at Preparation of the Gifts

❏ *Book of the Gospels*, if used and not carried in procession

❏ nearby: any candles, candlestands not carried in procession

❏ nearby: stand for processional cross

Credence Table:

❏ large spoon on dish (for mixing of fragrance and oil during rite)

❏ large chalice (can be covered by pall and/or white veil)

❏ purificator

❏ corporal

❏ book stand, if needed

❏ water in small cruet, if not in procession of gifts

❏ basin, pitcher of water, towel

❏ any bread, wine, not in procession of gifts

❏ additional chalices and purificators for the congregation (on tray)

❏ additional patens, bowls, or ciboria for the congregation

Cathedra:

❏ hymnal or booklet

❏ places nearby for ministers assisting with miter, pastoral staff, *The Roman Missal*

Seating for Concelebrants and Other Ministers:

❏ texts for concelebrants

❏ hymnals or booklets, if not carried in procession

Ambo:

❏ Lectionary with texts marked

❏ Psalm setting for cantor (unless carried there for this action)

❏ (there is no Universal Prayer at the Chrism Mass)

SACRISTY

❏ charcoal lit in thurible, then put by procession gathering

❏ extra charcoal (and tongs, matches) for adding during Mass

❏ controls set for air, sound, lights

❏ microphones put in places, turned on, and tested

VESTING ROOM(S)

❏ vesture (see page 131); chasuble, dalmatics of white; if many deacons and priests are vesting, several rooms may be necessary—arranged so that the procession is duly formed

❏ space for the Bishop to address priests after Mass (*Ceremonial of Bishops*, 294)

- space and equipment for the orderly distribution of oils (if not done during liturgy, may be in several rooms); for example, table for main vessels; pitchers for drawing off oils and setting up stations for distribution (at each station: table, three pitchers clearly labeled with oil's title, paper towels, trays for resting parish vessels and pouring, containers for receiving old oils, receptacles for paper towels, dishes of cut lemons for ministers' hands).

- hymnals or booklets for concelebrants

- lavaliere microphones, if any

- *Book of the Gospels* with texts marked, if carried in procession

- local texts (dismissal of elect and catechumens) prepared and other texts marked (blessing of oils) in *The Roman Missal* and *Roman Pontifical,* for review

- thurible, with lit charcoal

- vessel of incense, Lenten scent

- processional cross

- two or more candlesticks with lit candles

ENTRANCE

Table with Gifts:

- three large vessels of olive oil

- vessel with chrism fragrance, to be mixed with the oil that will be consecrated as chrism

- bread for all on in patens, bowls, or ciboria, if in procession

- wine for all, if in procession

Other

- collection baskets ready

- booklets, bulletins or other handouts

CATECHUMENEON

- opened, if dismissal is scheduled

The Sacred Paschal Triduum

Sacristans hardly need to be told of the Triduum's importance—or of its complexity! It is the privileged time for celebrating the primal event of salvation that is still present in our midst, still shaping us as Church. It is the center of our year; its preparation should never wait for late Lent. We will be less burdened when we recognize the Triduum events as annual repetitions of time-honored actions, not as fresh inventions each year. Notes from former years are enormously important as we enlist more volunteers and prepare requisites.

From the Evening Mass of Thursday of Holy Week through Evening Prayer on Easter Sunday, we will need to make changes in the physical environment of our buildings, utilize many implements seen but once a year, and serve more worshippers than at any other point in the year. Our responsibilities begin weeks or months ahead, making lists of requisites needed from careful reviews of the rites, and then finding or commissioning the most dignified materials possible. These artifacts are noted in the checklists that follow.

DECORATIONS   The church building is mostly bare for the first two days, then transformed with paradisal decorations at the Easter Vigil. There are some additional special arrangements:

Thursday evening at the end of Mass. The place for the transfer of the Holy Eucharist is the tabernacle used all year, presuming that this is separated from the altar. Its decoration this night should be simple but beautiful. A few flowers or small olive trees or branches can be combined with candles. Away from the chapel of reservation, everything is to be stripped or veiled following the Evening Mass: no crosses visible, no holy water in stoups or font, no covers or cloths on altar. Only permanent furniture like the altar and the ambo should be visible, and they should be barren.

Thursday midnight. The Blessed Sacrament is brought to a private place—usually a vault or safe in the sacristy. All candles are extinguished, and all decorations are taken from the Eucharistic chapel.

Friday of Holy Week [Good Friday]. Only those items of furniture needed are set out, then removed after the rite. All else is bare. Following the liturgy, the cross (which was carried in during the celebration) is placed with lit candles in a place conducive both to quiet prayer and to reverencing the cross with a touch or kiss.

Saturday. The many artifacts and furnishings of the Vigil need to be placed as early as possible, but if the office of Morning Prayer or the Office of Readings is prayed in the church, decorations should be delayed until after these prayers. The rubrics in the *Ceremonial of Bishops* (#48) ban the use of flowers "from Ash Wednesday until the *Gloria* at the Easter Vigil." For centuries, a reverent procession of flower bearers and veil removers took place at the Gloria of the Vigil. Where possible, this custom may be retained. Thus, the decorative tasks of Holy Saturday include the delivery of decorations, temporary placement to see how they will look, and then an immediate removal of them to some place where a procession of flower-bearers will form during the Vigil. For this procession, the flowers can be placed in clusters or zones so that the right pots end up in the planned positions. A rehearsal of procession leaders can take place as the flowers are delivered and set. Meanwhile, the cross remains in its place of honor. One other image can be introduced into the still-stripped environment: an image of Christ in the tomb, of the descent into hell, or of the sorrowful Virgin Mary.

Thursday of the Lord's Supper: At the Evening Mass

PLACE FOR EUCHARISTIC ACTION

Seating:

❏ hymnals or booklets

Open Space:

❏ chairs for those whose feet will be washed

❏ pedestals for the holy oils (after Entrance Procession)

❏ containers for gifts for the poor (unless at entrance)

Altar:

❏ covered with one white cloth, unless this comes at Preparation of the Gifts

❏ *Book of the Gospels* with text marked, if used and not carried in procession

❏ nearby: any candles, candlestands not carried in procession

❏ nearby: stand for processional cross

Credence Table(s), in Order of Usage:

❏ robe stand or place for resting chasuble during foot-washing

❏ linen apron (gremial), if used

❏ large pitcher(s) of warm water, basin(s), towels for drying feet

❏ basin with soap, pitcher of water, towel for hand-washing

❏ corporal

❏ large chalice (can be covered by pall and/or white veil)

❏ purificator

❏ book stand, if needed

❏ water in small cruet

❏ additional chalices and purificators for the congregation (on tray)

❏ additional patens, bowls, or ciboria for the congregation

❏ pyxes for hosts consecrated for the sick, unless these are held by the ministers who will leave from Mass for this ministry

❏ humeral veils

❏ candles and holders for all ministers to carry in procession at end

Priest Celebrant's Chair:

❏ *The Roman Missal* (after review in vesting room)

❏ hymnal or booklet, if not carried in procession

Ministers' Seats:

- ❏ texts for concelebrants, if any
- ❏ hymnals or booklets, if not carried in procession

Ambo:

- ❏ Lectionary with texts marked
- ❏ Psalm setting for cantor (unless carried there for this action)
- ❏ Universal Prayer (Prayer of the Faithful), if done here

Music Stand (or Secondary Podium):

- ❏ Universal Prayer (Prayer of the Faithful), if done here

SACRISTY

- ❏ charcoal lit in thurible, then put in vesting room
- ❏ extra charcoal (and tongs, matches) for adding during Mass
- ❏ second thurible with charcoal to be lit later in Mass
- ❏ controls set for air, sound, lights
- ❏ microphones put in place, turned on, and tested

VESTING ROOM

- ❏ vesture (see page 130); chasuble, dalmatic of white
- ❏ lavaliere microphones, if any
- ❏ *Book of the Gospels* with texts marked, if carried in procession
- ❏ local texts (reception of the holy oils, dismissal of catechumens and elect, intercessions) prepared and other texts marked in *The Roman Missal*, for review prior to placement by chair
- ❏ thurible, with lit charcoal
- ❏ vessel of incense
- ❏ processional cross
- ❏ two or more candlesticks with lit candles
- ❏ holy oils, in their vessels (for opening procession)

ENTRANCE

Exterior:

- ❏ bells ready for ringing during Gloria

Table with Gifts:

❏ bread for all in patens, bowls, or ciboria

❏ bread for all on Good Friday in large ciborium

❏ wine for all

❏ container for gifts for the poor, unless all in congregation bring their gifts up

Other:

❏ collection baskets ready

❏ booklets, bulletins or other handouts

❏ candles and holders for all, if used for procession at end

❏ Baptistry (or where repository of oils is located)

❏ repository open for reception of oils during introductory rites

CATECHUMENEON

❏ opened and prepared, if catechumens are present

CHAPEL OF EUCHARISTIC RESERVATION

❏ lamp removed

❏ tabernacle empty, unveiled, with doors open (and key at hand)

❏ simple decorations, unlit candles in place

Good Friday and Holy Saturday: *Tenebrae* Office of Readings Combined with Morning Prayer

Over the centuries preceding the Second Vatican Council, *Tenebrae* was the name given to the Office of Readings ("Vigils" or "Matins") combined with Morning Prayer ("Lauds") during which candles were extinguished as morning came. In recent centuries, despite the early-morning images, this was sometimes moved to Wednesday night, a sort of prelude to the Triduum. The reformed rites call for a return of the original *Tenebrae*. The combined office calls for these requisites:

PLACE FOR CONGREGATION

Seating:

❏ hymnals or booklets

Open Space:

❏ large candelabrum for *Tenebrae* can be positioned and lit, if used (old customs called for the extinguishing of candles at each Psalm, until only one was left)

Altar, if Hours Celebrated in Eucharistic Space:

❏ bare, nothing on it or near it

Priest Celebrant's Chair:

❑ ritual book (after review in vesting room)

❑ hymnal or booklet

Ministers' Seats:

❑ hymnals or booklets

❑ candle snuffer (if used)

Ambo:

❑ copies of the Liturgy of the Hours with texts marked, or passages marked in Bible (with passage from early Christian literature in separate book)

❑ text of intercessions, if done here

Music Stand (or Secondary Podium):

❑ text of intercessions, if done here

SACRISTY

❑ controls set for air, sound, lights

❑ microphones put in places, turned on, and tested

VESTING ROOM

❑ albs; stole for deacon/priest (red on Friday, violet Saturday)

❑ lavaliere microphones, if any

❑ texts marked in Liturgy of the Hours book or in special volume prepared with proper texts in correct order, for review before placement at chair

ENTRANCE

❑ booklets, bulletins or other handouts

Friday of the Passion of the Lord (Good Friday)

PLACE FOR CONGREGATION

Seating:

❑ hymnals or booklets

Open Space:

❑ space set for prostration of Priest Celebrant and others

❑ place set for later placement of two candles and cross (for example, processional cross base or simple stand for larger cross)

Altar:

- ❑ completely bare
- ❑ processional cross and stand put away

Credence Table:

- ❑ white altar cloth, to be placed before Communion Rite
- ❑ corporal
- ❑ plates or ciboria for the Communion of all

Priest Celebrant's Chair:

- ❑ *The Roman Missal* (after review in vesting room)
- ❑ hymnal or booklet
- ❑ nearby: robe stand for chasuble (if removed for adoration), shoe horn (if needed) for replacing shoes (if removed for adoration)

Ministers' Seats:

- ❑ hymnals or booklets

Ambo:

- ❑ Lectionary with texts marked
- ❑ Psalm setting for cantor (unless carried there for this action)
- ❑ books for singing the Passion or reading in parts, if used (secondary lecterns for those taking parts in proclamation of Passion, or reading desks added to large ambo area)
- ❑ text for the introduction or announcement of each intercession (unless announced from chair or music stand)

Sacristy

- ❑ controls set for air, sound, lights
- ❑ microphones put in place, turned on, and tested

Vesting Room

- ❑ vesture (see page 130); chasuble, dalmatic of red
- ❑ lavaliere microphones, if any
- ❑ Lectionary with texts marked, if carried in procession
- ❑ local texts (dismissal of catechumens and elect) inserted and other texts marked in *The Roman Missal*, for review prior to placement by chair

ENTRANCE

- ❏ cross (veiled or not, depending on ritual option selected)
- ❏ two candles, candlesticks (able to stand on floor by cross)
- ❏ matches
- ❏ collection baskets ready
- ❏ booklets, bulletins or other handouts

CATECHUMENEON

- ❏ opened and prepared, if catechumens and elect are present

CHAPEL OF EUCHARISTIC RESERVATION

- ❏ one candle lit by tabernacle
- ❏ key at tabernacle
- ❏ humeral veil (white or red)
- ❏ two candles, candlesticks, able to stand to side of altar
- ❏ matches

Holy Saturday: Preparation Rites for the Elect

The *Rite of Christian Initiation of Adults* (#185–192) calls for preparation rites this day: song and greeting, reading the Word of God and homily, and celebrating certain rites (Presentation of the Creed and/or the ephphetha rite).

CATECHUMENEON OR OTHER PLACE FOR CONGREGATION

Seating:

- ❏ hymnals or booklets

Open Space:

- ❏ stand with oil of catechumens, if anointing will take place

Altar, if Rites Celebrated in Eucharistic Space:

- ❏ bare, nothing on it or near it

Credence Table, if Infants Received:

- ❏ basin with lemon, pitcher of water, towel

Priest Celebrant's Chair:

- ❏ ritual book (after review in vesting room)
- ❏ hymnal or booklet

Ministers' Seats:

- ❏ hymnals or booklets

Ambo:

- ❏ Bible or Lectionary with texts marked
- ❏ Psalm setting for cantor, if Psalm used

Sacristy

- ❏ controls set for air, sound, lights
- ❏ microphones (if necessary) put in place, turned on, and tested

Vesting Room

- ❏ albs; violet stole for deacon, priest
- ❏ lavaliere microphones, if any
- ❏ texts marked in ritual book in correct order, for review before placing at chair

Entrance

- ❏ booklets, bulletins or other handouts

The Easter Vigil in the Holy Night

Place for Eucharistic Action

Open Space:

- ❏ dedication candles, pew candles in place; lit during service
- ❏ taper candles for the entire congregation, placed on seats (or in baskets at entrances)

Altar:

- ❏ covered with one white cloth, unless this comes at Preparation of the Gifts
- ❏ *Book of the Gospels* with text marked, if used (not carried in tonight)
- ❏ nearby: two or more candles, candlestands in place; lit in service
- ❏ nearby: processional cross in stand

Credence Table:

- ❏ large chalice (can be covered by pall and/or white veil)
- ❏ purificator
- ❏ corporal
- ❏ book stand, if used

❏ water in small cruet

❏ basin, pitcher of water, towel

❏ additional chalices and purificators for the congregation (on tray)

❏ additional patens, bowls, or ciboria for the congregation

Priest Celebrant's Chair:

❏ hymnal or booklet

Ministers' Seats:

❏ texts for concelebrants, if any

❏ hymnals or booklets

Ambo:

❏ Lectionary with texts marked

❏ stand for the Paschal candle

❏ text of *Exsultet* (in special book)

❏ Psalm settings for cantor (unless carried there each time)

❏ Universal Prayer (Prayer of the Faithful), if done here

Music Stand (or Secondary Podium):

❏ Universal Prayer (Prayer of the Faithful), if done here

SACRISTY

❏ unlit charcoal placed in thurible and taken to gathering place

❏ extra charcoal (and tongs, matches) for adding during Mass

❏ controls set for air, sound

❏ lights off (panel marked for times and numbers of changes)

❏ microphones put in place, turned on, and tested

VESTING ROOM

❏ vesture (see page 130); chasuble, dalmatic of white or gold

❏ lavaliere microphones, if any

❏ local texts (intercessions, introductions, dismissal of catechumens not being baptized tonight and ritual texts [initiation]) prepared; *The Roman Missal* and *Rite of Christian Initiation of Adults* marked for review prior to placement by fire or chair for carrying by assistant

❏ robes for neophytes; areas set for them for drying and vesting

❏ towels, clothes, and change of vesture for the Priest Celebrant if entering the font to baptize by immersion

ENTRANCE

Exterior:

- ❏ bells ready for ringing during Gloria
- ❏ signs directing congregation to special gathering place

  (see also "Other Gathering Place" below)

Table(s) with Gifts:

- ❏ flowers and other decorations to be brought in during the Gloria, set up in correct order
- ❏ bread for all in patens, bowls, or ciboria
- ❏ wine for all

Other:

- ❏ collection baskets ready
- ❏ booklets, bulletins or other handouts
- ❏ fire extinguishers near ushers

Baptistry:

- ❏ font full and warm
- ❏ chrism in vessel
- ❏ baptismal candles
- ❏ towels for neophytes
- ❏ basin with pieces of lemon, pitcher of water, towel (for washing of hands of priest after anointings)
- ❏ vessel(s) to be filled from font, and sprinkler(s)

CATECHUMENEON

- ❏ opened and prepared, if catechumens not being baptized are present

CHAPEL OF EUCHARISTIC RESERVATION

- ❏ lamp in place, lit after Holy Communion when Blessed Sacrament is placed here

OTHER GATHERING PLACE

- ❏ large fire (receptacle, fuel, matches); other lights out
- ❏ candles, bobeches, hymnals or booklets for all
- ❏ places set for congregation, Priest Celebrant, and ministers
- ❏ fire extinguishers nearby

On Table Near Place for Priest Celebrant and Ministers:

❏ Paschal candle (unless carried from vesting room)

❏ thurible with unlit charcoal

❏ vessel of incense, Easter scent

❏ material for decoration of candle (incense grains, stylus)

❏ wooden taper or other means of lighting Paschal candle from fire

❏ discreet book light for illuminating texts for the Priest Celebrant at the fire

❏ *The Roman Missal* or other ritual binder

❏ tongs for lighting charcoal

Easter Sunday of the Resurrection of the Lord: Evening Prayer

The Triduum is recalled and concluded by a joyous celebration of Evening Prayer late on Easter Sunday. In the spaces where the sacraments have recently been celebrated with such fervor, we gather to share once more in Easter light, psalms, and water. This list presumes that the liturgy begins by the candle in the main congregation space, moving to the baptistry during the liturgy. For references to this renewed custom, see the *Ceremonial of Bishops,* 371, the *General Instruction of the Liturgy of the Hours,* 213, and the official texts of the hours.

PLACE FOR EUCHARISTIC ACTION

Seating:

❏ hymnals or booklets

❏ candles and bobeches for all

Open Space:

❏ dedication and pew candles in place, lit in service

Altar:

❏ altar covered with white cloth as at Mass

❏ nearby: processional cross may be in place

Priest Celebrant's Chair:

❏ Priest Celebrant's or lay presider's book (after review in vesting room)

❏ hymnal or booklet

❏ candle and bobeche

Ministers' Seats:

- ❑ hymnals or booklets
- ❑ candles and bobeches

Ambo:

- ❑ nearby: Paschal candle still burning in stand
- ❑ cantor's setting of thanksgiving for light
- ❑ cantor's Psalm settings (unless carried there for that action)

SACRISTY

- ❑ controls set for air, sound
- ❑ lights off for beginning (panel marked with which lights to be turned on)
- ❑ microphones put in places, turned on, and tested
- ❑ charcoal lit in thurible (for use in later procession to baptistry and at the Gospel canticle)
- ❑ vessel of incense, Easter scent

VESTING ROOM

- ❑ vesture (see page 130); cope, dalmatic of white or gold
- ❑ lavaliere microphones, if any
- ❑ Bible or Liturgy of the Hours with reading marked, for review before placing in baptistry
- ❑ texts inserted (prayer over the blessed Easter water, solemn Easter blessing) and marked in Liturgy of the Hours, or all texts placed in correct order in special book for the Priest Celebrant or lay presider, for review before placing at chair

ENTRANCE

- ❑ candles and bobeches, booklets, bulletins or other handouts

Baptistry:

- ❑ another stand for Paschal candle
- ❑ stand for thurible and vessel of incense between uses

Podium:

- ❑ Bible or Liturgy of the Hours with passage marked
- ❑ texts of intercessions

Easter Time

THE LITURGICAL TIME   The Roman Calendar takes great care to show the unity of the days from Easter Day through Pentecost. (Easter Day is, uniquely, part of two liturgical times — Sacred Paschal Triduum and Easter Time.) The liturgical time is one great solemnity, one "great Sunday." It is the time for joyfully incorporating neophytes in the congregation, for singing Alleluia, for feeling the pull of the new Jerusalem. Within the 50 days, two special times provide heightened awareness of certain Easter realities. The octave of Easter highlights the wonders of initiation; the concluding days from the Ascension to Pentecost, the first novena, kindle the fire of the Spirit.

VESTURE   There should not be one set of vesture for Easter Sunday and another for the rest of the liturgical time. Let the vesture itself say that these days are one unit of time and celebration. The red days provide exceptions: apostles, martyrs and, of course, Pentecost.

DECORATIONS   The best decorations are not just pleasing ornaments. They are the central elements of our interaction, providing beauty and focus to our congregation. Thus, the principal decoration is neither flowers nor banners, but the large Paschal candle that was praised at Easter, that was plunged into the font, that provides light for all the baptized, that ties all the future days of this year to the Paschal Mystery. Nothing should compete with it or diminish it, especially by hiding or muting its verticality and brightness. It should be kept lit for every gathering, burning brightly even before people gather. Once the candle is lit during the Easter Vigil, it is never extinguished publicly. Other candles can be lit from it, a gracious gesture at the beginning of any liturgy.

The newly baptized and their sponsors should occupy special places in the congregation throughout Easter Time. Perhaps special seats could be reserved for them near the candle and ambo. Our tradition calls for using, throughout the liturgical time, the water blessed at the Vigil. Parishes with fonts in separate places sometimes display a large bowl of water somewhere near the front of the church. (Too often this looks like a punch bowl and not a sacred vessel.) It would be far more sensible to keep attention fixed on the font, no matter where it is located. During the sprinkling rite, maintain some association with the font, even if that means drawing Easter water from it and then carrying this water into the congregation for the prayer of thanksgiving over the water.

In an interesting parallel, synagogues follow a long tradition of using lilies for their 50-day celebration. Three other traditions of the Festival of Weeks may inspire Christian decorators. Texts highlight the apple tree with its beautiful blossoms (the tree is said to bear fruit 50 days after it blossoms); branches, boughs and greens are placed about the bema (ambo); and Torah scrolls are decorated with roses. Whatever patterns of decor are set on Easter Day, they should be followed with fresh blossoms throughout the 50 days.

With springtime wreaths on the church doors, with banners and bunting merrily waving, we announce our joy to the world.

Ordinary Time

ORDINAL TIME   Ordinary Time is not so much "ordinary" in the sense of undistinguished, but "ordinal" or counted time. It is simply the way that the Church organizes liturgical texts, assigning each Sunday a number, counting each week one after the other. These 225 or so days do not form a liturgical time in the same way as do the 43 or so in Advent-Christmas, or the 96 in Lent-Triduum-Easter. They form the regular flow of the year, so that the five principal liturgical times stand out in their exceptional characteristics.

These weeks fill the intervals from the day after the Feast of the Baptism of the Lord until the day before Ash Wednesday, and then from the day after the Solemnity of Pentecost until the eve of Advent. As the liturgical times of nature outside the church change from winter to summer and fall, the changing colors and flowers may play a part in decorations. These are far less important, however, than attention to Sunday and the marking of varied solemnities and feasts.

VESTURE   The portion of Ordinary Time in winter reminds us, in most climates, of the need for coat rooms, even temporary areas for the coldest months (see page 84). The liturgical color for priest and deacon on most Sundays is green, but on several Sundays, solemnities eclipse Ordinary Time and call for white (or gold and silver) or red. Some planners prefer to see the green chasubles and dalmatics shift from darker to lighter shades as the weather warms, perhaps to correlate with the month's flowers. There are no exact regulations here.

DECORATIONS   During this time between the principal liturgical times of the liturgical year, the decorations should be simple, opening our eyes to appreciate the inherent dignity of the space. Then, when the liturgical times of high decoration arrive, it will have much more impact. Even in the simplicity of Ordinary Time, flowers or other elements of color might be introduced, but "theme art" to display the given Sunday's scriptures should be avoided.

In the place where the Eucharist is celebrated, or in other parts of the church buildings, individual feasts and particular portions of Ordinary Time can be highlighted by temporary decor; for example, candles or flowers before images of saints on their feasts, special displays of volunteer opportunities in the entrance halls before Lent and Advent, the placement of a special book for inscribing the names of the dead near the baptistry in November.

On the exterior walls, or on surrounding grounds, the changing climate might suggest decorations. Especially recommended for any time of the year are those exterior embellishments that involve the participation of many members (ice sculptures or snow saints where winter reigns, doorways draped with festive colors for the dedication anniversary, gardens for flowers or vegetables). These should never become too contrived.

February 2, Feast of the Presentation of the Lord: Blessing of Candles and Mass

The first form of the procession given in *The Roman Missal* should be used in almost every circumstance, even when the feast falls on Sunday.

PLACE FOR EUCHARISTIC ACTION

Seating:

❑ hymnals or booklets, unless distributed in other gathering area

Open Space:

❑ dedication and pew candles lit

❑ taper candles for the entire congregation, if the first form is not used

Altar:

❑ covered with one white cloth, unless this comes at Preparation of the Gifts

❑ *Book of the Gospels* with text marked, if used and not carried in procession

❑ nearby: any candles, candlestands not carried in procession

❑ nearby: stand for processional cross

Credence Table:

❑ large chalice (can be covered by pall and/or white veil)

❑ purificator

❑ corporal

❑ book stand, if used

❑ water in small cruet, if not in procession of gifts

❑ basin, pitcher of water, towel

❑ any bread, wine, not in procession of gifts

❑ additional chalices and purificators for the congregation (on tray)

❑ additional patens, bowls, or ciboria for the congregation

Priest Celebrant's Chair:

❑ nearby: white chasuble, if cope worn at start

❑ hymnal or booklet, if not carried in procession

Ministers' Seats:

❑ texts for concelebrants, if any

❑ hymnals or booklets, if not carried in procession

Ambo:

❏ Lectionary with texts marked

❏ Psalm setting for cantor (unless carried there for this action)

❏ Universal Prayer (Prayer of the Faithful), if done here

Music Stand (or Secondary Podium):

❏ Universal Prayer (Prayer of the Faithful), if done here

SACRISTY

❏ charcoal lit in thurible, then put in vesting room

❏ extra charcoal (and tongs, matches) for adding during Mass

❏ controls set for air, sound

❏ lights turned off until after congregation's candles extinguished

❏ microphones put in place and turned on

VESTING ROOM

❏ vesture (see page 130); cope or chasuble, dalmatic of white

❏ lavaliere microphones, if any

❏ *Book of the Gospels* with text marked, if carried in procession

❏ local texts prepared (dismissal of catechumens, intercessions) and other texts marked in *The Roman Missal*, for review prior to placement in gathering area

❏ thurible, with lit charcoal

❏ vessel of incense

❏ processional cross

❏ two or more candlesticks with lit candles

ENTRANCE

Exterior:

❏ signs directing congregation to special gathering place

Table with Gifts:

❏ bread for all on one paten, bowl, or ciborium, if in procession

❏ wine for all, if in procession

Other:

❏ collection baskets ready, if used

❏ booklets, bulletins or other handouts

❏ opened and prepared, if catechumens present

Other Gathering Place

Table (Unless Held by Ministers):

❏ vessel of water and sprinkler

❏ *The Roman Missal*

❏ candles (as large as possible) for all, with bobeches

❏ lit candle(s) from which to draw flame

Other:

❏ hymnals or booklets for all

❏ space reserved for instrumentalists and musical leaders

❏ space reserved for Priest Celebrant and other ministers

February 3, Memorial of Saint Blaise: Blessing of Throats in a Liturgy of the Word

Texts for the blessing of throats are found in Chapter 51 of the *Book of Blessings*. This traditional sign of the struggle against illness can take place at Mass, at the Liturgy of the Hours, or in a Liturgy of the Word. This setup list is for the last of these options, a liturgy which can be led by a priest, a deacon, or a lay minister.

Place of Congregation

Seating:

❏ hymnals or booklets

Open Area:

❏ spaces designated for act of blessing

Altar, if Blessing Celebrated in Eucharistic Space:

❏ altar cloth may remain as at Mass

❏ candles can be lit in the area

❏ stand with processional cross in place

Credence Table:

❏ two candles, tied with red ribbon, for each minister who will assist with the blessing

Priest Celebrant's Chair:

❏ *Book of Blessings* (after review in vesting room)

❏ hymnal or booklet, if not carried in procession

Ministers' Seats:

❏ hymnals or booklets, if not carried in procession

Ambo:

❏ Bible or *Book of Blessings*, with reading marked

❏ Psalm setting for cantor (unless carried there for this action)

❏ intercessions on sheet or marked at #1645 of Book of Blessings, if done here

Music Stand (or Secondary Podium):

❏ intercessions on sheet or marked at #1645 of Book of Blessings, if done here

SACRISTY

❏ controls set for air, sound, lights

❏ microphones put in place, turned on, and tested

VESTING ROOM

❏ vesture (see page 131); cope of red (or white) possible for presider

❏ lavaliere microphones, if any

❏ *Book of Blessings* for review prior to placement by chair

ENTRANCE

❏ booklets, bulletins or other handouts

Solemnity of the Most Holy Body and Blood of Christ: Mass and Procession

PLACE FOR EUCHARISTIC ACTION

Seating:

❏ hymnals or booklets

❏ candles and bobeches for all, if carried in procession and if not handed out upon arrival

Open Space:

❏ dedication candles, pew candles may be lit

Altar:

- ❏ covered with one white cloth, unless this comes at preparation rite
- ❏ *Book of the Gospels* with text marked, if used and not carried in procession
- ❏ nearby: any candles, candlestands not carried in procession
- ❏ nearby: stand for processional cross

Credence Table:

- ❏ vessel of water, when Rite of Sprinkling occurs
- ❏ large chalice (can be covered by pall and/or white veil)
- ❏ purificator
- ❏ corporal
- ❏ book stand, if used
- ❏ water in a small cruet
- ❏ basin, pitcher of water, towel
- ❏ any bread, wine, not in procession of gifts
- ❏ additional chalices and purificators for the congregation (on tray)
- ❏ additional patens, bowls, or ciboria for the congregation
- ❏ monstrance and lunette (glass pyx in shape of host)
- ❏ humeral veil
- ❏ candles and bobeches for all ministers
- ❏ "torches" or mounted candles for accompanying the Eucharist

Priest Celebrant's Chair:

- ❏ *The Roman Missal* (after review in vesting room)
- ❏ hymnal or booklet, if not carried in procession
- ❏ nearby (on robe stand): white or gold cope, if used

Ministers' Seats:

- ❏ texts for concelebrants, if any
- ❏ hymnals or booklets, if not carried in procession
- ❏ nearby: white copes for additional priests participating in procession, if any

Ambo:

- ❏ Lectionary with texts marked
- ❏ Psalm setting for cantor (unless carried there for this action)
- ❏ Universal Prayer (Prayer of the Faithful), if done here

Music Stand (or Secondary Podium):

❏ Universal Prayer (Prayer of the Faithful), if done here

SACRISTY

❏ charcoal lit in thurible, then placed in vesting room

❏ extra charcoal (and tongs, matches) for adding during Mass

❏ second thurible prepared for closing procession

❏ controls set for air, sound, lights

❏ microphones put in place, turned on, and tested

❏ portable canopy for use in procession, if customary

VESTING ROOM

❏ vesture (see page 130); chasuble, dalmatic of white or gold

❏ lavaliere microphones, if any

❏ *Book of the Gospels* with text marked, if carried in procession

❏ local texts (dismissal of catechumens, intercessions) prepared, and other texts marked in *The Roman Missal*, for review prior to placement by chair

❏ thurible, with lit charcoal

❏ vessel of incense

❏ processional cross

❏ two or more candlesticks with lit candles

ENTRANCE

Exterior:

❏ arrangements made for procession: permit for use of streets or sidewalks, traffic guards, special parking regulations, etc.

❏ entire procession route cleared of any obstructions or litter

Table with Gifts:

❏ bread for all in patens, bowls, or ciboria, including host shaped to fit in lunette

❏ wine for all

Other:

❏ collection baskets ready

❏ candles and bobeches, booklets, bulletins or other handouts

CATECHUMENEON

❏ opened and prepared, if catechumens are present

OTHER GATHERING PLACE

❏ (destination of procession after Holy Communion: neighboring church, cemetery chapel, parish hall)

❏ space for the processions' participants

❏ altar covered, ready to receive monstrance

❏ text of prayer before Eucharistic benediction

❏ key available at tabernacle for receiving the lunette

November 2, Commemoration of All the Faithful Departed (All Souls): Mass and Visitation of a Cemetery

Cemeteries are privileged places for liturgical prayer (see page 91). The *Book of Blessings* has an order for a liturgical visit to a nearby cemetery (Ch. 57). This list is for the fullest form: Mass in church, procession, and Order for Visiting a Cemetery.

PLACE FOR EUCHARISTIC ACTION

Seating:

❏ hymnals or booklets

Altar:

❏ covered with one white cloth, unless this comes at Preparation of the Gifts

❏ *Book of the Gospels* with text marked, if used and not carried in procession

❏ nearby: any candles, candlestands not carried in procession

❏ nearby: stand for processional cross

Credence Table:

❏ large chalice (can be covered by pall and/or white veil)

❏ purificator

❏ corporal

❏ book stand, if used

❏ water in small cruet

❏ basin, pitcher of water, towel

❏ any bread, wine, not in procession of gifts

❏ additional chalices and purificators for the congregation (on tray)

❏ additional patens, bowls, or ciboria for the congregation

Priest Celebrant's Chair:

❏ *The Roman Missal* (after review in vesting room)

❏ hymnal or booklet, if not carried in procession

Ministers' Seats:

❏ texts for concelebrants, if any

❏ hymnals or booklets, if not carried in procession

Ambo:

❏ Lectionary with texts marked

❏ Psalm setting for cantor (unless carried there for this action)

❏ Universal Prayer (Prayer of the Faithful), if done here

Music Stand (or Secondary Podium):

❏ Universal Prayer (Prayer of the Faithful), if done here

SACRISTY

❏ charcoal in thurible lit, then put in vesting room

❏ extra charcoal (and tongs, matches) for adding during Mass

❏ controls set for air, sound, lights

❏ microphones put in place, turned on, and tested

VESTING ROOM

❏ vesture (see page 130); chasuble, dalmatic of white, violet or black

❏ lavaliere microphones, if any

❏ *Book of the Gospels* with text marked, if carried in procession

❏ local texts (intercessions) prepared and other texts marked in *The Roman Missal,* for review prior to placement by chair

❏ thurible, with lit charcoal

❏ vessel of incense

❏ processional cross

❏ two or more candlesticks with lit candles

ENTRANCE

Exterior:

❏ arrangements made for procession: permit for use of street, traffic guards, special parking regulations

❏ entire procession route checked for obstructions and cleared of litter

Table with Gifts:

❏ bread for all in patens, bowls, or ciboria, if in procession

❏ wine for all, if in procession

Other:

❏ booklets, bulletins or other handouts

Baptistry:

❏ book, on standing desk or stand, for parish members to inscribe the names of the deceased (in place from the eve of All Saints to the day before Advent)—can be located near lit Paschal candle in baptistry or elsewhere

❏ pens for inscriptions

Cemetery:

❏ scripture text marked in *Book of Blessings* or *Order of Christian Funerals* or Bible

❏ Psalm setting and litany text for cantor

❏ *Book of Blessings*, with texts marked

❏ vessel of baptismal water and sprinkler

❏ thurible with lit coals and vessel of incense (carried from Mass)

❏ additional booklets for those who join only at cemetery

❏ area designated for Priest Celebrant, musical leaders, other ministers (perhaps near cross at center or near entrance of cemetery)

Local Solemnities: Title of Parish, Anniversary of Dedication

THE DAYS   These wonderful celebrations help us feel more intensely these fundamental realities: that the local community, the people here gathered, are the holy people of God; that these buildings built by our ancestors and ourselves are privileged places of sacred mysteries; that our cherished patrons and parish names help to form us in the image of Christ. We are incomplete communities if we adhere only to the universal calendar, as wondrous as that might be. We need these local days to see our own particular living in sacramental unity.

Ideally, the anniversary of dedication is celebrated on the actual date of dedication, but in reality that happens more often in communities like monasteries, where the full congregation of members can gather even on weekdays. In parishes, the anniversary of dedication can be celebrated on the nearest Sunday (if this is a Sunday in Ordinary Time) or on the Sunday before All Saints. This latter day, the observed dedication anniversary for all churches whose date of dedication is unknown, shows the profound unity of the holy ones on earth and all the saints in heaven.

The solemnity of the title (name or patron) of the parish takes place in closer proximity to the date of the feast, because we celebrate this date in unity with many other churches. The actual date is more than likely related to the death date (birthday into heaven) of the saint or the dedication of an early church in honor of this title. If in Ordinary Time, parishes should move the observance to the nearest Sunday.

DECORATIONS   As always, the best decorations arise from or are deeply related to the actual rites being celebrated. Events unfolding on the local feast should be reviewed when considering the best decorations. An outdoor procession with an image of the patronal saint might suggest the strewing of the path with "seasonal" flowers. A procession of all to the font for a signing with baptismal water might indicate the hanging of fresh garlands over the entrance area of the baptistry. A candlelight vigil would require enough candles for the entire congregation. The intense interest of children (after preparing a skit on the history of the parish, or completing a catechetical unit on the life of the saint) also could be expressed by their work on a large, temporary mural celebrating local faith. In addition to events, the images presented by the dedication anniversary texts and by the title or saint can help form ideas for the decor.

These celebrations, especially the anniversary of dedication, should motivate us to look at the entire building. We need more than sanctuary flowers. Instead, we might concentrate on the walls and corners on the outlines of the building itself. Dedication candles (page 139) should certainly be lit at all local solemnities, for they provide the embrace of Christ's light for the whole people. The four corners of the congregation hall might be marked by brilliant arrangements of flowers.

A rediscovery of patronal or titular days should motivate a parish to review its iconography. Does the name of the parish find expression in a suitable image? Can one be commissioned? Can one owned by the parish be brought out of storage? Is it properly located to attract veneration but not to interfere with the celebration of the sacred mysteries?

Decorations should be provided outdoors—around doorways, to the outline of the structure, or to the tower. Everyone who passes it should know that this parish is celebrating. Luminarias (*farolitos*) might surround any outdoor image of the title at ground level.

Chapter Thirty-four
Checklists for Other Rites

Relationship to the Liturgical Year

Celebrations of the Mass and the Liturgy of the Hours are by far the most frequent actions prepared for by sacristans. Our liturgical heritage, however, provides us with many other rites to celebrate passages in human life, to maintain and deepen our life in Christ. The various lists in this section highlight the requisites for some of the most important rituals.

These other rites (Initiation, Marriage, Holy Orders, Pastoral Care of the Sick, blessings and funerals) often occur in the context of the Mass. Whether in or outside of Mass, they all should reflect our annual passage through liturgical time. To cite but two examples, a funeral in Advent can draw on the rich texts of Isaiah and the expectation of the final coming. Celebrations of Marriage in Easter Time can use texts about the wedding feast of the Lamb.

On some days, the importance of the solemnity or feast has brought about rules forbidding or restraining certain rites. These are usually listed in the *Ordo*, and can be ascertained from a careful study of the general introduction printed at the beginning of each of our ritual books. Days for the rites related to the catechumenate and adult initiation are generally set by the rite itself. On certain days, funerals may only take place outside of Mass (Holydays of obligation, Thursday of Holy Week and the Paschal Triduum, Sundays of Advent, Lent and Easter Time). On certain days, the Rite of Marriage is forbidden (for example, Holy Saturday); on several others, the prayers and readings must be from the "seasonal" day (for example, Pentecost). Many rites have particular texts identified for use during Easter Time; many other texts of scripture or prayers are easily related to particular liturgical times (for example, Isaiah in Advent, Revelation in Easter). These can be identified by reviewing the texts on surrounding days beside those in the ritual book.

In such ways, all of the rites in a parish show our tradition's enormous respect for liturgical times and solemnities. Our worship is not just a random grouping of nice texts. It is a liturgy of repeated days and liturgical times and rites and smells and sounds, so that its rhythm can become ours. In every way possible, we should collaborate with others who prepare the liturgy so that decorations and texts, music and vestments, altar cloths, and volunteer schedules work for the full experience of the liturgical year.

Using the Checklists

A general list for the Liturgy of the Hours, especially Morning Prayer and Evening Prayer, is given first. These important liturgies should be part of every parish's life, but in many parishes the offices are rarely, if ever, offered. The checklist for the Liturgy of the Hours is followed by several lists for actions found in the *Roman*

Ritual. (See page 100 for a list of all the ritual books grouped under the *Roman Ritual.*) Finally, there are checklists for some of the liturgies at which a Bishop presides. The events normally linked to a particular day in the liturgical year are found in the lists of the previous chapter; for example, the initiation of adults at the Easter Vigil.

Quite obviously, these are general charts, not local lists. A given celebration of Evening Prayer can involve 10 or 1,000 persons, with grand ceremonial or minimal action. The lists here presume the fuller forms of the rites, and simpler forms will simply mean the omission of certain elements from the lists (for example, incense). Local preparations and customs, and the particular circumstances of each rite, will always call for adaptations. The lists here are meant as starting points for local lists, which should be prepared in consultation with priests, deacons, and liturgists, long before the day of celebration.

Liturgy of the Hours

PLACE OF CONGREGATION

Seating:

- ❏ hymnals or booklets, with all appropriate texts for congregation
- ❏ flexible seating best arranged with congregation in facing rows
- ❏ (at Evening Prayer, with full service of light: candles, bobeches for all)

Open Space:

- ❏ at solemn Evening Prayer, with a service of light, especially on Sundays: the Paschal candle may be positioned so that all may light their candles from it; or Evening Prayer could be celebrated in the baptistry itself; or other candles may provide the light if the Paschal candle remains in the baptistry and the congregation is elsewhere. In Advent, the candles of the wreath provide light.

Altar, if Hours Celebrated in Eucharistic Space:

- ❏ the altar cloth may be removed
- ❏ nearby: processional cross may be in place, if not in procession

Priest Celebrant's or Lay Presider's Chair:

- ❏ Book for Priest Celebrant or lay presider (after review in vesting room)
- ❏ hymnal or booklet
- ❏ at Evening Prayer with full service of light: candle, bobeche

Ministers' Seats:

- ❏ hymnals or booklets
- ❏ at Evening Prayer with full service of light: candles, bobeches

Ambo:

❏ Bible or Liturgy of the Hours with reading(s) marked

❏ cantor's book with Psalms, if done here

❏ text of intercessions, if done here

Music Stand (or Secondary Podium):

❏ text of intercessions, if done here

SACRISTY

❏ charcoal lit in thurible, then placed in vesting room

❏ extra charcoal (and tongs, matches), if more to be added later; controls set for air, sound, lights

❏ lights off, if evening prayer begins with service of light

❏ microphones (if necessary) put in places and turned on

VESTING ROOM

❏ albs for ministers; stole if presider is ordained; feasts: cope/dalmatic optional

❏ lavaliere microphones, if any

❏ texts marked in Liturgy of the Hours or inserted in ritual book, for review prior to placement by chair

❏ thurible, with lit charcoal

❏ vessel of incense

❏ (at solemn celebrations: processional cross)

❏ (at solemn celebrations: two candles, candlesticks)

ENTRANCE

❏ booklets, bulletins or other handouts

❏ (at Evening Prayer with full service of light: candles, bobeches for all, if not placed in seats)

Rite of Acceptance

This list presents the general requisites for this rite when it is celebrated at the parish's Sunday Mass. This rite may also be combined with the Rite of Welcoming baptized but previously uncatechized adults.

Place for Eucharistic Action

Seating:

- ❏ hymnals or booklets, unless in other gathering place

Altar:

- ❏ *Book of the Gospels* on altar, if used
- ❏ covered with one white cloth, unless this comes at the Preparation of the Gifts
- ❏ nearby: any candles, candlestands not carried in procession
- ❏ nearby: stand for processional cross

Credence Table:

- ❏ Bibles or *Books of Gospels* for new catechumens (and candidates)
- ❏ large chalice (can be covered by pall and/or white veil)
- ❏ purificator
- ❏ corporal
- ❏ book stand, if needed
- ❏ water in a small cruet, if not in procession of gifts
- ❏ basin, pitcher of water, towel
- ❏ any bread, wine, not in procession of gifts
- ❏ additional cups and purificators for the congregation (on tray)
- ❏ additional patens, bowls, or ciboria for the congregation
- ❏ pyx or ciborium, if extra bread consecrated for the sick

Priest Celebrant's Chair

- ❏ nearby, on robe stand: chasuble, if cope worn at start
- ❏ hymnal or booklet, if not carried in procession

Ministers' Seats:

- ❏ texts for concelebrants, if any
- ❏ hymnals or booklets, if not carried in procession

Ambo:

- ❏ Psalm setting for cantor (unless carried there for this action)
- ❏ text of intercessions for the catechumens (and the candidates), if done here
- ❏ Universal Prayer (Prayer of the Faithful) if done here

Music Stand (or Secondary Podium):

❏ text of intercessions for the catechumens (and candidates), if done here

❏ Universal Prayer (Prayer of the Faithful), if done here

Sacristy

❏ charcoal lit in thurible, then put in vesting room

❏ extra charcoal (and tongs, matches) for adding during Mass

❏ controls set for air, sound, lights

❏ microphones put in places and turned on

Vesting Room

❏ vesture (see page 130); cope or chasuble, dalmatic of day's color

❏ lavaliere microphones, if any

❏ Lectionary with texts marked, for carrying in procession

❏ texts from the Rite of Acceptance or from the combined Rite of Acceptance/Welcome, and local texts (Prayer of the Faithful) inserted and other texts marked in *The Roman Missal*; or all texts placed in order in special Priest Celebrant's book—for review prior to placement at gathering area

❏ thurible, with lit charcoal

❏ vessel of incense, "seasonal" scent

❏ processional cross

❏ two or more candlesticks with lit candles

Entrance

Exterior:

❏ signs indicating area for initial gathering

Table with Gifts:

❏ bread for all in patens, bowls, or ciboria, more if needed

❏ wine for all

Other:

❏ collection baskets ready

❏ programs, bulletins or other handouts

Catechumeneon

❏ opened and prepared

Outside the Church, in the Entrance Hall or Elsewhere:

- ❏ *The Roman Missal*, plus ritual book, after review in vesting room
- ❏ hymnals for entire congregation, unless all will first gather in place of Eucharistic congregation and then go in procession with hymnals to this gathering area
- ❏ space set for candidates and sponsors
- ❏ space set for instrumentalists and other leaders of music
- ❏ space set for Priest Celebrant and other ministers

Rite of Baptism for Several Children

This list is designed for a Sunday afternoon celebration of the baptismal liturgy apart from Mass. This rite is for children younger than "catechetical age." (Those older take part in the stages of catechumenate described in the *Rite of Christian Initiation of Adults*.) This rite may also be celebrated at the parish's gathering for Sunday Mass, with ritual adaptations explained at number 29 of the rite.

PLACE FOR EUCHARISTIC ACTION

Seating:

- ❏ arranged as close to ambo as circumstances allow
- ❏ hymnals or booklets

Altar:

- ❏ altar cloth may be removed
- ❏ nearby: processional cross may be in place

Priest Celebrant's Chair:

- ❏ hymnal or booklet, if not carried in procession

Ministers' Seats:

- ❏ hymnals or booklets, if not carried in procession

Ambo:

- ❏ ritual book or Lectionary with texts marked
- ❏ Psalm settings for cantor (unless carried there for this action)
- ❏ nearby: stand with vessel of oil of catechumens, if used
- ❏ text of intercessions, if done here

Music Stand (or Secondary Podium):

- ❏ text of intercessions, if done here

Sacristy

- ❏ controls set for air, sound, lights
- ❏ microphones, if necessary, put in place, turned on, and tested

Vesting Room

- ❏ vesture (see page 131); cope, dalmatic of white or of day's color
- ❏ lavaliere microphones, if any
- ❏ local texts inserted (names of children for the invocation of saints) and other texts marked in *Rite of Baptism for Children*, for review prior to placement by entryway

Entrance

- ❏ space set for parents, godparents, children
- ❏ space set for instrumentalists and other leaders of music
- ❏ space set for Priest Celebrant and other ministers
- ❏ space set for rest of congregation
- ❏ hymnals or booklets for all
- ❏ table for checking names and detailed information
- ❏ ritual book for Priest Celebrant

Baptistry:

- ❏ font full of warm water
- ❏ Paschal candle lit
- ❏ spaces set for parents, sponsors, children, instrumentalists, other leaders of music, Priest Celebrant, other ministers
- ❏ table or other place set for drying and vesting (in christening clothes) of infants after immersion Baptism

Other Table:

- ❏ shell for pouring, if used
- ❏ towels
- ❏ baptismal candles
- ❏ candlelighter for passing light from Paschal candle
- ❏ vessel of chrism (unless in nearby repository)

Catechumeneon:

- ❏ provisions for the care of infants/children (*Rite of Baptism for Children*, 14, 43)

Devotional Areas:

- ❏ Marian shrine lit, if custom calls for bringing infants there

Reception of Baptized Christians

This rite, found at Part II:5 of the *Rite of Christian Initiation of Adults,* is usually celebrated at Mass. When it is part of the Easter Vigil, see the checklist on page 204. On other days, at a regularly scheduled parish Mass, or at another gathering for the Eucharist, the following list can be used.

PLACE FOR EUCHARISTIC ACTION

Open Space:

- ❏ place designated for the act of reception (and Confirmation)
- ❏ pedestal or stand with vessel of chrism (if Confirmation included in rite)

Seating:

- ❏ hymnals or booklets
- ❏ designated seating for those to be received and their sponsors, if reserved

Altar:

- ❏ *Book of the Gospels* on altar, if used and not carried in procession
- ❏ covered with one white cloth, unless this comes at the Preparation of the Gifts
- ❏ nearby: any candles, candlestands not carried in procession
- ❏ nearby: stand for processional cross

Credence Table:

- ❏ smaller vessel from which chrism can be administered (if Confirmation included in rite)
- ❏ basin, pitcher of water, towel (with lemon pieces if Confirmation included in rite)
- ❏ large chalice (can be covered by pall and/or white veil)
- ❏ purificator
- ❏ corporal
- ❏ book stand, if necessary
- ❏ water in small cruet, if not in procession of gifts
- ❏ any bread, wine, not in procession of gifts
- ❏ additional chalices and purificators for the congregation (on tray)
- ❏ additional patens, bowls, or ciboria for the congregation

Priest Celebrant's Chair

❏ *The Roman Missal,* after review in vesting room

❏ ritual book, after review in vesting room, unless copies of these texts inserted in *The Roman Missal*

❏ hymnal or booklet, if not carried in procession

Ministers' Seating:

❏ texts for concelebrants, if any

❏ hymnals or booklets, if not carried in procession

Ambo:

❏ Lectionary with texts marked

❏ Psalm setting for cantor, unless carried here for this action

❏ intercessions, if done here

Music Stand (or Secondary Podium):

❏ intercessions, if done here

SACRISTY

❏ charcoal lit in thurible, then put in vesting room

❏ extra charcoal (and tongs, matches) for adding during Mass

❏ controls set for air, sound, lights

❏ microphones put in place, turned on, and tested

VESTING ROOM

❏ vesture as on page 130; chasuble, dalmatic of day's color

❏ lavaliere microphones, if any

❏ *Book of the Gospels* with text marked, if carried in procession

❏ texts from the Rite of Reception and local texts prepared and other texts marked in *The Roman Missal*; or all texts placed in order in special book for Priest Celebrant; or both *The Roman Missal* and ritual book marked, for review prior to placement at Priest Celebrant's chair

❏ thurible, with lit charcoal

❏ vessel of incense, "seasonal" scent

❏ processional cross

❏ two or more candlesticks with lit candles

Entrance

Table with Gifts:

- ❏ bread for all in patens, bowls, or ciboria
- ❏ wine for all

Other:

- ❏ collection baskets ready
- ❏ programs, bulletins or other handouts

Catechumeneon

- ❏ opened and prepared, if catechumens present

Funerals: Vigil for the Deceased

Place of Vigil

Open Space:

- ❏ space arranged for placement of coffin on coffin stand, on bed of flowers or herbs, or on floor in place of honor
- ❏ Paschal candle or other candles placed nearby

Seating:

- ❏ for Priest Celebrant, ministers, congregation
- ❏ hymnals or booklets
- ❏ space for leaders of music

Altar (if Vigil in Eucharistic Space):

- ❏ nearby: processional cross may be in place
- ❏ nearby: candles may be lit

Ambo (or Other Lectern, if Vigil Not in Main Congregation Place):

- ❏ ritual book or Lectionary with texts marked
- ❏ Psalm setting for cantor (unless carried there for this action)
- ❏ text of litany/intercessions, if done here

Music Stand (or Secondary Podium):

- ❏ text of litany/intercessions, if done here

Sacristy

- ❏ controls set for air, sound, lights
- ❏ microphones, if necessary, put in place, turned on, and tested

Vesting Room

- ❑ albs; cope (white, violet, black), if used; stole for deacon or priest (white, violet or black)
- ❑ lavaliere microphones, if any
- ❑ local texts prepared and other texts marked in *Order of Christian Funerals* (82–97), for review prior to placement by entry (unless carried there)

Entrance

- ❑ hymnals or booklets for all
- ❑ area for Priest Celebrant, ministers, congregation to receive body
- ❑ vessel with baptismal water, sprinkler
- ❑ coffin pall, if coffin closed
- ❑ symbol of Christian life (*Book of the Gospels*, Bible, cross) if used
- ❑ ritual book for Priest Celebrant (unless carried there)

Funerals: Funeral Mass

Place for Eucharistic Action

Seating:

- ❑ hymnals or booklets, unless distributed at entrance

Open Space:

- ❑ space arranged for placement of coffin on coffin stand, on bed of flowers or herbs, or on floor in place of honor
- ❑ Paschal candle or other candles placed nearby

Altar:

- ❑ covered with one white cloth, unless this comes at the Preparation of the Gifts
- ❑ nearby: any candles, candlestands not carried in procession
- ❑ nearby: stand for processional cross

Credence Table:

- ❑ large chalice (can be covered by pall and/or white veil)
- ❑ purificator
- ❑ corporal
- ❑ *The Roman Missal,* after review in vesting room
- ❑ book stand, if used
- ❑ water in small cruet

❏ basin, pitcher of water, towel

❏ any bread, wine, not in procession of gifts

❏ additional chalices and purificators for the congregation (on tray)

❏ additional patens, bowls, or ciboria for the congregation

❏ pyx or ciborium, if extra bread consecrated for the sick

Priest Celebrant's Chair:

❏ hymnal or booklet, if not carried in procession

Ministers' Seats:

❏ texts for concelebrants, if any

❏ hymnals or booklets, if not carried in procession

Ambo:

❏ Lectionary with texts marked

❏ Psalm setting for cantor (unless carried there for this action)

❏ ritual book, or other sheet with Prayer of the Faithful, if done here

Music Stand (or Secondary Podium):

❏ ritual book, or other sheet with Prayer of the Faithful, if done here

SACRISTY

❏ charcoal lit in thurible, then placed in vesting room

❏ extra charcoal (and tongs, matches) for adding during Mass

❏ controls set for air, sound, lights

❏ microphones, if necessary, put in place, turned on, and tested

VESTING ROOM

❏ vesture (see page 130); chasuble, dalmatic of white, violet, or black

❏ lavaliere microphones, if any

❏ *Book of the Gospels* with text marked, if carried in procession

❏ texts marked in *The Roman Missal*, for review prior to placement on credence table

❏ local texts prepared and other texts marked in *Order of Christian Funerals*, before placement by entrance (unless carried there)

❏ thurible, with lit charcoal

❏ vessel of incense

❏ processional cross

❏ two or more candlesticks with lit candles

- ❏ hymnals or booklets for all
- ❏ area for Priest Celebrant, ministers, congregation to receive body
- ❏ vessel with baptismal water, sprinkler
- ❏ coffin pall, if used
- ❏ symbol of Christian life (*Book of the Gospels*, Bible, cross) if used
- ❏ ritual book for Priest Celebrant (unless carried there)

Table with Gifts:

- ❏ bread for all in patens, bowls, or ciboria, if in procession
- ❏ wine for all, if in procession

Cemetery:

- ❏ processional route cleared to parish cemetery
- ❏ spaces set at grave site for congregation
- ❏ burial plot prepared for committal
- ❏ shovels or other equipment for Rite of Committal (rite calls for this to occur during or at conclusion of rite)
- ❏ flowers or other materials for gesture of leave-taking
- ❏ hymnals or booklets, if not brought by congregation from church
- ❏ ritual book for Priest Celebrant, unless carried from church
- ❏ ritual book or other sheet with intercessions, for assistant

Funerals: Rite of Committal

It is highly recommended that this take place at the actual site of burial, so that the action of committal can occur as part of the service.

BY THE BURIAL SITE

- ❏ spaces set for congregation
- ❏ burial plot opened, prepared for committal
- ❏ shovels or other equipment for Rite of Committal (rite calls for this to occur during or at conclusion of rite)
- ❏ flowers or other materials for gesture of leave-taking
- ❏ hymnals or booklets, if not brought by congregation from church
- ❏ ritual book for Priest Celebrant unless carried from church
- ❏ ritual book or other sheet with intercessions, for assistant

Nearby:

- ❏ vesture, if used (alb for any minister; alb and stole, with optional cope for deacon or priest—white, violet, or black)

Rite of Marriage: Celebration during Mass

PLACE FOR EUCHARISTIC ACTION

Seating for Congregation:

- ❏ hymnals or booklets
- ❏ carpet/runner for aisle installed, if used

Open Space:

- ❏ pew candles lit, if customary
- ❏ space set for exchange of consent and rings
- ❏ seating and hymnals or booklets for bride, groom, witnesses (without turning their backs to congregation, perhaps just to one side or another, or near Priest Celebrant's chair, not necessarily a few feet in front of altar, since the ambo may not be visible from there); kneelers
- ❏ stand/pedestal with dish for holding rings

Nearby (or on credence table):

- ❏ vessel of baptismal water, sprinkler for blessing of rings

Altar:

- ❏ covered with one white cloth, unless this comes at Preparation of the Gifts
- ❏ *Book of the Gospels*, if used and not carried in procession
- ❏ nearby: any candles, candlestands not carried in procession
- ❏ nearby: stand for processional cross

Credence Table:

- ❏ vessel of baptismal water and sprinkler
- ❏ large chalice (can be covered by pall and/or white veil)
- ❏ purificator
- ❏ corporal
- ❏ book stand, if used
- ❏ water in small cruet
- ❏ basin, pitcher of water, towel
- ❏ any bread, wine, not in procession of gifts
- ❏ additional chalices and purificators for the congregation (on tray)
- ❏ additional patens, bowls, or ciboria for the congregation

Priest Celebrant's Chair:

❑ *The Roman Missal*, after review in vesting room

❑ hymnal or booklet, if not carried in procession

Ministers' Seats:

❑ texts for concelebrants, if any

❑ hymnals or booklets, if not carried in procession

Ambo:

❑ Lectionary with texts marked

❑ Psalm setting for cantor (unless carried there for this action)

❑ Universal Prayer (Prayer of the Faithful), if done here

Music stand (or secondary podium):

❑ Universal Prayer (Prayer of the Faithful), if done here

SACRISTY

❑ charcoal lit in thurible, then put in vesting room

❑ extra charcoal (and tongs, matches) for adding during Mass

❑ controls set for air, sound, light

❑ microphones put in places, turned on, and tested

VESTING ROOM

❑ vesture (see page 130); chasuble, dalmatic of white or day's color

❑ lavaliere microphones, if any

❑ sheet from planning meeting with list of selected texts

❑ *Book of the Gospels* with text marked, if carried in procession

❑ local texts (intercessions) prepared and other texts marked in *The Roman Missal*, for review prior to placement by chair

❑ local texts (words of welcome) prepared and other texts marked in *Rite of Marriage*, for review before placing at entrance

❑ thurible, with lit charcoal

❑ vessel of incense

❑ processional cross

❑ two or more candlesticks with lit candles

Entrance

- ❏ space set for Rite of Welcome (bride, groom, parents, witnesses, some or all of congregation)
- ❏ space set for Priest Celebrant, other ministers (cross-bearer, candle-bearers, incense-bearer)
- ❏ ritual book for Priest Celebrant (unless carried there)
- ❏ hymnals or booklets for all

Table with Gifts:

- ❏ bread for all in patens, bowls, or ciboria, if in procession
- ❏ wine for all, if in procession

Rite of Marriage: Celebration outside Mass

Place of Congregation

Place for Eucharistic Action, or Other Chapel

Seating:

- ❏ hymnals or booklets
- ❏ carpet/runner for aisle installed, if used

Open Space:

- ❏ pew candles lit, if customary
- ❏ space set for exchange of consent and rings
- ❏ seating and hymnals or booklets for bride, groom, witnesses (without turning their backs to congregation, perhaps just to one side or another, or near presider's chair, not necessarily a few feet in front of altar, since the ambo may not be visible from there); kneelers unnecessary
- ❏ stand/pedestal with dish holding rings
- ❏ nearby: vessel of baptismal water, sprinkler

Altar (if Rite Celebrated in Eucharistic Space):

- ❏ altar cloth may be removed
- ❏ *Book of the Gospels* with text marked, if used and not carried in procession
- ❏ nearby: processional cross may be in place, if not in procession

Priest Celebrant's Chair:

- ❏ hymnal or booklet, if not carried in procession

Ministers' Seats:

❑ hymnals or booklets, if not carried in procession

Ambo:

❑ Lectionary with texts marked

❑ Psalm setting for cantor (unless carried there for this action)

❑ Universal Prayer (Prayer of the Faithful), if done here

Music Stand (or Secondary Podium):

❑ Universal Prayer (Prayer of the Faithful), if done here

SACRISTY

❑ charcoal lit in thurible, if used, then put in vesting room

❑ controls set for air, sound, lights

❑ microphones put in place, turned on, and tested

VESTING ROOM

❑ vesture (see page 131); cope, dalmatic of white or of day's color

❑ lavaliere microphones, if any

❑ sheet from planning meeting with list of selected texts

❑ *Book of the Gospels* with text marked, if carried in procession

❑ local texts (words of welcome) prepared and other texts marked in *Rite of Marriage*, for review before placing at entrance

❑ thurible, with lit charcoal, if used in procession

❑ vessel of incense, if used in procession

❑ processional cross, if used in procession

❑ two candlesticks with lit candles, if used in procession

ENTRANCE:

❑ space set for Rite of Welcome (bride, groom, parents, witnesses, some or all of congregation)

❑ space set for Priest Celebrant, other ministers (cross-bearer, candle-bearer, incense-bearer)

❑ ritual book for Priest Celebrant (unless carried there)

❑ hymnals or booklets for all

Pastoral Care of the Sick: Holy Communion

This rite is chapter 3 of the *Pastoral Care of the Sick.* See number 74 of that rite and page 76 of this manual regarding bringing Communion wine to the sick.

PLACE OF GATHERING

Depending on the number and condition of the sick, this rite may take place in the sitting room of a nursing home or a similar gathering place within a hospital. There, several of the sick and their relatives and friends might gather.

Open Space:

- ❏ space designated and proper furnishings provided for the sick
- ❏ space for relatives, friends, and any representatives of the local church
- ❏ hymnals or booklets for all
- ❏ scripture text provided for reader (from #84 of rite or from Bible)
- ❏ text of intercessions, if these will be read by other minister

Small Table:

- ❏ (may be prepared by those who are with the sick, before the minister's arrival)
- ❏ linen cloth cover on table
- ❏ lit candles
- ❏ space designated for the dignified placement of pyx and/or vessel of Communion wine
- ❏ vessel of baptismal water, if used (may be in place or brought by minister)
- ❏ ritual book, usually brought by minister
- ❏ small container of water, if Eucharistic vessel(s) will be cleansed there

LOCAL CHURCH BUILDING

Before the Minister Departs for the Place of Celebration:

- ❏ texts marked in *Pastoral Care of the Sick*
- ❏ baptismal water in closed carrying vessel prepared, if used
- ❏ (if communal celebration in nursing home or hospital, minister may bring alb and, if ordained, stole)

Chapel of Eucharistic Reservation:

- ❏ pyx with Communion bread prepared, with sufficient amount for all the sick and relatives who will receive
- ❏ vessel with Communion wine prepared, if used (see page 76)

Pastoral Care of the Sick: Anointing

PLACE FOR EUCHARISTIC ACTION

Seating:

❑ hymnals or booklets

Open Space:

❑ space designated for the sick to step forward for anointing (or else their seating positioned with room for ministers to move among them)

❑ stand/pedestal with vessel of oil of the sick

Altar:

❑ covered with one white cloth, unless this comes at Preparation of the Gifts

❑ *Book of the Gospels* with text marked, if used and not carried in procession

❑ nearby: any candles, candlestands not carried in procession

❑ nearby: stand for processional cross

Credence Table:

❑ small bowls or other vessels for minister(s) of anointing to carry oil to sick

❑ cards with text for anointing action, for ministers

❑ basin(s) and lemon, pitcher(s) of water, towel(s) for ministers

❑ large chalice (can be covered by pall and/or white veil)

❑ purificator

❑ corporal

❑ book stand, if necessary

❑ water in small cruet, if not in procession of gifts

❑ any bread, wine, not in procession of gifts

❑ additional chalices and purificators for the congregation (on tray)

❑ additional patens, bowls, or ciboria for the congregation

❑ pyx or ciborium, if bread consecrated for the absent sick

Priest Celebrant's Chair:

❑ *The Roman Missal*, after review in vesting room

❑ ritual book, after review in vesting room

❑ hymnal or booklet, if not carried in procession

Ministers' Seats:

- ❏ texts for concelebrants, if any
- ❏ hymnals or booklets, if not carried in procession

Ambo:

- ❏ Lectionary with texts marked
- ❏ Psalm setting for cantor (unless carried there for this action)
- ❏ Litany (#138 in rite), if done here

Music Stand (or Secondary Podium):

- ❏ litany (#138 in rite), if done here

Sacristy

- ❏ charcoal lit in thurible, then put in vesting room
- ❏ extra charcoal (and tongs, matches) for adding during Mass
- ❏ controls set for air, sound, lights
- ❏ microphones put in place, turned on, and tested

Vesting Room

- ❏ vesture (see page 130); chasuble, dalmatic of white or day's color
- ❏ lavaliere microphones, if any
- ❏ *Book of the Gospels* with text marked, if carried in procession
- ❏ local texts (dismissal of catechumens) prepared and other texts marked in *The Roman Missal*, for review prior to placement by chair
- ❏ texts also marked in *Pastoral Care of the Sick*, 135–142, for review prior to placement by chair or assistant minister's chair or credence table:
- ❏ thurible, with lit charcoal
- ❏ vessel of incense
- ❏ processional cross
- ❏ two or more candlesticks with lit candles

Entrance

Table with Gifts:

- ❏ bread for all in bowls, patens, or ciboria, if in procession
- ❏ wine for all, if in procession

Other:

- ❏ collection baskets ready, if used
- ❏ booklets, bulletins or other handouts

Rite of Reconciliation

The Rite of Penance contains several ritual orders, with or without sacramental absolution, for a variety of pastoral circumstances. Each of these orders or rites is a liturgy, with particular artifacts and furnishings that facilitate the communal action. This is true even for the rite for reconciliation of individual penitents, what many commonly call "confession"—even with just two present, it is the act of Christ and his Church.

This list is for the order that is most often used in the United States, what has usually come to be called a "penance service."

PLACE OF CELEBRATION

Seating for Congregation:

- ❏ hymnals or booklets
- ❏ space designated for other priests to gather near the Priest Celebrant after individual confession and absolution

Altar (if Celebration is in Eucharistic Space):

- ❏ nearby: candlestands, if candles will be carried in procession
- ❏ nearby: processional cross may be in stand or may be carried in procession

Priest Celebrant's Chair:

- ❏ ritual book, after review in vesting room
- ❏ hymnal or booklet, if not carried in procession

Ministers' Seating:

- ❏ places designated for other priest confessors
- ❏ hymnals or booklets, if not carried in procession

Ambo:

- ❏ Lectionary or ritual book, with texts marked
- ❏ Psalm setting for cantor (unless carried there for this action)

Music Stand (or Secondary Podium):

- ❏ text of examination of conscience, if used
- ❏ text for general confession and litany, read by deacon or other minister

PLACES FOR INDIVIDUAL CONFESSION AND ABSOLUTION

This may be space designated within the main gathering place or regular chapels of reconciliation. At each designated place or chapel:

- ❏ chair for confessor
- ❏ text of absolution, if needed

- ❏ chair for penitent
- ❏ kneeler and, if possible, screen; arranged so that penitent approaches place and can choose kneeler or chair before the priest sees him or her

SACRISTY

- ❏ controls set for lights, air, sound
- ❏ microphones put in place and tested

VESTING ROOM

- ❏ vesture for Priest Celebrant: alb and stole (with cope), violet or color of day
- ❏ vesture for other priests: alb and stole, violet or color of the day
- ❏ lavaliere microphones, if any
- ❏ local texts prepared and other texts marked in the *Rite of Penance*, for review before placing at chair
- ❏ processional cross, if carried in procession
- ❏ two lit candles, if carried in procession

Rite of Eucharistic Exposition

Solemn or lengthy exposition should begin after the Prayer after Communion of the Mass at which the host for exposition is consecrated. This list is for exposition taking place at a time removed from the celebration of the Mass.

PLACE FOR EUCHARISTIC ACTION

Seating:

- ❏ hymnals or booklets

Altar:

- ❏ covered with one white cloth
- ❏ nearby: two or four candlestands, with lit candles
- ❏ nearby: processional cross may be in stand
- ❏ nearby: space set for Priest Celebrant and ministers to kneel and to incense the Eucharist
- ❏ nearby: ritual book, hymnal, after review in sacristy

Credence Table:

- ❏ monstrance
- ❏ stand with thurible and vessel of incense nearby

Priest Celebrant's Chair:

❑ hymnal or booklet, if not carried in procession

Ministers' Seats:

❑ hymnals or booklets, if not carried in procession

Ambo:

❑ Lectionary or ritual book (*Holy Communion and Worship of the Eucharist outside Mass*), with readings marked

❑ Psalm settings for cantor (or carried there for this action)

Music Stand (or Secondary Podium):

❑ texts of litanies, intercessions or other prayers used

SACRISTY

❑ thurible, with lit charcoal, ready for incensation near beginning and end of exposition (or on stand accessible from altar)

❑ vessel of incense

❑ controls set for air, sound, lights

❑ microphones, if necessary, put in place, turned on, and tested

VESTING ROOM

❑ vesture (see page 131); cope, dalmatic of white

❑ lavaliere microphones, if any

❑ local texts for exposition prepared and other texts marked in ritual book (*Holy Communion and Worship of the Eucharist outside Mass*), for review prior to placement either at presider's chair or in place for kneeling

ENTRANCE

❑ booklets, bulletins or other handouts

CHAPEL OF EUCHARISTIC RESERVATION

❑ lamp lit

❑ key at tabernacle

❑ lunette (glass pyx that fits monstrance) in tabernacle, holding host consecrated at prior Mass

❑ white humeral veil for transfer of Eucharist to altar

❑ two candlestands and candles to accompany transfer, then joining other two or four candles near altar

Blessings: Order for the Blessing of Animals

The *Book of Blessings* has 71 chapters with orders of blessing for families, buildings, objects, parish members, and more. Its introduction should be read for an appreciation of what "blessing" means here—praise of God and intercession for those who use elements of God's creation. Most of the rites contain a Liturgy of the Word before a prayer of praising God. The list given here presumes a large gathering of parishioners and animals in an outdoor place. The service is led by a priest, deacon, or lay minister.

PLACE OF CONGREGATION

Seating:

- ❏ folding chairs from parish hall, blankets or lawn chairs brought from homes, or no formal seating
- ❏ booklets for all
- ❏ room for pet carriers, or similar assistance for all animals

Priest Celebrant's Chair or Place to Stand:

- ❏ *Book of Blessings*, after review in vesting room
- ❏ booklet
- ❏ sound system, if necessary

Small Table:

- ❏ vessel of baptismal water and sprinkler (several, if other ministers will also circulate for full sprinkling action)

Ministers' Seats or Places to Stand:

- ❏ booklets

Lectern (reserved for readings, homily—Priest Celebrant's prayer should be from his position):

- ❏ Lectionary or *Book of Blessings*, with text marked
- ❏ Psalm setting for cantor (unless carried there for this action)
- ❏ intercessions
- ❏ sound system, if necessary

Place for Instrumentalists and Other Leaders of Music:

- ❏ sound system, if necessary
- ❏ music stands, as needed

VESTING ROOM

- ❏ albs for assisting ministers; alb, cope, and stole for Priest Celebrant
- ❏ lavaliere microphones, if usable with outdoor sound system
- ❏ texts marked in *Book of Blessings,* for review prior to placement

❏ signs directing participants to correct place

Devotions: Stations of the Cross

Because this devotional practice is not part of the liturgy, there are neither official texts nor exact lists of requisites. There are even different lists of the 14 (sometimes 15) stations. See page 37 for a description of the installation of crosses and images for this devotion.

This list is for a public gathering that includes hymn singing and the procession of participants from station to station.

PLACE OF CONGREGATION

At the Start of the Processional Route, Near Station One:

❏ hymnals or booklets for all

❏ places designated for musicians, leader, and other ministers (for example, cross-bearer and two candle-bearers)

Processional Route, by 14 or 15 Stations:

❏ lighting, as appropriate

❏ places designated for congregation and ministers

❏ 14 or 15 images or crosses set in place, if not permanently positioned

SACRISTY

❏ controls set for lights, air, sound

❏ microphones put in place, if used

VESTING ROOM

❏ vesture: alb for any leader; alb and stole (and cope) for ordained leader, in red or color of day

❏ lavaliere microphones, if used

❏ texts marked or inserted in appropriate books for all who will read or lead prayer

❏ processional cross, if used in procession

❏ two lit candles, if used in procession

ENTRANCE

❏ sign indicating location of celebration, if in separate or outdoor place

Chapter Thirty-five

Checklists for Rites at which a Bishop Presides

Pastoral Visitation of the Bishop

The *Ceremonial of Bishops* (#1177) emphasizes to Bishops that their visits to parishes should never be purely an administrative duty. The visitation should allow parishioners to interact with the chief herald of the Gospel in the local Church, their shepherd and loving teacher. Sacristans sometimes focus on the Bishop not as administrator or shepherd, but as the man whose presence brings unusual and often confusing demands on the sacristy. This need not be so. The rites at which the Bishop presides usually involve larger assemblies, but this can be seen as an opportunity to involve more volunteers in the sacristy. Some rites might be unfamiliar (for example, an Ordination), but the representatives of the Bishop (and he himself) will usually want to plan details far in advance. With adequate preparation, the Bishop's visit does not need to burdensome, and can in fact be what it should be: a joyful moment for the entire community.

A formal visitation by the Bishop might include any of these events: a formal Rite of Welcoming (see below), Dedication of the Church (list at page 256), Mass (same as any celebration of the Eucharist), Liturgy of the Hours, Confirmation (list at page 247), Ordination (lists on pages 249–256) visits to the sick (list at page 238), celebration of the word of God, and a liturgical visit with parishioners to the cemetery (list at page 233).

SPECIFIC CUSTOMS   A visitation that begins with a formal reception or liturgical welcome (*Ceremonial of Bishops,* 1180) may require these items:

VESTING ROOM

❏ cope, stole, alb for pastor

Entrance Hall:

❏ space for congregation

❏ space for pastor and Bishop

❏ a crucifix (or processional cross) for veneration

❏ vessel of baptismal water and sprinkler

Priest Celebrant's Chair:

❏ *The Roman Missal* with texts marked

Rite of Confirmation within Mass

Those baptized as infants are normally confirmed by the Bishop, at their first Holy Communion or at some later time (the age is determined by the local Bishop). (See the Easter Vigil list, page 204, for the Confirmation by presbyters of adults baptized or received into the church.)

PLACE FOR EUCHARISTIC ACTION

Seating:

- ❏ hymnals or booklets
- ❏ designated seating for candidates and sponsors

Open Space:

- ❏ pedestal or stand with vessel of chrism
- ❏ space designated for candidates and sponsors when called forward

Altar:

- ❏ covered with one white cloth (if a festive colored cloth is used, the topmost cloth should be white)
- ❏ *Book of the Gospels* with text marked, if used and if not carried in procession by deacon or lector or reader
- ❏ nearby: any candles, candlestands not carried in procession
- ❏ nearby: stand for processional cross, if it is to remain near the altar

Credence Table:

- ❏ smaller vessel(s) from which chrism can be administered
- ❏ basin(s) with lemon pieces, pitcher(s) of water, towels
- ❏ large chalice (can be covered by pall and/or white veil)
- ❏ purificator
- ❏ corporal
- ❏ water in small cruet, if not in procession of gifts
- ❏ book stand, if necessary
- ❏ additional chalices and purificators for the congregation (on tray)
- ❏ additional patens or bowls or ciboria for the congregation

Priest Celebrant's Chair:

- ❏ nearby: seats for servers assisting the Bishop
- ❏ nearby: the server assisting with the book has the *The Roman Missal* and ritual book (*Roman Pontifical* or the *Rite of Confirmation* excerpted from it)
- ❏ hymnal or booklet

Ministers' Seats:

- ❏ texts for concelebrants, if any
- ❏ hymnals or booklets

Ambo:

- ❏ Lectionary with texts marked
- ❏ Psalm setting for cantor (unless carried there for this action)
- ❏ intercessions from the *Rite of Confirmation*

Music Stand (or Secondary Podium):

- ❏ names of candidates to be presented

SACRISTY

- ❏ charcoal lit in thurible, then placed in vesting room to be ready for Entrance Procession
- ❏ extra charcoal; tongs, matches for adding during Mass
- ❏ controls set for air, sound, lights
- ❏ microphones put in places, turned on, and tested

VESTING ROOM(S)

(Several rooms may be necessary, especially if candidates will wear robes or albs and if they will be in opening procession.)

- ❏ robes for candidates, set up in order agreed at rehearsal, preferably albs, the baptismal garment
- ❏ space set for candidates' gathering before the procession
- ❏ albs (with cinctures and amices, if necessary) for all ministers, stoles and chasubles for concelebrants (red, if a Votive Mass of the Holy Spirit is used, with chasubles if available)
- ❏ stoles and dalmatics for deacons, normally red
- ❏ stole, chasuble, zucchetto (skullcap), miter, pastoral staff for Bishop, plus pallium for Archbishop
- ❏ lavaliere microphones, if any
- ❏ Lectionary with texts marked
- ❏ *Book of the Gospels* with texts marked, if carried in procession
- ❏ local texts (dismissal of catechumens, intercessions) prepared in binder and other texts marked in *The Roman Missal* and in ritual book, for review prior to placement by chair
- ❏ thurible, with lit charcoal
- ❏ vessel of incense
- ❏ processional cross
- ❏ two or more candlesticks with lit candles

Table with Gifts:

- ❑ paten with hosts, including large concelebration host, if used, with additional patens or ciboria containing hosts for the entire congregation
- ❑ wine in cruet or carafe for pouring into chalices at the Preparation of the Gifts

Other:

- ❑ collection baskets ready, if used
- ❑ booklets, bulletins or other handouts

CATECHUMENEON

- ❑ opened and prepared, if catechumens present

Ordination of Deacons

PLACE FOR EUCHARISTIC ACTION

Seating:

- ❑ hymnals or booklets
- ❑ reserved seating, if necessary, kept to a minimum, must be well marked

Open Space:

- ❑ seating for candidates (not blocking sight lines between members of the congregation, between congregation and altar)

Altar:

- ❑ covered with one white cloth (if a festive colored cloth is used, the topmost cloth should be white)
- ❑ nearby: any candles, candlestands not carried in procession
- ❑ nearby: stand for processional cross

Credence Table(s):

- ❑ Sunday: vessel of baptismal water and sprinkler, if used
- ❑ stoles and dalmatics for newly ordained (arranged with names if in specific sizes)
- ❑ *Book of the Gospels* with text marked
- ❑ large chalice (can be covered by pall and/or white veil)
- ❑ purificator
- ❑ corporal
- ❑ book stand, if necessary

- ❏ water in small cruet
- ❏ basin, pitcher of water, towel
- ❏ additional chalices and purificators for the congregation (on tray)
- ❏ additional patens, bowls, or ciboria for the congregation

Priest Celebrant's Chair (Cathedra):

- ❏ nearby: chairs for assistants who will miter, pastoral staff, books (hymnal or booklet, *The Roman Missal*, *Roman Pontifical*)
- ❏ space nearby where candidates can stand without blocking sight lines of congregation, and can prostrate themselves

Ministers' Seats:

- ❏ special seating for vested deacons
- ❏ texts for concelebrants
- ❏ hymnals or booklets

Ambo:

- ❏ Lectionary with texts marked
- ❏ Psalm setting for cantor (unless carried there for this action)
- ❏ Music Stand (or Secondary Podium):
- ❏ names of candidates to be called
- ❏ text for presentation of candidates
- ❏ Litany of the Saints text for cantor, with interpolations (patrons, titular, petitions)

SACRISTY

- ❏ charcoal lit in thurible, then put in vesting room
- ❏ extra charcoal; tongs and matches for adding during Mass
- ❏ controls set for air, sound, lights
- ❏ microphones put in place, turned on, and tested

VESTING ROOM(S)

(The vesting can take place in any room(s) of the complex, as long as it is large enough.)

- ❏ albs (with cinctures and amices, if necessary) for all ministers, including those to be ordained
- ❏ stoles and dalmatics for those who are already deacons (vesture in color of day or white)
- ❏ stoles (and chasubles) for concelebrants

- ❏ stole (dalmatic), chasuble, miter, pastoral staff for Bishop, pallium for Archbishop
- ❏ lavaliere microphones, if any
- ❏ *Book of the Gospels* with text marked
- ❏ texts marked in *The Roman Missal* and in *Roman Pontifical*, for review prior to placement by chair
- ❏ thurible, with lit charcoal
- ❏ vessel or "boat" of incense
- ❏ processional cross
- ❏ two or more candlesticks with lit candles
- ❏ place for ministers to gather for procession

ENTRANCE

- ❏ paten with hosts, including large concelebration host, if used, with additional patens or ciboria containing hosts for the entire congregation
- ❏ wine in cruet or carafe for pouring into chalices at the preparation of the altar

Ordination of Priests

PLACE FOR EUCHARISTIC ACTION

Seating:

- ❏ hymnals or booklets
- ❏ reserved seating, if necessary, kept to a minimum; must be well marked

Open Space:

- ❏ seating for candidates (not blocking sight lines between members of the congregation or between congregation and altar); may be seated with other deacons
- ❏ stand or pedestal for vessel of chrism

Altar:

- ❏ covered with one white cloth (if a festive colored cloth is used, the topmost cloth should be white)
- ❏ nearby: any candles, candlestands not carried in procession
- ❏ nearby: stand for processional cross

Credence Table(s):

- ❏ vessel of baptismal water and sprinkler, if used

- ❏ stoles for presbyters not concelebrating who will lay on hands

- ❏ chasubles and stoles for newly ordained (arranged with names if in specific sizes)

- ❏ linen apron (gremial) for Bishop

- ❏ vessel for anointing with chrism

- ❏ basin(s) with lemon pieces, pitcher(s) of water, towel(s) for newly ordained and Bishop

- ❏ purificator

- ❏ corporal

- ❏ book stand, if necessary

- ❏ additional chalices and purificators for the congregation (on tray)

- ❏ additional patens, bowls, or ciboria for the congregation

Priest Celebrant's Chair (Cathedra):

- ❏ nearby: chairs for assistants who will miter, pastoral staff, books (hymnal or booklet, *The Roman Missal*, *Roman Pontifical*)

- ❏ space nearby where candidates can stand without blocking sight lines of congregation, can prostrate themselves, and can kneel for presbyters to lay on hands

- ❏ space for all presbyters to gather about the Bishop after laying on of hands

Ministers' Seats:

- ❏ for newly ordained during preparation of altar and after Holy Communion

- ❏ for vested priests, texts for concelebrants

- ❏ for deacons of the Mass (usually one or two)

- ❏ hymnals or booklets

Ambo:

- ❏ Lectionary with texts marked

- ❏ Psalm setting for cantor (unless carried there for this action)

Music Stand (or Secondary Podium):

- ❏ names of candidates to be called

- ❏ text for presentation of candidates

- ❏ Litany of the Saints text for cantor, with interpolations (patrons, titular, petitions)

SACRISTY

- ❏ charcoal lit in thurible, then put in vesting room
- ❏ extra charcoal; tongs, matches for adding during Mass
- ❏ controls set for air, sound, lights
- ❏ microphones put in places, turned on, and tested

VESTING ROOM(S)

(The vesting can take place in any room(s) of the complex, as long as it is large enough.)

- ❏ albs (with cincture and amices, if necessary) for all ministers
- ❏ diaconal stoles for all to be ordained (vesture in color of day or white)
- ❏ stoles and dalmatics for deacons of the Mass
- ❏ stoles (and chasubles) for concelebrants
- ❏ stole (dalmatic), chasuble, miter, pastoral staff for Bishop, pallium for Archbishop
- ❏ lavaliere microphones, if any
- ❏ *Book of the Gospels* with text marked
- ❏ texts marked in *The Roman Missal* and in *Roman Pontifical*, for review prior to placement by chair
- ❏ thurible, with lit charcoal
- ❏ vessel of incense
- ❏ processional cross
- ❏ two or more candlesticks with lit candles
- ❏ place for ministers to gather for procession

ENTRANCE

- ❏ large chalice with water and wine, with paten holding large concelebration host, to be prepared before Mass begins for presentation to ordinands during the rite
- ❏ additional patens or ciboria containing hosts for the entire congregation
- ❏ additional wine in cruet or carafe for pouring into chalices at the Preparation of the Gifts

Ordination of a Bishop

PLACE FOR EUCHARISTIC ACTION

Seating:

- ❏ hymnals or booklets
- ❏ reserved seating, if necessary, kept to a minimum; must be well marked

Open Space:

- ❏ stand or pedestal for vessel of chrism

Altar:

- ❏ covered with one white cloth (if a festive colored cloth is used, the topmost cloth should be white)
- ❏ nearby: any candles, candlestands not carried in procession
- ❏ nearby: stand for processional cross

Credence Table(s):

- ❏ vessel of baptismal water and sprinkler, if used
- ❏ linen apron (gremial)
- ❏ vessel for anointing with chrism
- ❏ basin with lemon pieces, pitcher of water, towel
- ❏ ring, pastoral staff, miter for Bishop-elect
- ❏ large chalice (can be covered by pall and/or white veil)
- ❏ purificator
- ❏ corporal
- ❏ water in small cruet, if not in procession of gifts
- ❏ book stand, if necessary
- ❏ additional chalices and purificators for the congregation (on tray)
- ❏ additional patens, bowls, or ciboria for the congregation

Priest Celebrant's Chair (Cathedra):

- ❏ nearby: chairs for assistants who will miter, pastoral staff, books (hymnal or booklets, *The Roman Missal* and Roman Pontifical)
- ❏ space nearby where Bishop-elect can stand without blocking sight lines of congregation, can prostrate himself, and can kneel for laying on of hands

Ministers' Seats:

- ❏ near the *cathedra:* prominent chair for use by newly ordained Bishop or by principal consecrator after the ordination
- ❏ near the *cathedra:* chairs for other Bishops (a minimum of two), with copies of the consecratory prayer
- ❏ for the Bishop-elect, and two assisting priests
- ❏ for priest who will present Bishop-elect
- ❏ for concelebrating priests
- ❏ for vested deacons
- ❏ for assisting ministers
- ❏ for lectors or readers
- ❏ for college of diocesan consultors and chancellor
- ❏ for ecumenical and interfaith representatives
- ❏ hymnals or booklets at all these chairs

Ambo:

- ❏ Lectionary with texts marked
- ❏ Psalm setting for cantor (unless carried there for this action)
- ❏ the apostolic mandate (letter of appointment from the Holy Father)

Music Stand (or Secondary Podium):

- ❏ text of presentation
- ❏ Litany of the Saints text for cantor, with interpolations (patrons, titular, petitions)

SACRISTY

- ❏ charcoal lit in thurible and then put in vesting room
- ❏ extra charcoal; tongs, matches for adding during Mass
- ❏ controls set for air, sound, lights
- ❏ microphones put in places and turned on

VESTING ROOM(S)

(The vesting can take place in any room(s) of the complex, as long as it is large enough.)

- ❏ albs (with cinctures and amices, if necessary) for all ministers
- ❏ stoles and dalmatics for deacons of the Mass (vesture in color of day or white)
- ❏ stoles (and chasubles) for concelebrating priests

- ❏ stoles and copes for priests assisting Bishop-elect, if they do not concelebrate
- ❏ pectoral cross, stole, dalmatic, chasuble for Bishop-elect
- ❏ stoles, chasubles, miters for concelebrating Bishops
- ❏ stole (dalmatic), chasuble, miter, pastoral staff, (and pallium if Archbishop) for principal consecrator
- ❏ hymnals or booklets for all
- ❏ lavaliere microphones, if any
- ❏ *Book of the Gospels* with text marked
- ❏ texts marked in *The Roman Missal* and in *Roman Pontifical*, for review prior to placement by *cathedra*
- ❏ thurible with lit charcoal
- ❏ vessel of incense
- ❏ processional cross
- ❏ two or more candlesticks with lit candles
- ❏ place for ministers to gather for procession

ENTRANCE

- ❏ paten with hosts, including large concelebration host, if used, with additional patens or ciboria containing hosts for the entire congregation
- ❏ wine in cruet or carafe for pouring into chalices at the preparation of the altar

Dedication of a Church

PLACE FOR EUCHARISTIC ACTION

Open Space:

- ❏ dedication candles on walls, unlit
- ❏ small table for resting reliquary, if needed
- ❏ altar, completely bare (with aperture for relics)

Credence Tables:

- ❏ vessel of water and sprinkler
- ❏ sealant or cement to close the cover of the aperture in the altar (over relics)
- ❏ linen apron (gremial)
- ❏ vessel of chrism (with smaller bowl if necessary)
- ❏ basins with lemon pieces, pitchers of water, towels

- ❏ brazier with charcoal briquettes, and vessel of incense; small candle and matches
- ❏ several thuribles and charcoal, with vessel of incense
- ❏ linen towels for altar (and waterproof cover, or cerecloth—linen waxed on both sides)
- ❏ altar cloth
- ❏ four, six, or seven candlestands and candles
- ❏ stand for processional cross
- ❏ small candle, matches to begin lighting of altar candles, then dedication candles
- ❏ candlelighter, if needed
- ❏ large chalice (can be covered by pall and/or white veil)
- ❏ purificator
- ❏ corporal
- ❏ water in small cruet
- ❏ book stand, if necessary
- ❏ additional chalices and purificators for the congregation (on tray)
- ❏ additional patens, bowls, or ciboria for the congregation
- ❏ ciborium for use during procession to the Blessed Sacrament chapel after Mass
- ❏ humeral veil

Priest Celebrant's Chair:

- ❏ nearby: seats for ministers assisting with miter, pastoral staff, books (dedication rite, *The Roman Missal*, hymnal or program)

Ministers' Seats:

- ❏ texts for concelebrants, if any
- ❏ hymnals or booklets

Space for Leaders of Music:

- ❏ Psalm setting to be carried by cantor to ambo
- ❏ special text of litany of the saints with local interpolations
- ❏ ambo, completely bare

SACRISTY

- ❏ controls set for air, sound, lights (generally off, until lighting of the altar rite)
- ❏ microphones put in place, turned on, and tested

ENTRANCE

Exterior:

- ❏ signs that direct congregation to preliminary congregation place
- ❏ procession route arranged: permits for use of streets or sidewalks, traffic guards.

Doors:

- ❏ closed; no one enters church building before procession

Table with Gifts:

- ❏ paten with hosts, including large concelebration host, if used, with additional patens or ciboria containing hosts for the entire congregation
- ❏ wine in cruet or carafe for pouring into chalices at the Preparation of the Gifts

CHAPEL OF EUCHARISTIC RESERVATION

- ❏ lamp in place, unlit
- ❏ tabernacle open and empty until ciborium is placed here after Holy Communion

VESTING ROOM

(Room is distinct from church, near gathering place.)

- ❏ albs (with cinctures and amices, if necessary) for all ministers
- ❏ stoles and dalmatics of white for deacons (red, if carrying martyr's relics)
- ❏ stoles and white chasubles for priests
- ❏ stole (dalmatic), white chasuble, miter, pastoral staff (pallium) for Bishop
- ❏ lavaliere microphones, if any
- ❏ Lectionary with texts marked, to be carried by lector or reader
- ❏ texts marked in *The Roman Missal* and in dedication ritual book, for review prior to carrying by assistant
- ❏ processional cross

OTHER GATHERING PLACE

(A neighboring church or other suitable place will do.)

- ❏ relics of saints in reliquary, with flowers and candles
- ❏ booklets for all
- ❏ space for entire congregation
- ❏ spaces set for instrumentalists, other leaders of music, Bishop, other ministers

Index